D1621857

The

Hunter's Guide
to **Montana**

The
Hunter's Guide
to **Montana**

by Mark Henckel

Falcon Press Publishing Co., Inc.
Billings and Helena, Montana

Manufactured in the United States of America.

Library of Congress Catalog Card Number: 85-080603

ISBN 0-934318-69-7 (clothbound)
    0-934318-56-5 (softbound)

Falcon Press is continually expanding its list of recreational guidebooks.
You can order extra copies of this book and get information and prices by
writing Falcon Press, P.O. Box 1718, Helena, MT 59624. Also please ask for
a free copy of our current catalog listing all Falcon Press books.

Cover photo: Mike Logan, author of *Montana Is. . .* and *Yellowstone Is. . . .*

This book is dedicated to my parents:

Arthur R. Henckel,

a hunter who instilled a love for fish and wildlife both in and out of season and taught me that the way a person spends his days in the field is far more important than how many tags he fills or bag limits he brings home, and

Rose E. Henckel,

a woman who actually enjoys reading dictionaries and has contributed so much to my own efforts at using the written word to communicate a love of the outdoors to others.

Acknowledgements

Pity the poor spouse of a writer driven by a deadline. And pity the poor children, too, who must learn to tread lightly as that dark deadline day draws ever nearer.

In Carol, Andy, and Matt, there are three relieved individuals who have weathered a storm that swept through the household like an equinox blast in the high country, except that this fury lasted for months instead of days. Perhaps now that the copy deadline has passed and this book is finally in print, they can resume a more normal lifestyle that doesn't include whispering whenever father is on the telephone and steering clear when he's pounding the keys of his computer. At least, that's what I promised them time and time again as this book ground out of the printer. And I can tell them, too, that their tolerance was appreciated and their support kept me going.

There are others who lent support to the writing cause, not the least of them Warren Rogers and Dick Wesnick at the Billings Gazette, who have been responsible for giving their outdoor writer the freedom to learn about hunting in Montana over the years and develop the expert sources it takes to produce both a weekly outdoor page and a book like this one.

Special thanks, too, should go to Ralph Saunders, who went over the manuscript and offered his suggestions and enthusiasm along the way, and John Potter, whose lifelong love of wildlife shows through in his illustrations for The Hunter's Guide.

In terms of personal development in hunting which provided the background for this book, there are John Kremer and Jack Tanner, who enjoyed the boom times and endured the busts on trips all around Montana, and Jay Archer, who must have been born with a rifle in one hand, shotgun in the other and his instincts already in tune with the game species of the Treasure State. There's Vince Yannone, whose wealth of knowledge on all wildlife is so generously shared with anyone who cares to ask. And there's Frank Martin, who shoots straight, casts a fine fly line, and endures my endless questions about hunting and fishing.

Within the Montana Department of Fish, Wildlife and Parks, Charlie Eustace has been more than generous with his knowledge and humor, Roger Fliger has shared his expertise, and Bill Pryor has been a good friend, source, and traveling companion on late-night drives. Others whose contributions go beyond this book for their accumulated assistance over the years include Harley Yeager, the late Buck Compton, Ken Walcheck, Alberta Francis, Shawn Stewart, Claire Simmons, Tom Butts, Heidi and Clif Youmans, and Mike Aderhold.

Thanks, too, to publishers Mike Sample and Bill Schneider, whose collective boot in the rear was entirely responsible for making this book happen, and to Russell B. Hill for his editing pencil.

And, of course, appreciation goes to all the wildlife biologists and information officers of Fish, Wildlife and Parks and the hunters you'll learn about in the pages to come. Sitting for interviews and taking phone calls at odd hours, they have been an extremely patient and helpful panel of experts who have shared their time and experience to help you, the reader of *The Hunter's Guide to Montana.* — Mark Henckel

Contents

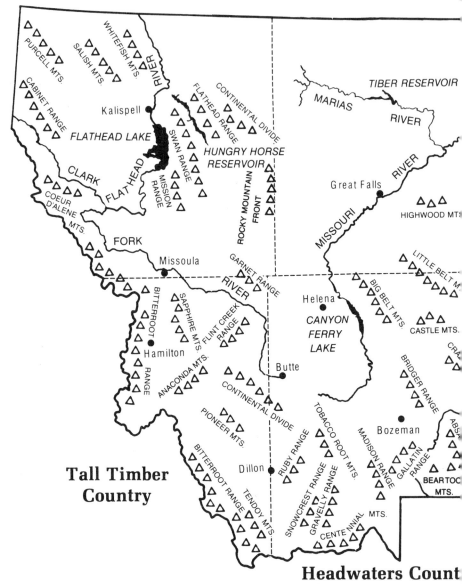

Tall Timber Country

Headwaters Country

Breaks Country

Farm Country

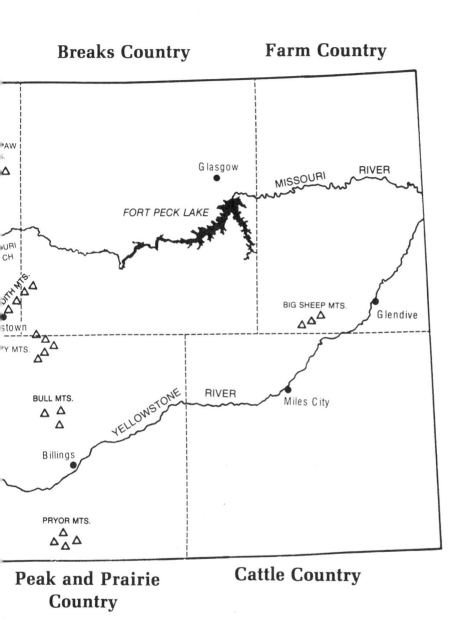

AW
.
△

Glasgow

MISSOURI   RIVER

FORT PECK LAKE

URI
CH

JTH MTS.
△ △
△

stown

'Y MTS.
△
△
△

BIG SHEEP MTS.
△ △ △

Glendive

BULL MTS.
△   △
△

YELLOWSTONE   RIVER

Miles City

Billings

PRYOR MTS.
△
△ △ △

Peak and Prairie
Country

Cattle Country

Elk are a big attraction in Montana from the Bitterroot Valley to the Missouri Breaks. Michael Sample photo.

Foreword

Look at *The Hunter's Guide to Montana* as an autumn odyssey from Alzada to Yaak with the wildlife of the Treasure State. That's the way it was written.

It takes you from the elk country of the Gallatin and Gravellies, past the mountain goats of the Rocky Mountain Front, the whitetails of the Lewistown area, sharptails of the Missouri Breaks, geese of the Medicine Lake region, antelope of the Ekalaka area and on to the unlimited bighorn sheep districts of the Beartooths, the highest mountain range in Montana. Though any book about hunting should deal with the taking and tagging of animals in all those places, this book will take you a little further.

The Hunter's Guide was designed to give readers an insight into the habits and lifestyles of the animals they're after. In that regard, it should be a valuable tool for the serious wildlife photographer, the active naturalist who just wants to go out and observe wildlife and the armchair bird and big game watcher who revels in learning a little more about the animals of the Treasure State. The book will also provide the beginning hunter with the savvy of countless years of hunting experience and offer the veteran some new fields of operation in parts of the state he might not know so well.

It has always been my contention that more than half the pleasure of being a hunter was learning the year-long habits of the species that I hunted. It stretched my fun far beyond the all-too-narrow parameters of opening day and closing day in fall and gave me an excuse to visit the big game winter ranges in January, the grouse dancing grounds in April and the mountain trails in summer. If a person learns enough about the way wildlife lives and the tactics it takes to find them in all seasons, it will also make him a more productive and appreciative visitor to the field in the fall.

As a result, this book is tailored to those ends rather than to the nuts and bolts approach of exactly where to pitch your tent when hunting season arrives. You won't read instructions that tell you to turn right at the cow, left at the horse, and shoot the elk standing in the middle of the road. Instead, you will read about the differences among such things as hunting elk in the Missouri Breaks in archery season, the Bob Marshall Wilderness when they're bugling, the thick timber of southwestern Montana, and the winter migrations of the Gallatin River drainage. It will tell you about differences in terrain, and the animals that live in it, from one end of the state to the other. Given that knowledge of the animals' habits and an insight into how to hunt them, the details of exactly where a hunter should go after them is left up to the individual.

There's no way any one individual could provide that kind of knowledge of wildlife and tactics in hunting country so large and diverse as Montana. Certainly, I couldn't. So this book has been the product of many hunts by many people over many years. There are the collective experiences of 120 sources within the pages of *The Hunter's Guide to Montana* and, for the most part, the advice they so willingly shared has been put in their own words. The reader will learn about big game and small from wildlife biologists, outfitters, outdoor writers, university wildlife professors, and hunters from one end of the state to the other. While some of the names may be familiar ones, others are just hunters like you and me who have loved their chosen game and have put in the time to get to know it on an intimate basis over the years.

In a state like Montana, coming up with that many sources really was no problem. There are excellent hunters residing in every part of the Treasure State. All but a very few are happy to share with the beginner or those new to the area.

The end result is to paint a true picture of hunting in Montana today with the help of those who know it best.

To make the wildlife picture a little easier to understand, the state has been divided into eight regions based on habitat types and the species that live there. Simply for the convenience of the writer, each of these regions has been given a name and if you've never heard them called that name before, rest assured that no one else has, either. It was just much easier to call it Breaks Country rather than East-North-Central Montana, and Peak and Prairie Country instead of East-South-Central Montana.

Among the other things that readers won't find much mention of in this book is information on license fees, drawings, and deadlines. In truth, they change every year and a letter or phone call to the Department of Fish, Wildlife and Parks will give a person all he needs to know. Suffice it to say that residents can purchase deer, black bear, elk, upland bird, waterfowl, and sportsman's licenses over the counter, while species like antelope, mountain goats, bighorn sheep, and moose are awarded through computer drawings during the summer before the season. Nonresidents who want to purchase the combination sportsman's license had better do so early in the license year because their number is limited and they always sell out long before the season starts. All big game and upland bird hunters during rifle season must wear at least 400 square inches of hunter orange. And everyone, residents and nonresidents alike, should remember to punch the month and date on their big game tags immediately after making the kill and attach the tag to the carcass right away. Failure to do so is the most common hunting violation in Montana, the one most easily avoided, and the major culprit in producing citations, fines, and confiscated big game animals.

You also won't read much about rifle calibers for big game hunting or shotgun gauges for birds and waterfowl unless there is a specific need. For the most part, any of the standard rifle calibers like the .270, .30-06, .308, or 7 mm. magnum can be considered adequate for most hunting situations. And getting into arguments over the relative benefits of the .243, 6 mm., or .257 Roberts in a particular situation presents problems that will never be resolved and, frankly, aren't worth the space they would take up in the book. As for the shotguns, a 12-gauge can take down anything that flies in Montana, many hunters have found true bliss in the 20-gauge, and there is a growing legion of wingshooters on the prowl for 28 and 16-gauge shells as well. For rifles and shotguns alike, it all boils down to personal preference and the ability of the hunter to use his chosen weapon.

As one final word of advice to anyone who plans to head for the high ground or open range of Montana in hunting season, remember to tread lightly and enjoy your surroundings. The Treasure State offers some of the most beautiful and unspoiled hunting country to be found in the United States to look for the Pope and Young Club trophies of the bowhunter or the Boone and Crockett Club dreams of the rifleman. As visitors to it, we all share the responsibility for keeping it that way. That means asking permission when hunting private lands, which is the law. It means honoring road closures and walk-in areas. And it means leaving the field at the end of the day or season in a condition at least as good as you found it.

With those things in mind, the wildlife waiting, and 120 hunting partners ready to walk beside you in the pages ahead, let the odyssey begin — *Mark Henckel*

Montana—Hunting Country

The mystery of where to hunt in Montana was summed up so easily by
Vince Yannone, a hunting partner from Helena, when asked about big
game in the mountains of the Treasure State a few years ago.

"Mule deer are high.

"Whitetails are low.

"And elk? Elk are where you find them," Yannone said.

If only hunting was that simple. Then there really wouldn't be a need for
a book like this one. Everyone would fill every tag every year. And, I'm
afraid, some of the fun would be gone from a sport so easy to unravel.

The truth of the matter is that hunting in Montana is as diverse as the
eastern prairie, the river breaks, mountain valleys, and alpine high country which can be found in various parts of the state. All of it is hunting
country in one form or another, and each has its attractions for the person
who packs a gun or bow in autumn and chooses to explore it.

But there is more to the diverse hunting in Montana than just the variety
of terrain that can be found here. There are all those species of wildlife
which can be chased in season. There are ten big game species in all, including elk, mule deer, white-tailed deer, antelope, bighorn sheep, mountain goat, moose, mountain lion, black bear, and grizzly bear. Add to that
upland bird species like pheasants, blue grouse, spruce grouse, ruffed
grouse, sage grouse, sharp-tailed grouse, Hungarian partridge, chukar partridge, and turkeys. Then consider the fall flights of ducks, Canada geese,
snow geese, cranes, and tundra swans which include Montana on their
migration paths.

The end result is hunting country so rich in opportunity that no hunter could taste all its pleasures, in all its locales, in the course of a single season. But it sure would be fun to try.

This promise of varied hunting is certainly nothing new in Montana. The state has a long tradition of bountiful wildlife dating back to the buffalo days of the nineteenth century. Though the big buffalo herds disappeared due to the guns of market hunters and changing land practices more than a century ago, there were still plenty of species to go after.

According to the book *Game Management in Montana*, edited by Tom Mussehl and F.W. Howell, the earliest laws governing hunting included outlawing the taking of introduced game birds in 1869; setting a grouse season in 1870; closing the hunting from February 1 to August 15 each year of buffalo, moose, elk, deer, sheep, mountain goats, antelope, and hares in 1872; and ending market hunting for birds in 1877.

By 1895, season bag limits of three bull elk, one hundred grouse, eight deer, eight sheep, eight mountain goats, and eight antelope were set and the first Board of Game Commissioners was organized. The first game warden was hired in 1901 to enforce those laws and the first licenses were required. Those licenses, for nonresidents only, cost $25 for big game animals and $15 for game birds. The first resident license was enacted for the 1905 season at the cost of $1 per season per family.

The 1907 hunting season in Montana was from October 1 through December 1 with a three-deer limit, limits of one each for elk, sheep and goats; an upland bird daily bag limit of five of any species; and a water-fowl bag of twenty ducks.

Hunting in Montana began to fall on hard times through the homestead years and the dry and dusty times of the 1930s. Deer all but disappeared from much of their historic range, seasons were closed on antelope and moose statewide, and hunting for other species was severely restricted.

It wasn't until the 1940s that Montana enjoyed the statewide rebirth in hunting opportunity that continues to the present day. Due to better understanding and management of game species, introductions of animals into new areas, and the acquisition of critical habitat, it can be said that, in many ways, hunters in the Treasure State are better off now than their great-grandfathers were.

Seasons are long, limits are generous, and the wildlife is protected much better in Montana today than at any time in the state's history. Not that there aren't problems facing big game and bird populations here. Hunting pressure is increasing every year. People pressures on wildlife winter ranges have reached critical proportions in many areas. Lack of access to some private ground and too much access to some public ground is a recurring nightmare. And changing land use practices continue to pose threats to certain species.

But the hunting still holds up season after season, and the pressures on wildlife here pale in comparison to what has happened in most other parts of the country.

It's still possible here for anyone to purchase a bighorn sheep tag for certain hunting districts and take his chances in the high country. A hunter can take several deer in some seasons and stay within the limits of the law. And bird hunters who vary their targets can fill up a game pouch on one kind of grouse in the morning, top it off again in the early afternoon on a second, and have hunting until sunset on a third species.

By 1907, hunters had to be satisfied with taking only one elk each year. Michael Sample photo.

The extent of a person's hunting is limited by his available time in the field and his willingness to move on to another species, rather than by his ability to keep up his interest after bagging just a few available birds and big game animals.

The general rule of thumb remains: the hunter who puts in the most time in the field learning an area will have the best results when it comes to punching tags or filling game pouches. But this book can give you a running start when it comes to getting acquainted with the diverse hunting opportunities that Montana has to offer.

It would be virtually impossible to give a complete rundown on every species in every area of Montana, simply because there are so many species in so many areas of this, the fourth-largest state in the union. But building your own experience on the knowledge of others can cut into the years of trial and error that it usually takes for a hunter to become proficient at the game.

To make the picture complete, the habits and lifestyles of the animals and the tactics of people that go after them in one part of the state should be compared to what goes on in another region. While there are individual differences, there are insights to be learned in all areas that can help a person become a successful hunter no matter where he goes.

It's a pleasant thought that hunting in Montana could be as simple as mule deer being high, whitetails living low, and elk being where a hunter finds them. But Yannone, a most successful hunter himself, knows things are never so cut and dried.

Good hunting in Montana is a recipe of timing, experience, equipment, and environment. Put them all together in the proper proportions, pick your country carefully, and you can cook up the hunting memories of a lifetime.

Terrain is varied and in some places a horse can be a valuable friend to pack out game. Mark Henckel photo.

Montana has the hunting country which provides those rich, sensual memories and the wildlife that most hunters, in most other places, can only dream about. If you don't believe it, just read on.

Headwaters Country

This is the heartland of the elk range in Montana. It offers some of the few hunting districts available anywhere where all a hunter has to have is a desire to hunt bighorn sheep and he can go after them. And no matter what species of bird or big game animal strikes your fancy, you can rub shoulders with them in Headwaters Country.

Headwaters Country is made up of the big, broad valleys of the headwaters of the Missouri River, the pristine waters of the upper Yellowstone, and myriad smaller rivers and streams which are famous only to those who return to the country around them each fall to set up hunting camps.

It has such fabled place names as the Gallatin, Gravelly, Absaroka and Little Belt Ranges and lesser-known but equally rich mountains in between. There is one last look at the Continental Divide in the western reaches of Headwaters Country and the first glance at the prairie on the east.

A hunter can find almost every game animal and bird that Montana has to offer in some part of Headwaters Country. There is the trophy hunter's Big Ten: mule deer, white-tailed deer, elk, moose, bighorn sheep, mountain goat, black bear, antelope, mountain lion, and even grizzly bear, though there's no season on them here. As for upland birds, hunters test their proficiency against pheasants, sharp-tailed grouse, sage grouse, Hungarian partridge, blue grouse, spruce grouse, and ruffed grouse. In fact, the only missing attraction of the bird group is good populations of the elusive chukar partridge, which is a foreigner to most other parts of the state, as well.

Headwaters Country is a land of mixed access for hunters. In some parts, there is too much access and it's too easy, to the point that game herds can be endangered by hunters able to move about too freely. In other areas, access is limited by the availability of horses or a person's stamina to reach hunting country far from the end of the road. In still other parts, it's private ground locked up so tight that it comes down to not just who you know, but how long you've known them or how close a relative you've married in the family, which will decide whether or not you'll get on to hunt.

Just as its hunting offers a mixed bag, its terrain is equally diverse. It can be as rugged as the mountain goat ranges of the Absarokas or as easy as the open elk ground of the Gravelly Range. There are hikes up steep mountain ridges in the Elkhorns in search of blue grouse and walks across the flat prairie of Park County for Hungarian partridge. It has bountiful white-tailed deer populations on the Musselshell and rich mule deer numbers in the Bridgers.

In short, there is everything a hunter would want in Montana in some part of Headwaters Country, just as long as he knows where to look. But be aware that it's traditional country, too. Elk camps that have occupied the same piece of real estate every fall for years are apt to get into the big bulls most often. Bird hunters whose dogs run over the same ground each autumn will get the most feathers by the end of the day. And deer hunters who know where the deer are likely to be when rutting time arrives will come away with the biggest bucks.

Headwaters Country is indeed the heartland of Montana hunting. But just as in any dealings of the heart, a person has to shake hands and get acquainted first before the labors of love begin to pay off.

Elk

Mike Fillinger has no illusions about the natural ability of elk to detect danger. "All you have to do is remember they can hear everything within a mile, even a whisper. They can see everything at five miles, including the ants. And they can smell everything in the state of Montana," the Helena hunter said.

With those kinds of defenses, it's a wonder that anyone ever bags a bull. But it does give the hunter a look at what he's up against and shows why those who work the hardest and longest at the game have the best chance of ending their hunts with smiles on their faces and bulls in the back of their pickup trucks.

In Headwaters Country, the hunter has another advantage as well. The area is so diverse and the season so long that he can choose the time and place where his methods can best be put to use. Whether it's the bugling time of the archery season, the first weeks of the general season, the mid-season doldrums or the late migrations from the high country, the hunter can take his pick and try his luck.

So let's follow the seasons and see where the elk take us. It's a journey that most mountain elk make each autumn, following traditions that have been formed over centuries and defenses they have added in more recent times as hunters have increasingly moved in on them.

Just remember that the ground rules are the same, no matter what the season. An elk needs food, water and shelter. It's just the places they find them that change.

Early in the rut, bugling for elk is the most effective tactic for a bowhunter. Mark Henckel photo.

"There are two kinds of places I've consistently found them in the archery season," said Rob Seelye, a bowhunter from Laurel who journeys to the southwestern Montana mountains near Dillon each fall to bugle big bulls. "One place is the head end of the creek bottoms. Most of the time, that's where the bulls hang out in the moist, boggy areas. The other place is on the high grassy ridges. If they're there, they're close to good black timber. It's hot weather at that time of year and elk don't like sun," he said. "They tend to bed in the dark, deep timber where it's cooler, away from the flies."

His September-October tactics rely on making the most of the rut and

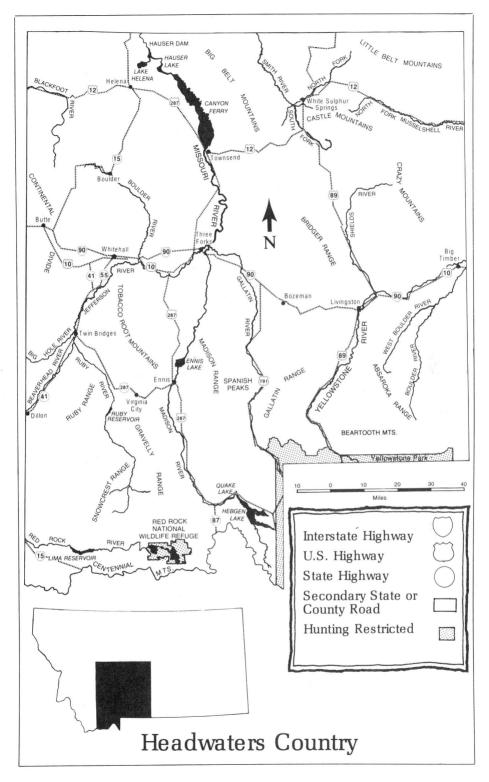

Headwaters Country

Open parks and ridges make it possible for hunters to spot elk from a distance. Michael Sample photo.

bringing in bulls with bugling. "It's pretty damn tough to walk up on an elk in the woods. Unless you can ambush him coming to and from his feeding grounds or bring him in with bugling, your chances of getting them are slim.

"The best time to bugle a bull is the earlier part of the rut because at that time, they're trying to establish their dominance and their harems. There's a lot of bugling going on later in the rut, but they're not going to come in as readily. Early in the rut, you get most of your aggressiveness," Seelye said.

The rut lasts about three weeks, but it's an uneven event with cows in different drainages and mountain ranges coming into heat at different times. As a result, bulls may fill the air with their bugled challenges at every turn in one drainage and yet be silent in the next.

"I'll bugle two or three times with a mouth diaphragm and tube from one area and if I don't get an answer, I'll move three hundred to four hundred yards and try again," Seelye said. "What really worked well for me last year was bugling with a partner. Sometimes a certain call will excite a bull and other times a different call will work. Both of us would bugle maybe seventy-five yards apart. One would bugle and the other would answer. It would excite an elk to think there was two other bulls in the neighborhood.

"My hunting partner had a call that was really a low, deep-sounding bugle, and it seemed to excite this one bull. Then he shut up and I kept calling but by that time, he was excited enough to answer anything," he said. "We moved to him, a little closer. If they feel challenged they seem to come a little more easily than if you're four hundred or five hundred yards away. You get as close as you possibly can without spooking him. It challenges him to defend his harem.

"That tactic worked twice for us last year. Both of them were five-point bulls and we got them both, the first one with a shot at twenty yards and the second one at less than fifteen yards," Seelye said. "That double bugling really works well if you're in an area with a lot of sign, a lot of feed and a lot of rubs. When you have that feeling you're into them but they're not answering, it might be enough to get them interested."

Elk hunting changes with the beginning of the gun season in late October. For most bulls, the passions of the rut are gone and survival and trying to regain poundage lost to the breeding season are their main concerns.

On opening day of the gun season, hunting can be as simple as following up preseason scouting by being at a meadow's edge at dawn and shooting the elk that graze there. It can be knowing where the escape routes are when the opening-day arrival of hunters in elk country push them through traditional passes where the bulls can be ambushed. That early-season approach gradually changes, however, as the bulls get more pressure and move to select hiding places where the hunters can't reach them. Yet hunters in Headwaters Country have an advantage: there are open parks and ridges in most of its mountain ranges and glassing with binoculars or a spotting scope can be an ally in bagging a bull. Just as long as you put in the days to make the system work.

"I like to glass early in the morning, see where the animals are going to bed, and then figure out an approach," said Fillinger, who works several mountainous areas out of his home in Helena. "You have to hunt country you know the elk are in and then put in the time and wait for the two to come together. Seeing an elk and getting a shot are in direct correlation to time. Elk take a lot of time. I've thought that for twenty years. It's a rare instance where a guy can take two or three days and get a shot at them. When I hunt a week or ten days, I know I've got time. They come with persistence."

Fillinger goes to areas he has come to know over the years and lets his binoculars do much of the preliminary work for him. Getting on a high point and panning across the clearings, he can spot grazing elk from a long way off and watch where they disappear into the thick timber to bed down. Then he can go in after them, moving slowly and quietly to hunt them in their beds.

"You have to go in with the wind right and hopefully from above them. I've walked away from them when they're bedded if the conditions are wrong. You'll just spook them. If you don't spook them, they'll probably be there again tomorrow and you can work on them when the conditions are right," Fillinger said. "Most of the time, people try to hurry on them. If you do that, you're going to make a mistake. You have to go slowly. I think another mistake people make in the thick stuff is to not use their binoculars. I use glasses wherever I go. They can triple what you see and force your eyes to see a small area. I have seen animals bedded down with them. Of all the elk I've taken over the last seventeen or eighteen years, I've shot three nice bulls in their beds at less than seventy-five feet. It was strictly because of using binoculars in thick stuff."

As the hunting season progresses, the elk move deeper and deeper into security areas where the hunters are less likely to bother them. In some cases, it's simply a roadless area too far back for most hunters on foot to reach. In other cases, it might be a draw or a canyon that's overlooked in the rush to hunt other areas nearby.

"I sometimes think they hire bears in the summertime to dig holes for them to hide in when the hunting season arrives," Fillinger quipped.

In truth, this part of the season, before the snow arrives, can be the most frustrating of all for the hunter. He knows the elk are somewhere in his chosen patch of mountains, but not exactly where that somewhere is. It's a time for some long, tall walking to locate the hiding places and possibly some research to provide a clue.

"You need some body conditioning," said Vince Yannone, assistant administrator of the Conservation-Education Division for Fish, Wildlife and Parks in Helena. "Hunting is a physical thing. You've got to be in condition to hike and climb mountains. You have to know your physical ability and then find an area where there are elk. You have to learn your area and go there. Most people that screw up, they jump around and jump around and jump around. They don't get to know an area."

Yannone carried that knowledge of an elk area one step further. In addition to his own hikes there in all seasons, he relied on the successes of others to build his expertise on the Elkhorn Mountains near his home.

"Anytime I ever heard of a kill in the Elkhorns, I made a record of it. You have to develop a trend of where the animals are going and what they're doing. You keep a notebook on where an animal was shot, when it was shot and the weather," he said. "I put it on a map. I color-coded my pins. Red were positive where I talked to the guy and got a good location. Green was an animal I had pretty good information on. Yellow was a suspected kill based on third- or fourth-hand information. I took it for six or seven years and I noticed a trend of where the animals were taken. Also, if I wanted to go where there wouldn't be other hunters, I could find those areas, too. Over those years, I had about 120 pins in my map and over half of them were red."

Yannone also put in the time and had the persistence necessary in accumulating his record of sixteen bulls in seventeen years, nearly all of them off public land.

"I followed an elk one time for four days," he said. "I always pack a sleeping bag, stove, and some food and I just told myself this was the bull I wanted so I got a wild hair and kept after him. He was pretty distinctive, a five-by-six that had one brow tine that came down in front of his face. I kicked him out of his bed several times, but he always managed to stay out in front of me. There was a light snow, though, and I could keep track of him. He kept circling within five or six miles of the area where I jumped him and finally, on the fourth day, I headed him off and I caught him out in the open looking down to where I should have been. From where I jumped him to where I shot him was about a half-mile. I saw other animals, other bulls during those four days, but that was the one I wanted."

Knowing an area can also pay off in the late season when snow and cold begin to move elk out of their summer ranges and start the migrations that will carry them to their wintering grounds.

One of the more famous elk migrations in Headwaters Country occurs on the Gallatin where the big bulls will move out of Yellowstone National Park to the low country near the river.

A combination of snow and cold triggers the elk migration to winter ranges. Michael Sample photo.

Each November, Bob Jensen, of Circle, is there to witness the passage as he has over the past eighteen seasons from a high-country camp. Hunting from horseback, he has watched the seasons change from the bluebird early days to the onset of winter.

"I've hunted as many as thirty days in a season in there and it's kind of a split deal," he said. "You have the native elk that are there all summer. They'll be in there the first couple weeks of the season. They'll move out if there's enough pressure. Then you may have a lull. Then you'll have the elk coming in out of Yellowstone. It's a traditional migratory route for those elk and later in the year, you're going to see a lot of elk."

Elk movements are triggered by deepening snows and the onset of subzero cold in the high mountain nights. As Graham Taylor, wildlife biologist for Fish, Wildlife and Parks at Bozeman, puts it, "It's the temperature that's the final straw and makes a difference in beginning the elk moving out of the park. The stage has to be set with the snow, but you've got to have that cold snap."

Jensen feels the horse always gives him a distinct advantage in putting together the pieces of the puzzle that elk often present to a hunter, but a horse is never more valuable than during those final weeks of the season when the migration has begun. "It varies from heavy timber to a lot of high meadow country in the Gallatin and there's a lot of good grass in there. If you're in there with a horse and especially if you've got snow, you can cover a lot more country as daylight breaks and before daylight," he said. "Once the horse knows the trail, you can be four or five miles from camp before light ever breaks. That first hour of daylight is worth the rest of the day on those elk. Elk are an animal that survives by eating. As it gets colder, they'll feed later in the morning. But you still have to catch them out and a horse can cover three or four times the area of a man on foot. Or, if you're hunting the timber, you can take a horse and get to the top of the ridge, have someone else take the horses back and you can hunt down from the top on foot. A horse also gives you another hour of hunting in the evening. If the horse knows where the trail is, he can take you home in the dark.''

Knowing where the elk are going to go, through watching them over the years, is a second piece of the migratory puzzle that Jensen puts to work for him. "If you hunt it steady, you know where they're going to come. They have migratory paths they're going to take. They'll go as low as they can to get over the high ridges,'' he said. "I'd rate knowing an area as worth about everything. Once you know where the elk are going to go, it's just determination after that. But you have to be willing to pace yourself. People tend to hunt harder physically than they're capable of. It takes about four or five days to get used to altitude. If you're going to hunt late when the snow is a foot deep, you've got to pace yourself. If not, the altitude will get you.''

While having a horse, a knowledge of the country, and a snug backcountry camp with a wall tent and warm stove will help a hunter in his quest for a bull, it still takes persistence and with it the puzzle is complete. The year Jensen took his biggest bull, a 10½-year-old six-point with a wide, heavy rack, it came on his seventeenth straight day of elk hunting. As he

An outfitter can provide the equipment to live comfortably in the back-country, even in bad weather. Mark Henckel photo.

put it, "You can see a lot of elk in there, but big bulls are always scarce, no matter where you hunt them. It always takes some time."

While Headwaters Country offers an elk hunter perhaps the most bountiful herd of any part of Montana, don't get the mistaken impression that all parts of this area are created equally or that there aren't any threats to the elk population which annually provides about half the state's total harvest.

"In terms of elk numbers and harvest, it's as good as it has ever been. That's in terms of total animals killed and if that's how you measure goodness, we have good hunting," said Taylor. "We're killing as many or more branch-antlered bulls as we've ever killed on the Gallatin, but the average age is declining. It's a reflection of demand outstripping supply. With the amount of pressure being put on these elk herds, we're right at the edge of seeing some drastic changes taking place."

Those drastic changes have come about because of several factors including increasing hunter pressure, the cumulative effects of logging over the years, more access on logging roads into previously roadless areas and better vehicles at a hunter's disposal to get into areas that were impossible to reach years ago.

"It's no different than pheasants or anything else," said Terry Lonner, wildlife biologist for Fish, Wildlife and Parks in Bozeman. "If you start reducing the cover, the predators are going to get them. In elk, those predators are humans."

The results of those pressures have been a younger and younger harvest on elk in Headwaters Country. "It's something that's been occurring more and more in recent years. Ten years ago, it was around fifty percent of the harvest was spikes. Now it's probably sixty-five percent. In the mid-'50s, it was thirty-five percent. It's slowly going up and up, indicating a high turnover rate among the bulls through hunting."

For the most part, the pressures haven't cut into total numbers of elk. In Fish, Wildlife and Parks Region Three, for example, there was still an actual count of 27,000 elk in 1984 which was regarded as an absolute minimum for the total elk herd there. But if the heavy harvest of mature bulls is allowed to continue, it could begin to affect the breeding potential of the herd.

"The Gravelly-Snowcrest area was one of the first areas to go to a branch-antlered bull regulation because of low productivity in our elk herds," said Howard Chrest, wildlife biologist for Fish, Wildlife and Parks at Sheridan. "We had a real heavy turnover on the bulls because of an open habitat type. We were down to two or three percent bulls, and most of them would be yearlings. Now we've got most of those yearlings surviving. They go into the hunting season as raghorns at 2½ years old. We're finding that gradually some of those animals that get to 2½ seem to do things a little differently than the yearlings. They make it to the winter ranges after the season. It's a slow process, but you're getting a few of them that go into the 3½ and older year classes."

Not all populations have been hit as hard as those in the Gravelly-Snowcrest. "In the Little Belts, our long-range data for the Judith Game Range shows the harvest is about 50 percent spikes, 50 percent branch-antlered bulls," said Dick Bucsis, wildlife biologist for Fish, Wildlife and Parks at White Sulphur Springs. "There's no real evidence that we're down low enough in bulls that it's affecting the quality of the calf crop. But the branch-antlered bulls go to the more rugged areas in the season and they're harder to get. Where there's less vulnerability to the gun is where the better bulls are."

In Headwaters Country, the survival of bigger bulls and their availability to hunters seems to be directly tied to security habitat, with logging and roading the biggest long-term culprits.

"It boils down to slowing down logging," said Lonner. "We have to manage elk from year to year. They manage timber on a hundred-year cycle. In a sense, all this logging in the last forty years has been cumulative in terms of reduction of hiding cover. A forty-year-old clearcut, something that was cut in 1945, maybe is just now coming back to some decent hiding cover. That's something that's been a very subtle change over the years."

The answer has been closing some of the roads that logging has opened to slow the steady influx of hunters into these areas. That won't make the cover grow back any faster and these road-ends do create something of a trailhead effect which invites access, but at least the hunting pressure can be cut to some degree.

"The amount of road closures has increased dramatically and most people are glad to see it," Lonner said. "The best example is on the Beaverhead in the Gravelly-Snowcrest Mountains. People still have to have access, but at one time, you could drive to every square mile. Now, it's to every three to four square miles."

Hunting success requires a mixture of timing, experience, equipment, and environment. Mark Henckel photo.

If those kinds of forced security measures aren't put in force, the animals will certainly find a different, at times more maddening, method to elude hunters. "In the Little Belts, there's so much activity on the forest that the elk have picked up that they can move down lower and get away from people," Bucsis said. "There's been a noticeable change in elk habits over the past five or six years. A lot of elk that are normally in the mountains are not available to the public now. When the shooting starts, instead of finding tracks going up, they're going down to the private land. It's frustrating to the hunters. They've been beating the brush all day up high and drive home and see all these elk lying along the highway on posted land. Elk are very, very adaptable animals. It's where they're not bothered that you'll find them."

The challenge of the future in Headwaters Country will be to protect those security areas for elk while trying to give hunters the greatest opportunity to go after them. While the situation is indeed changing, hunters shouldn't get the impression that the big bulls are gone and that all the security areas have disappeared.

"We're still sitting good in terms of numbers," Lonner said. "But as habitat security starts to decrease because of roads, cover is removed on top of that, and on top of that, you have more hunters, you have to do something in terms of seasons. The main thrust of our future action will be trying to maintain hunter opportunity.

"Elk are the phantoms of the forest. That's the challenge. And that's the way we'd like it to remain for all time."

Whitetails and Mule Deer

Bagging a nice mule deer in Headwaters Country can boil down to a simple matter of timing and knowing where the bucks are at a particular stage of the season. Distribution patterns change as the hunting year moves from the bow season of September through the opening of the general season in October and on to the rut of late November.

"When I was running a check station in Bridger Canyon in 1975, a lot of guys would go up bowhunting and they would see all sorts of deer in September and come back to the same areas in the first week of the rifle season and wouldn't see a track. They'd come back cussing and moaning," said Dave Pac, wildlife biologist with Fish, Wildlife and Parks in Bozeman who has studied mule deer extensively in the Bridger Mountains.

Mountain mule deer have certain summer areas, traditional wintering areas and well-defined migration paths in between. Not every deer in Headwaters Country falls into this category, of course. There are resident mule deer of the foothills and valleys which spend the entire year in the same haunts. And there are whitetails which inhabit the brushy bottoms throughout their lives.

But the mountain mule deer provide a special opportunity for hunters here because they can be counted on to make the same migrations each fall. "A hunter should know as much as he can about these general distribution patterns so he doesn't go into a summer range area where the deer pull out early," Pac said.

The upper edge of the winter range can be a super spot for mule deer bucks late in the season. Michael Sample photo.

Snow is the stimulus that gets the deer moving, but it doesn't have to be an accumulation of several feet. It may just be several inches. Mule deer that must cross a high divide to get from summer areas to winter areas will often move as early as September to insure their seasonal crossings can be made.

"For one that summers on the west side of the Bridgers and winters on the east side, for example, those early snows make them move over the top and stage above the winter ranges," Pac said. "One that summers on the west side and winters on the west side often won't move a lot with those early storms. They basically just move down the hill toward the winter ranges when the snow piles up in late November. If a hunter knows the direction they're moving and when they move, he can go to the areas just above the wintering areas and find good concentrations of deer. If a guy knows what's he's doing, he can use it to his advantage."

Locating the wintering grounds and using them as guides to determine hunting areas in fall is relatively easy for the hunter who spends time outdoors in all seasons. Early spring fishing trips will often turn up concentrations of deer at the edge of the mountains, and these areas can be scouted again in the fall to determine when deer begin arriving. While it may take a season or two to pinpoint the time of arrival, it's certainly easier than trying to key in on the summer areas where deer which migrate to different wintering areas are often mixed.

"In the Bridgers, there are actually seven different population units. Three go to wintering areas on the west slopes and four go to the east side," Pac said. "They'll all pull out of those summer areas at different times, depending on where they're going."

So Pac waits until late in the season, when a combination of snow and cold has moved the deer into position to move onto the winter ranges and the onset of the rut has made the big bucks both active and a bit foolish.

"I go to a winter range that I know and hunt the upper edge in November after we get some cold temperatures and snow and the rut is really on," he said. "You get into the stands of Doug fir and walk really slow. You'll be into a lot of deer and you just let the bucks bump into you. All you have to do is know enough to put yourself in the general area where they're at."

Hunting the rut accounts for most of the big bucks taken in the mountains. But hunters looking for a genuine Boone and Crockett buck should know how tall the odds are against it.

"I'd say the Bridgers are good big buck country. There may be better places in the state but it's certainly better than average," Pac said. "Based on the ones we see in the helicopter survey in fall, we probably look over twelve thousand deer in the Bridgers. Of that, we're looking at two thousand antlered bucks. Out of those two thousand, you're looking at only about three Boone and Crockett bucks, if that. We average eight hundred to a thousand antlered bucks shot in that area each year. We turn them over at a rapid rate. Even if you didn't hunt them, there wouldn't be a great number because they just don't grow that big that often."

Hunting pressure and the ability of the mule deer to escape it are the keys to getting into big bucks in Headwaters Country. In the Dillon area, for example, open terrain and an abundance of roads combine to have an effect on the bucks. "It's generally low security habitat. We get lots of people down here hunting elk and that puts a lot of pressure on the mule deer," said Joel Peterson, wildlife biologist for Fish, Wildlife and Parks at Dillon. "You can drive almost anywhere to a certain degree. There are areas where you can road hunt and it's fairly open. But there are some areas where it's steep, rugged terrain and hunters have to walk. You have to pack back in there and that's where you'll find your larger bucks."

In the Gravelly-Snowcrest Ranges, hunting pressure has also taken its toll. "It's more open, rolling grassland habitat with a lot of access," said Howard Chrest, wildlife biologist for Fish, Wildlife and Parks at Sheridan. "We're looking right now at the age structure in the deer and finding it's declining over the past ten or fifteen years."

The increasing pressure, younger age structure, and the end result of fewer mule deer bucks growing to be trophy class animals has changed the approach of some hunters.

"When I first started hunting, there were all kinds of mule deer. You didn't just go out and shoot a four-point buck, you waited for a big one," said Dave Sorensen, of Harlowton. "I can remember going up with my dad when I was old enough to hunt and there were hundreds of deer on the creek. The big bucks would go up on the mountains during the day and they'd come down to the creeks at night to get the does and we'd intercept them on the way back up in the morning. But there's not very many of them anymore. The whitetails, as far as the trophies, outnumber the mule deer now."

Hunting for big whitetails has increased in popularity over the years, not just in the Harlowton area, but throughout Headwaters Country in places like the bottomlands of the Beaverhead, Jefferson, Madison, Yellowstone, and Missouri Rivers.

"The whitetail seem to be expanding their range. They're definitely in more areas over the past ten to fifteen years. All the major tributaries have whitetails to one degree or another," said Claire Simmons, wildlife biologist for Fish, Wildlife and Parks at Big Timber. "It's tougher hunting and it's tough to get permission to hunt because it's usually on private land, but people are becoming more aware of them."

Hunting tactics vary, but suffice it to say that methods used for mule deer don't work very well on whitetails. "A hunter who just walks through whitetail cover doesn't see ten percent of the deer he is pushing around," Simmons said. "You can hear deer going out in front of you, but you can't see them. And you never see the good bucks. They don't get that big by being dumb."

More productive methods include staging drives, sitting in tree stands, or slowly walking and standing near deer trails.

"Most of the people use drives," Sorensen said. "You get four or five guys and post somebody on the end and drive the deer toward them. The deer are there and they get into that thick cover and you just have to move them out of it. I also hunt the prairie quite a bit for those whitetails. They get pushed out there and nobody else goes out there after them."

Pac prefers to work the deer trails in the bottomlands and take advantage of these travel routes to bag his bucks. "Whitetails are more traditional than mule deer in the sense of using deer trails. They're more predictable in that sense," he said. "I wait for the rut and I do a fair amount of sitting. If you put things together and get between bedding and feeding areas, they'll come to you."

But though a fair amount of mule deer hunting can be had on national forest and BLM lands in Headwaters Country, whitetail hunters almost invariably have to contend with gaining access to private ground first.

"The ranchers will let in a certain few people that they know," Sorensen said. "In this country you know the landowner first."

"It's tough getting permission in the river bottoms around here," echoed Pac.

And Simmons added, "It's definitely tough to get access because of private land, buildings and livestock."

So it's up to the individual to pick his species, pick his hunting time, and pick his area in Headwaters Country. If he's willing to put in the effort to gain access to private land, whitetail hunting can provide a genuine trophy. If he wants to wait for the final weeks of the season and locate a good wintering area, he can take advantage of mountain mule deer migrations and hunt them in the rut.

No matter which species is chosen, Headwaters Country offers some excellent deer hunting opportunities which get better and better the more a hunter learns about the mule deer and whitetails which call this part of Montana home.

Bighorn Sheep

Total the legal take of bighorn sheep allowed from the 300 series unlimited hunting districts and it isn't a very impressive sum, just fourteen rams in the 1984 season. Yet in terms of hunter impact, those four hunting districts are as important as any in the United States.

Anyone who wants to hunt bighorn sheep is assured of getting their chance in Headwaters Country. Michael Sample photo.

Hunting Districts 300, 301, 302, and 303 stretch from the Absaroka Range on the east to the Spanish Peaks and Madison Range on the west. Together, they make up four of the seven unlimited bighorn sheep hunting areas found anywhere in the country today. If a hunter wants to go after bighorns here or in Hunting Districts 500, 501, or 502 further east, all he has to do is apply for a permit. In these areas, the number of permits issued is unlimited, everyone who applies draws one, and the hunt is run until the quota for that district is reached and the season is closed.

"It's the only place in the United States you can hunt bighorn sheep without drawing a special permit," said Jon Swenson, wildlife biologist for Fish, Wildlife and Parks at Livingston. "One thing about having an unlimited sheep hunt is a lot of people hunt it and a lot of people have a stake in it."

Not that the hunting is easy. The unlimited areas, in fact, offer some of the more difficult bighorn sheep hunting to be found in Montana.

"We're dealing with some fairly rugged, physical areas," explained Arnold Foss, regional wildlife manager for Fish, Wildlife and Parks at Bozeman. "They're fairly hard to get to. The odds of you exterminating the older-age males is a slim possibility."

The four hunting districts can be roughly divided into 300 and 303, which rely heavily on sheep based in or near Yellowstone National Park and 301 and 302, which hold resident herds in rugged country. "On both sides of the Yellowstone drainage, we've got sheep moving in and out of Yellowstone Park. In two of our other units, between the Gallatin and Madison, there's no association with the park," Foss said.

While Districts 300 and 303 have populations of resident sheep, it's the migrants out of the park that generally provide the most opportunity for the hunters. "Early in the season, they get into the sheep that are straddling the divide. Then, later in the season, it will be a story of whether the weather brings them out. At the end of the season is just when they're starting to move to the winter areas for the rut, and we close the season to minimize the chance of having a big bunch of rams come out and get wiped out on the way to the winter range," Swenson said. "In 300, getting a ram often depends on what side of the ridge they're on at any particular moment. In 303, the thing that limits the harvest there is the fact they spend so little time out of the park."

In Districts 301 and 302, hunters don't have to rely on such fickle movements but are looking at sheep which have adapted to the pressure of the hunting season. "They've become habituated to the hunting pressure that's in there. They have found some secure pieces of habitat where they can exist and still escape hunters," said Graham Taylor, wildlife biologist for Fish, Wildlife and Parks at Bozeman.

Those survival tactics include using timber much more heavily than bighorns in other parts of Montana where hunting pressure is limited by the luck of the draw. "The sheep use the timber more than anybody would ever guess. They use some heavy timber at high elevations," Taylor said.

"There's more timber hunting than what I thought there was," admitted Foss. "If you go up and watch the sheep in the summer, there are a lot that are in alpine habitat. They're operating at about timberline. But from what I can tell from where hunters get sheep, you've got quite a bit of hunting going on in the timber. When they get some activity up high, the sheep move down to where the alpine meets the timber. It's timber pockets where you're coming out of the alpine. When they're harassed, that timber affords them a lot more protection."

The unlimited nature of the hunt attracts quite a few sheep hunters of all types to this part of Headwaters Country but it's still an equal-opportunity venture in many respects. "We get backpackers in there. We get guys who take in a little camp and pack it on their backs. We get guys who rent a horse or borrow a horse. We have others that go in with outfitters. And we have people who just drive up the Yellowstone and do some glassing every morning," Foss said. "You've got the extremes from the guy who takes his little mountain tent and toughs it out for 15 days to the ones who just drive their cars."

In some parts of the bighorn sheep range, it can also get relatively crowded. But hunters who are willing to go further than the beaten path can still find solitude, according to Taylor. "There are drainages and certain trails that get a lot of hunter use. But if you're willing to bushwhack a little bit and set up a spike camp, you can have a basin to yourself," he said.

In terms of management philosophy, the unlimited districts operate under a different rationale than many of the limited districts where old, old rams are the object of hunting regulations. "The tradition goes back to the hunter," Foss said. "On the Sun River, they're used to seeing a lot of sheep and a lot of big sheep. What you have here is a fairly young male population. In most of our areas, they're 4 1/2 when they're hunted. What we're dealing with is a ram that is legal when a line started at the base of the horn and going through the eye cuts through any portion of the horn. You can get a sheep that's 3 1/2 years old that's a legal ram. But realistically, we've got lots of places where we're shooting bull elk where there aren't a lot of bulls over 2 1/2 years old after the season and we're still surviving. It's tradition in terms of what hunters consider an acceptable animal."

There are some older animals taken, of course, up to 9 1/2 years old, but hunters here are as much interested in the opportunity to hunt as in taking a trophy ram.

"We get as many letters in the fall from sheep hunters as we do for any other type of hunting and they say whatever you do, don't get rid of this unlimited hunt," Foss said. "Even though it doesn't offer much opportunity to get a sheep, it gives them the opportunity to go out and try."

Mountain Goats

Hunters in Montana these days seem to take goats for granted. If there's a tall mountain range nearby, they figure that mountain goats always roamed its high peaks.

In truth, the historic mountain goat range in Montana was severely limited. It's only in recent times that they have been available over a wide area in the state.

"They were primarily on the Continental Divide, the east front of the Rockies, in the Cabinets, the Bitterroots, all the way down to Beaverhead County," said Jon Swenson, wildlife biologist for Fish, Wildlife and Parks in Livingston. "In the Absarokas, Beartooths, Crazies, Bridgers, Snowies, Elkhorns, Spanish Peaks, and the Madison Range, those are all introduced populations."

A transplanting program for mountain goats began in 1941 which spread the species into suitable habitat elsewhere. That opened up new

Transplanting programs have spread mountain goats into many new areas of Montana. Michael Sample photo.

fields of operation for hunters in Headwaters Country and other parts of Montana. But it also set up a boom and bust pattern which is only now beginning to be understood.

The old Crazy Mountains herd, for example, which was among the first of the transplants, provides a lesson that Swenson is trying to avoid with the newer Absaroka Range herd. "They were put into some good habitat in the Crazies, but it was limited," he said. "The population literally exploded and far exceeded the amount of forage. The department came in and hunted them very hard but it was too late because they were already starting down. The population went from over three hundred goats to where now we see about thirty-five goats. We stopped hunting them in about 1976 and they have not changed since then. They have remained stable at about thirty-five since 1976."

In the fragile alpine country that mountain goats call home, the environment recovers slowly and damage to the range can last a long time. "With 20-20 hindsight, we should have started hunting them a lot sooner and we should have hunted them hard to keep them from peaking and crashing," Swenson said. "When you have an alpine range that has been overutilized, it is probably degraded and takes a long, long time for that to turn around. I don't know when we'll hunt goats in the Crazies again."

In the Absarokas, on the other hand, the goat herd is still on the rise and the permit situation has been looking better in recent years as management strategies have increased the harvest to keep it from peaking. "We're trying to reduce the population by twenty-five percent. They're approaching the peak now and we've increased the harvest rate to avoid a peak because we know we're getting close," Swenson said. "We've seen what happens already, so we don't want it to happen again."

Swenson figures the population of mountain goats between 175 and 250 in the Absarokas and knows the herd is a dynamic one. Annual kid production is still high, survival is good, and the herd is moving into new areas. "A native population, you can say, is one that has already crashed. It's not nearly as productive," he said. "If you go out and shoot out an area, it takes a long time for them to come back. Here, if you introduce them into new areas that are very favorable, they expand readily into new areas. They don't scatter right away like bighorn sheep do, but they do colonize new areas. The entire Beartooth and Absaroka was populated with plants in just two areas."

Trying to keep the population below peak levels should mean more hunters in the field in years to come in the Absarokas. But even without that boost, the transplant program begun more than four decades ago has already provided bountiful mountain goat hunting throughout Headwaters Country.

In each new area in this part of Montana, the goats have found good homes in the high country. But even in the most plentiful herds, mountain goat hunters here shouldn't expect to simply head into the mountains and begin bumping into goats wherever they happen to wander.

"You've got to know a little bit about where the goats are, in the first place. In most cases, Fish, Wildlife and Parks people can put you onto a drainage or two," said Claire Simmons, wildlife biologist for Fish, Wildlife and Parks at Big Timber. "In the summer, you'll find them in those high basins, the cirque basins, and on the headwalls. In the winter, those basins fill up with snow and they're forced onto the steep, real rocky south slopes or down into the timber."

Going for goats is no hunting for the faint of heart or the weak of leg and lung. "Our goat seasons open about September 15 and they can be up at 10,000 feet of elevation at that time of year, depending on the snow conditions," Simmons said. "A good spotting scope or a pair of binoculars is important. You spend a lot of time glassing. Even though they're white and you'd expect they'd stand out well, it can be difficult. Early in the season when you may not have snow, they're easier to spot, but a good pair of glasses really helps."

"You pack a camp in and get out where you have a good view and start glassing the meadows and cliffs," added Swenson. "It's almost all in the alpine zone but they sometimes are at tree level."

As in other parts of Montana, hunters should try to key in on the billies in the population while leaving the nannies to tend their present young and provide future kids for the herd.

And hunters should be prepared for the rigors of a high mountain adventure whenever they go into goat country. But if the country is rough and the elevations are tough on the legs and lungs, the hunters should be happy to have goats in there to go after in the first place. Headwaters Country offers an opportunity to go after mountain goats today, that old-timers in this part of Montana never had.

Moose

Historical fact proves that moose hunting was not allowed in Montana for nearly half a century, spanning the years from 1897 until a season was

Wet or boggy areas at the heads of drainages are the best places to find moose. Michael Sample photo.

reopened in 1945. Yet there are still some hunters today who would argue that it never really reopened at all. The elusive moose permit, they say, is just something on the books to lure hunters into sending in their drawing fees, thereby raising more money for the Department of Fish, Wildlife and Parks.

If Fish, Wildlife and Parks really issues moose tags, why is it so hard to find one with your name on it? Why does it often take years and years and years of sending in those drawing fees with no tag coming back in the mail? In fact, some would go so far as to say that the only reason moose are doing so well in Headwaters Country these days is because the moose tags are really a mythical creation of some budget planner. It's the only way they can balance the books in Helena and when inflation begins to worsen again, they'll probably add another line to the application forms that says they're issuing rhinoceros tags, too.

"The odds of getting a moose permit are pretty long," admitted Arnold Foss, regional wildlife manager for Fish, Wildlife and Parks in Bozeman, who went on to explain that the tags really do exist. "At one point in time, there were almost astronomical odds and they're still pretty tough. I never have drawn one. But my son, the first year he was old enough to apply, he got one. That about did me in."

That's the bad news about moose hunting in Headwaters Country, and everywhere else in Montana for that matter. The good news is that if a hunter is among the lucky few to draw one, he stands an excellent chance of getting a moose. "Once you get a moose permit, the hunter success is up to the seventy to seventy-five percent category," Foss said.

This part of Montana is loaded with moose, and the hunting districts which stretch from the Absaroka-Beartooth on the east to the Dillon country on the west do provide good hunting opportunities for them. "We contribute probably sixty percent of the statewide harvest," Foss said. "In our area, we feel we're holding pretty stable in terms of numbers. We've got a pretty intensive management program. We've just about got the permits down to a drainage by drainage basis."

The word "drainage" seems to be the key to finding moose once a hunter has done the hard part of drawing a moose permit. "I look specifically for the drainage ways. If you get a boggy meadow in the head of a drainage, that's a good place to start looking for moose," he said. "They're highly associated with willows and willow bottoms. That doesn't mean they don't get them out in the lodgepole or the timbered areas, but I try to get in the drainages when I'm looking for moose."

Phil Schladweiler, a research biologist for Fish, Wildlife and Parks at Bozeman, found willows to be extremely important to the region's moose population during a study between 1968 and 1974. "Their habitat varies, but they do like the big willow swamps," he said. "They mostly browse but use a lot of forbs in the summertime. Willows are an important food and dogwoods are important. But they can be found anywhere as long as there is forest habitat. They're not up in the goat rocks, but they can use various forest types."

Hunters looking for a bull would be well-advised to take advantage of the early opening of the season, which generally starts on September 15. "The rut is in late September to mid-October and the males are apt to move a fair amount during that time," Schladweiler said. "In Canada, they call them in during the rut a lot but I've never heard of anyone doing that here. Most people around here just hunt near the roads. I don't understand why people go to a lot of effort to get elk but they don't for moose."

Charlie Eustace, regional game manager for Fish, Wildlife and Parks in Billings, turned the tables on this standard moose hunting tactic, however, when he shot his Boone and Crockett bull in 1979. "Our plan on those moose was the same plan we use on elk," he said. "We found the sign of the areas they were using and were there a half-hour before daylight."

Eustace took his bull off the face of the Absaroka-Beartooth Range and followed the rule of thumb to look to the wet areas for his sign. "You don't get the typical lake and lily pad situation in there but they still were at some fairly moist sites," he said. "We could see quite a few areas where they were browsing. There was a lot of moose sign, a lot of moose browsing, you could smell the beasts, but we couldn't run onto them."

Eustace found his way into a likely-looking area the day after the season opened with the help of a flashlight. "We walked in in the dark and when it started to get light, we glassed and there he was. He was coming out of a drainage swale. He was probably four hundred yards away when I shot him and that surprised us. We didn't take it to be quite that far until we got over there. They're a big animal and it's a good thing that moose was big, that's a long ways to shoot."

Eustace's bull had a rack with a fifty-three-inch spread and scored 163 2/8 to earn it a spot in the record book.

"A fellow who gets out there in the earlier part of the season, during the rut, has an advantage," he said. "They're much more visible than later in the year. After the rut is over, they become more solitary. They're really quite a seasonal beast. We've seen them back in some horrendous places."

But don't worry too much about where you'll find the big bulls just yet. There's the little hurdle of drawing the permit to get over first. And even for Headwaters Country, where moose are relatively abundant, those permits with your name on them can be awfully scarce.

Black Bears

Black bears are at something of a crossroads in Headwaters Country. It's not like the bear-rich areas of northwestern Montana where the cover seems endless and the food sources are limitless. Instead, it's a more tenuous existence that the black bears live here, with habitat that's generally more wide open, food supplies which are less dependable, and, just to make things tougher on the bears, hunting pressure which has grown more intensive in recent years.

"We do not have the densities of bears they have in the Northwest," said Jon Swenson, wildlife biologist for Fish, Wildlife and Parks at Livingston. "It's a different kind of hunting, too, where you glass open slopes and stalk bears. They have a lot more cover up there. They don't have the big grassy slopes like we do. And, there are more people discovering that there's a spring hunting opportunity here and outfitters are promoting spring hunting in order to have some clients in spring."

All that has put enough stress on the black bear population in Headwaters Country that moves have been made in recent years to restrict what had been a long season here. In some areas now, the spring hunt has been cut short and the fall season has been delayed until the start of the general big game season.

"In Region Five, it's over eighty percent of the harvest which has been taken in spring by people who are definitely hunting bear," said Claire Simmons, wildlife biologist with Fish, Wildlife and Parks at Big Timber in speaking of his part of Headwaters Country. "The fall harvest is pretty much incidental. A guy that's hunting elk runs onto a bear and shoots it. We don't have that many elk hunters out here so the chances of running into a bear is less. The bears are generally pretty widely dispersed. A guy is pretty lucky to run onto a bear in the fall."

The problem facing black bears in Headwaters Country has been that the take of sows has been increasing over the past decade and the ages of the boars taken has been declining. Considering the low reproductive potential of black bears here, a situation like that which goes on too long can cut too deeply into the population in a hurry and create setbacks which can take many years to remedy.

"In this part of the state, we don't have near the nutritional base they have in the Northwest so we have a lower reproductive rate," Swenson said. "They eat a lot of pine nuts here in the fall and that's a variable food source compared to the big berry crops up there."

"A lot of it has to do with the condition of the animal," Simmons agreed. "A lot of the bears around here aren't reproductively active until their fifth spring. Alternate year breeding is common in most bear populations but here and in western Montana, they don't produce but maybe every third year. The reproductive potential of bear isn't like deer or elk, the average production per year is pretty low. The fact hunters weren't killing as many big males, males seven or eight years old or older, made us believe we were hitting that bear population quite hard."

Cutting back on the seasons really hasn't hurt the hunter looking for the big old boars, however. The seasonal patterns of their movements just insure that it's generally the older boars that will be taken while the younger boars and sows will be less likely targets.

"The boars apparently come out the earliest in spring," Simmons said. "They might come out of their dens from early to late April. Sub-adults, both males and females, are generally the next ones out and females with cubs are the last to emerge and that may not be until early May or even mid-May except in the very, very high country."

During that spring season, hunters can find them by glassing the big open slopes where black bears will be out grazing on the newly-sprouted grass. "Well through the month of June, vegetation of one sort or another is going to make up the bulk of the diet," Simmons said. "In this part of the state, any place you would expect to find elk in the spring is a good place to look for them. An area that greens up early and is providing a lot of good, lush forage is an area that's going to be attractive to a bear.

"As for their fur, most of your bears are going to be in good shape through May," Simmons added. "From early June on, a hunter should look at a bear fairly closely because they're going to start rubbing and their hide won't be as good."

Hunters out in the general big game season in fall are also more likely to run into a boar because the bears have generally moved into the high country by that time and have begun their progression toward hibernation which will carry them through the winter. "In early fall was when the bears would come down into the creek bottoms and the berry patches along creeks," Swenson said. "During that period, the females were much more vulnerable to being killed. Later, you can still find some in the chokecherry patches but a lot of them will be pretty high in the whitebark pine nuts. Finally, they'll be getting into the heavier timber and on the north slopes looking for places to den up." Generally speaking, they'll move back into the dens in reverse order of how they came out, with the pregnant females going in first and the big boars denning up last.

In both spring and fall, hunters can expect the bears to be active at most any time of day. "When you get into May and June, you're probably going to have a better chance at seeing more bears in the early morning and evening, but I suspect they do a lot of feeding all day long," Simmons said. "A bear is interested in filling his stomach all the time. I know that's the case in the fall when they're really putting on that weight. You can see bears out in the middle of the day. They may be there at any time when they find a food source."

But hunters looking for a really big black bears will have to look further than Headwaters Country. In fact, they'll have to look further than Montana.

"Pennsylvania has the heaviest bears in the country," Swenson said. "They have cubs that den up in the fall that are a hundred pounds. They get six hundred-pound males. The females there breed a lot earlier, they have larger litter sizes, and they breed more often. In Montana, the average-size sow is a hundred twenty to a hundred fifty pounds. A big sow would be two hundred pounds in the fall. In spring, a big boar is two hundred fifty pounds and a very nice adult black bear male in fall is three hundred fifty pounds. They're not big bears at all."

But they've certainly been big with the hunters in recent years. Perhaps too big. With black bears at a crossroads of hunter pressure and population stress, it's likely that the seasons will be fine-tuned again in the near future in Headwaters Country to protect the species here. "We've looked at the relationship between hunter effort and hunter harvest and found increasing effort, lower harvest and the average age of the black bears taken has been declining," Swenson said. "It's still good black bear hunting, but you can sustain less exploitation here because of the country they live in. And we've simply had to restrict our seasons because of that."

Upland Birds and Waterfowl

The early mornings of September are a special time in the mountains of Headwaters Country. It's the time of year when the hardwood leaves are turning from green to gold, when there's a dusting of frost on the grass and when the first seasons of fall beckon a hunter away from the fishing rods and garden tools of summer and carry him back to the high country.

The upland bird and archery big game seasons are the traditional first openers for hunters in Montana. And though the camouflage suit and compound bow may be the lure for many, there's a growing legion which prefers instead to try their hand at mountain grouse with a bird dog out in front of them and a shotgun cradled in their arms.

Bob Eng, director of the Fish and Wildlife Program at Montana State University in Bozeman, is among the hunters who look forward to those days in September when blue grouse beckon. Over the years, many of these mountain grouse have fallen to his 20-gauge and his methods are well worth mentioning in any hunting guide to Montana.

"You can find blues throughout this whole district," he said. "I hunt them by starting out at the bottom and walking up the ridges until you find them. You may find them high, you may find them low."

Blue grouse are among the rare creatures of this earth that actually move up the mountain with the onset of winter and come down again to raise their young in the lowlands in spring and summer. "The migration isn't all that consistent," Eng said. "It's tied to the vegetation and the berry crop. Usually, if you find some low, you can depend on some others being there, particularly if it's hens and young. The single birds will be the cocks. They never come down as far. They come about halfway down the mountain. They breed there and then start moving up."

Food habits of blue grouse can be varied in the fall, depending on the availability of individual favorites. They'll take berries, particularly snowberry and bearberry. They'll feed on clover as well. And, if the frost hasn't gotten to the grasshoppers yet, these too will go into the birds' daily diet.

"You quite often will hunt them around the edges of clearings and the hens and broods will be working the grasshoppers," Eng said. "That's the only time you can catch them dead to rights, when they're out away from the timber. If you're shooting them up in the mountains, nine out of ten

Blue grouse can be found at the edges of clearings in September, feeding on berries or grasshoppers. Michael Sample photo.

times, they'll be along the edge of the ridge and fly downhill which means you've got to put the lead underneath them, something which is hard to do. Normally, you're shooting at a flushing bird which is rising which means you're shooting above them."

It's on those downhill flushes that Eng's golden retriever comes into play. "When they're flying downhill, you'll hit them and they'll roll for fifty yards," he said. "I just use the dog mostly for retrieving."

The heads of drainages are other good places to look for blue grouse, especially if there's some water or moist areas to be found there.

While the mountain grouse season runs through the end of the big game season in late November, the best hunting is to be had before the snow flies. "Once you get snow, they take to the trees and they're tougher," Eng said. "They're hard to flush. You can't work them with a dog. They'll sit real tight. And they'll start switching to their winter diet which is conifer needles. The birds, before they go into the conifers, are as good as anything when it comes to eating, but when they start on the conifer needles, they get a little resinous."

By that time of the season, most hunters have moved on to something else whether it's pheasants and ducks for the shotgunners or deer and elk for the riflemen. Even before the switch, grouse hunting in Headwaters Country remains an activity with a limited following.

"There's a fair amount of bird hunting on opening day, but they don't get a lot of pressure after that," said Joel Peterson, wildlife biologist for Fish, Wildlife and Parks in Dillon. "Some people drive mountain roads for them. A lot of people walk open ridges. But the interest after opening day is pretty limited."

There are other bird species to be had in Headwaters Country besides blue grouse, of course.

"There's a fair number of spruce grouse in the Big Hole and adjacent areas," Peterson said. "They're pretty habitat specific, though. They're into more heavily timbered country."

"There are some pheasants through all these valleys, but it's very spotty," Eng said. "Usually you don't have the good food and cover together in most areas.

"And there are some ruffed grouse scattered wherever you've got aspen draws," he added. "There are some people that shoot a few but there are very few people that go out selectively for ruffs."

There are also sage grouse south of Dillon and in the Centennial Valley which are available early in the season. "It isn't a bad population of sage grouse, but it's spotty," Eng said. "But the elevation is really too high for them. They probably migrate thirty or forty miles out into Idaho during the winter. There are some banding records to show that."

As a hunter heads toward the eastern end of Headwaters Country, prairie grouse species like sage grouse and sharptails increasingly come into play in a bird hunter's season. And, there are those wonderful speedsters, the Hungarian partridge.

Ben Williams, of Livingston, describes himself as a Hun hunter first, then a school teacher, and has racked up figures on the species over the past twenty-five years that few other hunters could match anywhere.

"I shoot more Huns than anyone else in Montana," he stated flatly. "The best year I had was two hundred. I average a hundred forty to a hundred fifty Huns a year. I have my Hun hunting coveys marked that I hunt year after year after year. I can almost tell you exactly where they're going before they get up."

Williams doesn't key in on the stubble fields, however, like many other hunters do. "I hunt in the prairie country. Ninety percent of my hunting is on good rangeland, cattle land," he said. "As long as the land isn't overgrazed, you have some good grazing practices and forbs for the birds, it will produce. Water isn't extremely important but brushy areas are good.

"It's wide country and I cover lots of miles. On a slow day, I'll cover six miles. On a good day, twelve," he added. "I have a kennelful of Brittany spaniels and I usually hunt with four of them and my dogs hunt very, very wide also. On a good cast, I'll get them out a quarter of a mile."

Williams picks up sharptails on his Hun hunts as well. "If it's a good sharptail year, you can predict where the sharptails will be. They'll be around those dancing grounds they use in spring. In a poor year, you really have to work for them."

But despite his successes on sharptails and his trips eastward to go after pheasants, Huns remain his passion. "Huns are super for pointing dogs even though they don't hold as well as quail unless you break the coveys up," Williams said. "They make you walk a long ways but they're the toughest upland bird a hunter can go after in Montana. I'm a Hun hunter like other guys are sheep hunters."

Just as there is a small cadre of dedicated upland bird hunters which revels in the grouse seasons of September, there is a group that keys in on the waterfowl hunts of October through December. In many parts of

Ruffed grouse can be found in the aspen draws of the mountains of Headwaters Country. Frank Martin photo.

Headwaters Country, gunning is limited to jumpshooting on the creeks or setting decoys in the spring ponds or sloughs along the big rivers. But the public land waterfowl hunter got a big boost when the Canyon Ferry Wildlife Management Area came into being in the early 1970s.

Spawned by a dust abatement project on the south end of Canyon Ferry Reservoir, it provided a series of dikes, ponds, and islands which have been developed into waterfowl nesting habitat in the years since then.

"We're looking at about two thousand acres inside the dike system in terms of development for waterfowl and an additional five thousand acres of uplands which offers pheasant and white-tailed deer hunting," said Jeff Herbert, wildlife biologist for Fish, Wildlife and Parks at Townsend. "As far as work on the waterfowl is concerned, the greatest results to date have been on Canada geese but it's going to provide more of a duck area as time goes on."

The limitation has been nesting cover and geese seem to be more willing to nest in open sites than the ducks are. But even if the area never develops into a top-notch duck production area, hunters will be more than satisfied with the number of goslings reared there.

Canada geese have benefitted from island-building on the south end of Canyon Ferry Reservoir. Michael Sample photo.

"We've gone from zero nests in 1973 to two hundred active nests on that pond system in 1984," Herbert said. "We're over one thousand goslings a year at the time of hatching. We're shooting more and more geese locally each year. You're talking about everything from pits in the fields to island shooting over decoys. Then you throw in the opening weekend shooter who sits on a fenceline and pass shoots over the willows and you've got the full range."

Herbert feels that the duck production will begin to come around as cover improves. "We're primarily raising mallards right now," he said. "There have been mallards, some gadwall, pintail, and teal, and redheads have been the first diver. We also released some young bluebills there last year to get that species started."

It's the kind of program which should do more than just improve hunting at Canyon Ferry. It can be expected to bolster the duck and goose flight throughout the drainages to the south as well, and provide the nucleus for goose nesting in other suitable sites in the Missouri River valley.

The boost in waterfowl hunting in the years to come should contribute to making already good shotgun hunting country even better. From the blue grouse and Huns of September through the duck blinds of December, Headwaters Country offers as much action as any wingshooter could handle, and as much variety as there is to be found anywhere in Montana.

Tall Timber Country

Tall Timber Country can't boast the tallest peaks in Montana, but they are pretty tall. It doesn't hold the thickest forests, but they are pretty thick. And it can't lay claim to the most public land in the state, but there is a lot of it.

Rather than claiming the tallest, thickest and most, it's in the mixture of these ingredients that Tall Timber Country takes on a personality all its own. Its mountain country offers something of a blend of the more open peaks found further to the east and the thick timber which is the rule in northwestern Montana. In this transition zone which takes a hunter from the big mountain meadows of southcentral Montana to the brink of the Pacific Northwest rain forest, there is an opportunity for the hunter to find the type of country and type of hunting of his dreams.

There are vast tracts of unbroken mountain timber which is too steep to log and forms a dense black forest for the hunter on foot. These thick stands provide some excellent habitat for elk. But there are other places where logging and logging roads have made access too good and some roads must be closed to provide security for elk.

To find out how rugged this country can get, just ask anyone who has driven over Skalkaho Pass between Rock Creek and the Bitterroot Valley and let them tell you about a road clinging to the side of the mountain for mile after white-knuckled mile. Or simply talk to the mountain goat hunters who can converse with the clouds as long as they keep one eye on their footing while they're doing the talking.

Tall Timber Country has bighorn sheep herds, both old and new, and good moose numbers which prompt hunters to test their fates in the special permit drawings each summer.

Historically, it was good big buck country for mule deer, too, and white-tailed deer are on the rise in the valleys. It had pheasants in the lowlands which have faced some tough times in recent years and waterfowl hunting which seems to be enjoying a rebirth.

In short, Tall Timber Country is a prime area for the mountain hunter where access for species like elk, mule deer, bighorn sheep, moose, mountain goat, and mountain grouse isn't much of a problem. And it's country where a hunter who can gain access to private ground in the valleys can add white-tailed deer, pheasants, and waterfowl to his hunting plans.

You can find them all here, just as long as you can get lucky in the draw, scale the high peaks, climb the steep slopes, hike the dark timber, gain access to the bottomlands, and find the time to do it all. That's a mighty tall order for any hunter anywhere, but a taller one yet in Tall Timber Country.

Elk

When the first gunshots boom through the mountains of Tall Timber Country on opening morning, elk hunting quickly becomes a game of trying to think like an elk. Up to that point, the elk are relatively easy to find as they feed in the open parks and meadows. But all that's changed now and the elk will rely more heavily on the thick timber to elude people packing guns.

The open parks and meadows where lush grass has provided feed during the weeks and months before the season are still important. But hunters will find that they're used far more secretively. It's in the timber where elk will spend most of their daylight hours, and unless a hunter heads in there after them, his chances of downing a bull will diminish considerably.

"During the hunting season, they won't come out in the open very frequently if they've been pressured," said Mick Iten, of Hamilton, a lifelong resident of the Bitterroot Valley. "If you just look at the open parks, they're usually sterile. The first activity of the hunting season and they're gone."

Iten bags a bull every year by heading into the brush after them, finding the high security areas where elk will hide until snow forces them out of their hideaways and into the low country late in the season.

"I'm a brush hunter," Iten said. "I like to get in where you can't see very far and get up on them. I don't hunt bad deadfall. But I like to hunt the alder and thick lodgepole. It's something the average human doesn't like. When I'm in the brush, I never run into a hunter or a hunter's track or a sign of a hunter.

"There's one place I hunt where people hunt all around it. It's a half-mile long and quarter-mile wide and it's thick and the elk are in there all the time," he said. "It's steep, rocky and undesirable to walk in. It's too thick. But if you're looking for a mature bull, that's where to look."

Not that the open parks and meadows are abandoned entirely. Larry Clark, a guide living on Rock Creek near Philipsburg, said the elk are still tied to them because they provide the grass these big grazers need to survive while grass in the timber is harder to come by. You have to get there at the right time, however, if you're going to catch elk out in the open.

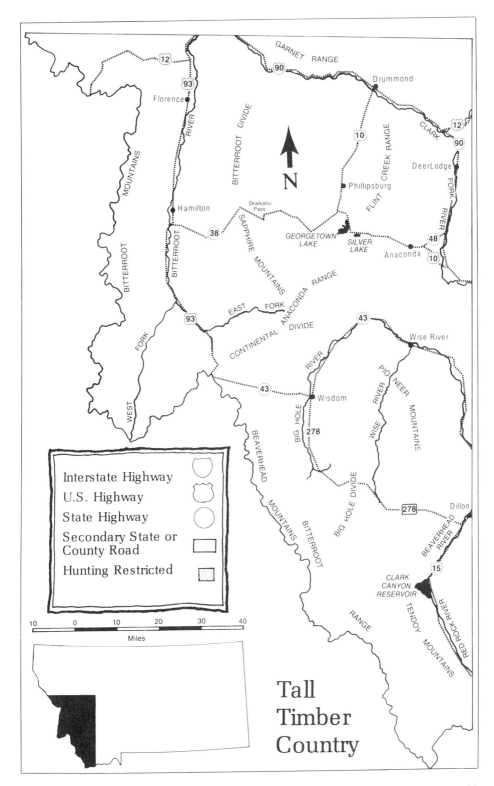

Tall
Timber
Country

Elk are still tied to the open parks in hunting season, but become more wary and secretive. Michael Sample photo.

"You can go through these parks day-in, day-out, and there's always fresh tracks in them," Clark said. "They pass through them every night. They know where they can get a bellyful of feed. They feed in the timber, too, but it's not as good as the parks. You hike in there early with flashlights and try to be there right at daylight. Quite often, we catch them in the open.

"These parks and meadows are not all that big, two or three acres to twenty-five to thirty acres in size, and they're almost all surrounded by timber," he added. "These animals will move two to three miles from these parks to an area where they bed. You'll get on a set of tracks and follow them that far."

But once again, if you don't catch them out in the open at first light, you're bound to go after them in the timber. "Probably eighty percent of our hunting is in timber," Clark said.

Hunting elk in the timber takes some specialized techniques and the ability to move slowly, v-e-r-y s-l-o-w-l-y, and quietly, v-e-r-y q-u-i-e-t-l-y, through the country the bulls call home.

"I like to hunt the timber, to me it's real challenging," said Lyn Nielsen, wildlife biologist for Fish, Wildlife and Parks at Deer Lodge. "But most people don't know how to hunt the timber. They're just flat too noisy. They stumble over the logs and brush. They just aren't ready. Good timber hunters don't cover very much country. They move real slow, look through binoculars constantly and can pick out a patch of elk hair in the trees."

Iten and Clark also emphasized the need to move slowly, and the difficulty of doing battle with bulls on their own turf, on their own terms. "Elk don't have a tendency to stand around long enough for you to get a shot at them. There's many times I feel I could successfully kill an elk and one of my hunters doesn't have a chance," Clark said. Added Iten, "If they're bedded down, you have to be pretty lucky and pretty sneaky to get up on a bull. And if you jump them, a trophy hunter often doesn't have the time to see if it's an eight-point or a two-point."

While snap-shooting at a fleeing bull or busting them in their beds are two possible methods to take them in the timber, Nielsen has a different approach which has proven to be very successful over the years.

"To me, once you know how to hunt elk, you can get almost every elk you jump," he said. "Most people say that they jumped elk out of their beds and trailed them for five miles. But that's very rare. Normally, every elk you jump won't go over a quarter-mile before they stop. They'll get up and go, usually a few hundred yards, then they'll get on a vantage point and stare back down their tracks. The very slightest movement on their back trail and they're just gone."

The tendency of most hunters is to immediately follow the tracks of the just-jumped elk in hopes of catching up with him. But that plays right into the defenses of the elk watching his trail and the hunter isn't likely to see the bull again.

"What you have to do is sit down a minimum of a half-hour. Just sit there," Nielsen said. "Then the trick is figuring out where the elk went and where they stopped. Usually, it's three hundred yards and maybe four hundred yards. You absolutely cannot go on the tracks. You have to make a big half-circle and come back in to where you guess he went. You come in from at least ninety degrees off where he's looking. If you're quiet, you'll see him standing there, staring back at his tracks."

Knowledge of the country you're hunting helps in situations like these. Having jumped elk there before and knowing their likely escape routes is valuable information to have. But there are some common tendencies among elk when they're jumped, and even in a new hunting area, there are some clues to where the elk will be.

"It's usually after they've gone through some open country and where it gets thick again, that's where they'll stop," Nielsen said. "They'll go over a ridge and stop, especially where they'll have a good vantage point looking back. You'll probably get to the point where you think the elk are, about an hour after you jump them. I've had several instances where they were just standing there a good hour after they've been jumped. Occasionally, they're bedded down looking back at their tracks. For thick timber elk, ones that are bedded, it's ninety percent odds you can get it if you do it this way."

There are some prerequisites to Nielsen's method. One of them is to have quiet walking conditions. Another is a sharp pair of eyes to see the elk standing there. There is also a great need for patience. And a hunter has to be able to find the bedded elk in the first place.

"I cover a lot of country until I jump a bull," he said. "Then I hunt them the fun way. Every year it works if the walking conditions are right."

It's understandable why the elk are found in these areas of dense brush and timber. They are the high security areas where few hunters go. But security is becoming more of a problem for elk in Tall Timber Country as more and more logging roads are punched into previously roadless areas.

"I started hunting elk in the Bitterroot back in the 1950s and there wasn't the roads in there," said Frank Tanner, of Corvallis. "They've done a lot of clear-cutting over there and that made it so people could get into the elk." That has changed the complexion of elk hunting, not just here, but in other parts of Tall Timber Country as well.

"Back then, there wasn't the roads in there. You'd drive as far as you could, but then you had to get out and go after them on foot. You had to hunt them. You couldn't road-hunt them. You tracked your elk, went after them and hunted them all day," Tanner said. "Now, there are more people hunting them, too. We could go out and hunt all day and never see more than one or two guys.

"You'd hunt along a ridge and there would be some open meadows where they came out and fed. If somebody got to chasing them, they'd be right in the lodgepole. Then you might as well leave them alone. If they're in the lodgepole, you've got to earn them. I've earned them," he said.

It's the higher hunter numbers in combination with the increase in logging roads and clear-cuts which have changed the situation over the years. Hunters have to hit the timber more these days to get an elk and game managers have to worry about preserving areas for the elk to hide when they're pushed.

"We have quite an access problem," said John Firebaugh, regional wildlife manager for Fish, Wildlife and Parks at Missoula. "There are a lot of roads. We figure seventy-eight percent of the region is within one mile of some type of road. Hunters are getting into these more remote, previously roadless, security areas."

As a result, road closures have been necessary to give the elk someplace to get out of the reach of hunters. It's also meant that seasons which used to offer either-sex opportunities have gone to bulls-only status on general licenses, with cow permits available to control the kill on that segment of the herd.

"We have a little more security than some regions. We have heavy timber, steep terrain. There is some fair security left for big bulls. But we're seeing a trend to more smaller bulls in the harvest. This relates to fewer security areas," Firebaugh said.

Big kills can also be counted on in the years when snow cooperates with hunters and moves the elk out of their timbered sanctuaries and within reach of waiting guns. "Snow makes quite a difference," he said. "The majority of our elk are migratory, particularly in the Bitterroot. You get dry years that don't have much snow and the elk harvest is practically nil. You get a good snow year and they really get into them."

Nielsen said the best time to catch the elk out in the open is right after a big snowstorm. "Snow is one of the most critical factors for getting elk for the average hunter. If the hunter doesn't have good snow conditions, the hunters don't get too many elk in this part of the country," he said. "Snow conditions have to be right. To me, the ideal time to hunt elk is if it's storming for two days and it clears off in the middle of the night. You want to be hunting the parks the next morning. Even until 9 a.m., they'll be out in the parks."

But the consistent method for locating elk still rests in the timber, work-

After being jumped, elk may move through some open areas before stopping to check their back trail. Mark Henckel photo.

ing through thick cover slowly and quietly. It's not the easiest elk hunting to be found in Montana, but it can be the most productive year-in and year-out in Tall Timber Country. All a hunter needs is plenty of patience and the courage to go into areas where other hunters rarely dare to tread.

"There's a lot of this country that's rugged and rough that the hunters just don't go into," Clark said. "But the elk go there when they're pressured and there are a lot of areas that still have some good bulls."

As Iten put it, "If you want that out of hunting, you go in there—the thicker, nastier, remote areas. It's that simple. A mature bull? That's where they're at."

Whitetails and Mule Deer

Jim Gransbery can remember the big mule deer buck vividly despite the fact it fell to him more than two decades ago. It was in the Big Hole country late in the season and as an Anaconda teen, he had gone out early that day with his cousin.

"The time I killed that big buck was the morning after a big storm. There was fresh snow and the morning was bright, crystal clear and cold," said Gransbery. "My cousin Red and I were in snow up to our knees. We cut his tracks and followed him for about a mile. It was in real thick timber and steep so it was very slow going. Then he stepped out from behind a tree and I nailed him."

The shot was only about fifty yards but the sight of that five-point mule deer buck with a heavy rack and spread of twenty-seven inches is still with him. It's a memory which he brings back each fall. Though he lives in Billings now, he goes back to the Big Hole country when hunting season beckons, to hunt once again with his brothers and friends. While he hasn't stopped looking for a bigger buck, Gransbery said mule deer hunting isn't what it used to be.

"There used to be some big deer in there. I don't think you'll see the size of the big bucks anymore," he said. "It could be there are more deer, but I don't think there are as many big deer anymore."

The same thing could be said of mule deer hunting throughout Tall Timber Country. Hunting pressure, even though it's often indirect hunting pressure, has hurt them. So has increased access through abundant logging roads which have cut into the security areas for the deer and allowed people to road hunt for them.

"It's mostly hunters driving nowadays," Gransbery said. "To hunt elk, people will get out and walk. But they drive for deer. My own personal feeling is that deer hunting in the Big Hole is also mostly secondary and accidental. When you're hunting up in the Big Hole, you're looking for elk and you just pick up deer along the way."

Because of the easy access and increased hunting in recent years, it shouldn't be surprising that the best bucks will be found beyond where the road ends. "I would try to find areas that have good, sound road closures in them," said Kurt Alt, wildlife biologist with Fish, Wildlife and Parks in Missoula. "We've got a fair number of road closures. Get a mile or a couple miles from the end of that road then get down off the top of the ridges and hunt the upper two-thirds of the slopes."

The best bucks in Tall Timber Country are found a few miles beyond the end of the road. Michael Sample photo.

Alt said hunting pressure has cut into the number of big bucks available in some areas. "With the access and the openness, they hit some of the old bucks pretty heavily," he said. "These road closures have helped improve the age structure of our bucks." Alt added that trophy bucks are hard to come by here, but there are some good bucks to be found. "You're not going to get the real big bucks, but you do get a chance at nice four-points."

While mule deer can be taken throughout the season, the best hunting for the big bucks undoubtedly comes in the final weeks when the rut and ever-deepening snows in the high country combine to push deer within the reach of hunters' guns.

"Snow is pretty important in terms of pushing those deer down that are migratory. It does push them into more accessible country where the hunters are," said John Firebaugh, regional wildlife manager for Fish, Wildlife and Parks in Missoula.

"Snow pushes them right down," added Gransbery, in speaking of the Big Hole. "Snow in the Big Hole gets mighty deep, pretty quick."

Muleys still provide the bulk of the deer hunting opportunities in this part of Montana, but whitetails seem to be on the rise. "It's been running about two-thirds mule deer," said Firebaugh. "But over the last few years, I think it's been running a little more to whitetails. They're found pretty much in the riparian habitats along the creek and river bottoms, but it has been increasing up into the foothill type of habitat. It may be a response to the increase in the population. They saturate these core areas and we see the spill-over into these more marginal areas."

One hunter who became a whitetail specialist even before the current upsurge in their numbers is Gene Wensel, a Hamilton bowhunter who has written a book on the finer points of his methods entitled *Hunting Rutting Whitetails*.

"I respect them more than any other big game animal in America," he said. "There are a lot of guys in Montana who are elk-oriented or are mule deer-related, but on a nationwide basis, the whitetail is the most popular because it's the most civilized big game animal in that they can adapt to man and coexist with them."

Wensel has hunted trophy-class whitetails throughout the U.S., has a number of them in the Pope and Young Record Book and has logged countless hours studying them in Montana. As he put it, "I spent more time in one year studying white-tailed deer than most guys do in a lifetime. It's not just the hunting season for me, it's a 365-days-a-year thing. At one point in my life, all I did was study white-tailed deer. They're just a fascinating animal."

He has learned how the trophy bucks move ("The biggest bucks won't follow the runs, they'll go parallel to the runs"). He discovered how they rely on other deer to protect themselves ("They'll use other deer as decoys. If anything spooks those other deer, you won't see the big ones"). And he knows the big old bucks are in a different league than the does and smaller bucks ("I classify the big buck as a whole different species than other whitetails. If you go out and hunt normal-size deer, you're doing exactly the opposite of what you should do for big whitetails").

With his twin brother, Barry, who lives in Whitefish, Wensel scouts and studies whitetails in the off-season and hunts as long as there's an unfilled tag in his pocket. But one of his favorite times to hunt big whitetails is in

Big whitetail bucks should be treated as an entirely different species of deer. Frank Martin photo.

the rut and one of his favorite methods is rattling antlers to bring them within bow range, a technique that is popular in other parts of the country but rarely used in Montana.

"Rattling works super," Wensel said. "It's no different than calling elk, calling turkeys or calling coyotes. Sometimes it works; sometimes it doesn't. But between the 12th and the 16th of November last year, we rattled in at least thirty bucks. Some we rattled in more than once, so it was probably fifty sightings. On the 17th, 18th, 19th and 20th, you could still rattle in deer, but they were younger, up to 3 1/2 years old. The big bucks all had does."

The rattling simulates two whitetail bucks fighting and other bucks will come in to check out the action. "The best place to rattle is where you know the deer are moving. You want to get in a rutting area," Wensel said. "Get on a stand before daylight and then let things settle down, wait an hour. In the evening, get in an area where you know they're moving and wait a while before you start.

"Everybody does the rattling different. You can lay six sets of rattling horns out and every set will sound differently. The tone isn't that important as long as the antlers are hard and not bleached out, just good, hard, fairly fresh antlers. Other than fire or theft, they'll last forever," Wensel said.

"It doesn't matter how you hold the antlers. The first thing is to make as much noise as you can. The initial thing is, I want them to hear me. I take it for granted the deer is quite a ways off. I smash them together as hard as I can, mesh them together, just pretend that two bucks are fighting. I stomp my feet and rake them up and down a tree. Just picture for yourself all the noise that's going on when two deer are fighting. I go as loud as I can for probably forty-five seconds to a minute. Then I'll stop, hang up the antlers. I've had deer run right in then, but for the most part, they won't come in until the second sequence," he said. "After two minutes, I'll rattle again, mesh them together. In the second sequence, you want them to get a line on you. Then wait and watch for five to seven minutes. On the third sequence, rub the beading down at the bottom and tickle the tines for fifteen or twenty seconds. Then hang them up quietly because the deer are going to be close."

Wensel said the bucks will pinpoint the sound and move in on it. Because of that fact, as soon as he sees a buck, he'll quit the rattling and wait for the buck to come closer.

"If the timing is right and there's competition between mature bucks, it can be great. The biggest bucks will try to circle," he said. "If you've got a buddy with you, have one do the rattling and have the shooter get twenty-five or thirty yards downwind. The bigger bucks will circle downwind from the rattling."

Wensel uses other hunting methods including drives, stands near primary scrapes, and morning and evening tree stands near trails, but none of them provide the excitement of rattling. "The ideal time is just a few days before the peak of the rut. Some bucks will walk directly in, some will come in downwind. Sometimes, they'll run in," he said. "But I hunt them a lot of different ways. As long as I have a tag and there's a season open, I'm going to be hunting."

With whitetail numbers on the rise in Tall Timber Country and in other parts of the Treasure State as well, it's a certainty that methods to hunt them will become more refined in the years to come and more hunters will become attuned to what Wensel already has accomplished successfully. It's also worth a bet that while this part of Montana still holds some fine mule deer bucks, the true trophy hunter will begin to concentrate more of his time on whitetails simply because the wise old bucks can withstand more hunting pressure and closer association with man.

But no matter which way a hunter decides to go, Tall Timber Country offers some good opportunities for both whitetails and mule deer. And for either species, there's no better time than late in the season when the first snows of winter and the coming of the rut can combine to put a big set of antlers in your sights and plenty of venison in your freezer.

Bighorn Sheep

Bighorn sheep hunting is more than just filling tags. It's where a hunter chooses to wander, when he decides to pursue them, and how much time he is willing to put in at the game.

For some, it's the experience of hiking the high country in autumn, panning binoculars across broad vistas and living, even if just for a time, in the company of bighorn sheep. At least, that's the way Jim Ford views it.

Ford, regional supervisor for Fish, Wildlife and Parks in Missoula, believes that if you're going to hunt bighorn sheep, you should do it on their terms. "I like to hunt early in the season," he said. "When you're talking about hunting them late, it's down on the winter range and it's like shooting them off the road. I don't like that. I don't think it's a quality experience. The sheep is an animal that deserves better."

Ford prefers to go after them in the high meadows, and Tall Timber Country offers some hunting districts to do it in. "I like to hunt them back in the high meadows and cirques. They summer way back up in the mountains," he said. "You spend lots and lots of time glassing. You'll find them where they have water and feed and some escape cover. It's tough the way I hunt sheep. The last permit I had in Montana was up on the Sun River and I spent thirty-one days hunting sheep," he said. "I never did shoot one but I saw a hundred and six legal rams. I was looking for a real good ram."

His drive to get "a real good ram" is understandable. Not only is it every true sheep hunter's dream, but he figures that with two rams to his credit already, it's the challenge of going for the big ram that's as rewarding as bringing one home.

These days in Montana, the best rams are coming from the herds with either the most diverse breeding potential or from the transplanted herds which are experiencing new vigor on their new home ranges. One perfect example of the latter is the Rock Creek herd. The area once held a herd that underwent periodic die-offs until the late 1960s when remnants remained.

"There was an old native herd on Rock Creek," explained Lyn Nielsen, wildlife biologist for Fish, Wildlife and Parks at Deer Lodge. "One of the landowners said he felt there was one ram left when they made the plant. But they had real small horn growth. They had real small body size."

That changed when bighorns were reintroduced into Rock Creek in 1975 with the release of twenty-nine head from the Sun River herd. In the years since then, the Rock Creek sheep have thrived. "It has to be nutrition. It has to be good nutrition for sheep," said Nielsen. "These are sheep from another range that doesn't have as good horn growth as we have. We just ran blood profiles on sheep we transplanted from here. It had much higher levels of different substances compared to those in Gardiner, for example."

That nutrition has translated into big body size and perhaps the best horn growth in the state, taking over top billing from the Thompson Falls herd as the top producer of trophy rams. "We've had 17 5/8-inch bases on six-year-old rams and forty-inch length on their horns which is an awful huge sheep," Nielsen said. "If that had been a ten-year-old ram, it would have been a world record. Just guessing, it would have had 18 or 18 1/2-inch bases which there never has been on a sheep."

A transplant operation near Anaconda at about the same time has produced a huntable herd there, too, with about an equal number of sheep as on Rock Creek. "But they don't have as good of growth as the Rock Creek herd," Nielsen said. "There are a lot of rams, about a hundred in each bunch. There are some big rams there, too, but the Rock Creek sheep are bigger."

Hunting the Rock Creek herd presents different problems for the bighorn sheep hunter than in the other herds of Tall Timber Country. The

Nutrition has produced big body size and the best horn growth in the state for the transplanted Rock Creek herd. Michael Sample photo.

Bitterroot herd is made up of native sheep with many years of tradition behind them and long migration paths from their high country summer ranges to winter ranges below. The Anaconda herd inhabits relatively low and open country which makes them highly accessible throughout the season. But the Rock Creek herd uses timber more and has an earlier season to protect them during the rut of late November.

"The big rams run together in bunches. There are lots of times you'll see fifty or sixty legal rams in one bunch. At other times, you'll see four or five together with a couple of little ones tagging along," said Larry Clark, a guide who lives on Rock Creek. "The rams summer in the hogback country where there's a lot more sliderock and timber. The ewes are in more grassy, open country. The rams start leaving that country in the middle of October and start to mix with the ewes. In November, they'll start pairing off and fighting with one another.

"You can walk right up to them when they're fighting. It would be no challenge to get a good trophy ram at that time. When these animals are in the rut, they throw all caution to the wind. That's why we asked to have the season closed during the rut to protect some of those big rams," Clark said.

Their tendency to use the timbered slopes during the season creates some special problems, according to Nielsen. "It may require a lot of timber hunting to get a good ram. They stick in the timber pretty tight," he said. "There are real steep slopes. It's very noisy walking so you can't be quiet. They're difficult to hunt.

"At Anaconda, they're in more open country. They're quite easy to hunt there. You can go up in there early and they're in open country and you can glass them," he said. "It's not the typical sheep where you're way above timberline. They're below timberline. That's because they're new herds and haven't established long migration routes into the high country. But the best way to get a big ram is to wait until the rut starts. By then they're really down low. If you want to wait for a trophy, you'd better wait until the rut."

When talking about bighorn sheep hunting in Tall Timber Country and singing the praises of the prolific and vigorous herd on Rock Creek, it should be pointed out that this is just the latest in a line of hot sheep herds in Montana. The same thing was said about Thompson Falls' herd not too many years ago. Yet the factor at work remains the same for both herds.

When you transplant sheep into a new area which holds good food and habitat for them, bighorns will thrive. You get big rams in a hurry. But hunters should remember that they can get a good sheep in any hunting district that offers permits for them and that the hot herds will change over time. Just as Thompson Falls has given way to Rock Creek, it's a good bet that Rock Creek will eventually give way to another herd which no one could even guess at today.

The tough part of bighorn sheep hunting in districts where only a limited number of tags are issued is still drawing a tag to hunt them in the first place. Wherever anyone is lucky enough to draw that tag, they should realize that it could be the opportunity of a lifetime. They should be prepared to put in all the time it takes to hunt for the ram they want and they should put in some thought beforehand as to exactly how they want to hunt for that ram.

Few people could fault Ford's argument that there's a certain thrill to heading into the high country for big rams and glassing the summer ranges when the hunting is tough. On the other hand, the easier way to get a ram and the surest way to get a big ram is to wait until they come down on the winter ranges during the rut. And, of course, there are the hot herds in places like Rock Creek where the rams can grow some impressive headgear in a short period of time.

The choice is up to the hunter as to how he wants to do it and where he wants to apply. And, of course, it's up to the fickle fates of the draw as well, in permitting a person to go after big rams at all, in the course of a hunter's lifetime.

Mountain Goats

Mountain goat hunting is not for the faint of heart. It's not for the out of shape, either. And for those who really want the most out of their goats, there's no room for a fear of snow.

"I see people hunt them in the fall of the year right when the season opens. It's kind of silly to do that. The goats prime up later and you should probably wait a little later in the season to hunt them," said Vince Yannone, assistant administrator of the Conservation-Education Division with Fish, Wildlife and Parks in Helena.

Yannone followed that advice when he hunted in the Pioneer Range of Tall Timber Country a few seasons back, endured the tougher conditions, and was richly rewarded with a fine billy.

"A person that gets a goat permit should try to put it off as long as possible. The hair is longer on the goats and it's fuller. I shot mine with one week left in the season and the hair on some of it is eight inches long and real full," he said.

His goat hunt in Tall Timber Country with Tom Greenwood provides a good look at what late season journeys into the high country are all about and what a hunter can expect to face. "If you're going to hunt after mid-season, you are hunting in the snow. The goats are more difficult to spot and it makes the trip more rigorous because of difficulty in climbing," Yannone said. "It's dangerous up high then. I wouldn't recommend anyone who waits until late in the season to go alone. The snow fills crevices and there are cornices. The sun hits the rocks, melts the snow, then it freezes again at night. If it snows, you've got a real dangerous situation.

"I fell and busted a couple ribs when I was hunting there. I fell off a cliff area. There was ice under the snow and I fell about twenty-some feet but I was in rocks," he said. "I was lucky. I knew I had busted ribs, but I could have busted a leg, busted an arm. That's why it's always good to have someone along with you."

But even earlier in the season, a hunter should be prepared to withstand the rigors of a journey to the mountaintops. "You need to be able to do some walking," said Bob Crick, an outfitter who works the Bitterroot Range that rises behind his home in Victor. "The better the physical condition you are in, the better off you are. It's rugged country."

Unlike Yannone, who backpacked into the Pioneers for his hunt, Crick uses horses to get back into the mountains, then hunts on foot from there, glassing the cliffs, grassy pockets, and areas of sparse timber. "Usually, the bigger billies are off by themselves and they're probably higher," Crick said. "If you're wanting a big trophy, you're looking for an old loner by himself. You can tell him, too, because he's got a little bit of yellow to him, a dirty type of yellow. You look the area over good and get a route you think you can go in on him. If you can work in above him, fine, that's an advantage but it doesn't work that way all the time. They're always looking down for danger. The only time they look up is if you get too close and make some racket."

It's the type of hunt where planning is as important as the stalk itself. It takes plenty of glassing with a good pair of binoculars or a spotting scope. It takes careful calculation of the route of the stalk. And it takes the realization that the easiest path between hunter and goat isn't always the best.

"It seems like goats use their natural ability and good hearing and

Going after mountain goats late in the season, when weather can turn severe with little warning, presents special problems for hunters. Michael Sample photo.

eyesight and sense of smell to protect themselves," Yannone said. "They're not a running type of animal. What they do if you approach them from below is just climb out of your reach. When you hunt them from above, they don't spook as much."

That was the approach that paid off for Yannone in a fine billy with horns measuring nine and three-quarters and ten inches. "I spotted the animal from a long ways off and I knew it was a billy. He was urinating and rolling in it which is something they'll do in the rut," he said. "I planned a route and had pinpointed some trees and predominant points to guide me. I got to where I knew I was above him and started creeping down. He was laying down when I spotted him and I crept and he heard me and stood up. I had a really good shot at him, he was probably within twenty to twenty-five feet. Tom Greenwood, the fellow with me, saw the whole thing unfold. It was unbelievable."

Shot placement wasn't difficult at that close range and the importance of rifle caliber didn't really come into play. But both are considerations when hunting mountain goats in most situations.

"They're a tough animal. They're all muscle inside," said Crick. "You need a caliber big enough to break them down. You're looking for them on a flat place where they won't kick themselves off and fall and break their horns. I like something .270 caliber or better. You can do it with a lighter caliber but they're a real tough son of a gun."

To break them down, many hunters including Crick, believe in hitting them in the front shoulders. But gauging exactly where the shot should be placed can be difficult for a newcomer at hunting goats. "Goats are very heavily muscled and it's a deceptive thing with shooting a goat. There are tendencies that people aim high," Yannone said. "It's the humped characteristic in front. If you aim or shoot high, there are no vital things there. You're shooting large muscles in the shoulder. A good heart or lung shot is the best but you have to think about where that is on a goat."

Yannone skinned out his goat on the spot, quartered it, and he and Greenwood packed it four and a half miles out of the mountains on their backs. "If I hadn't quartered him right away, I would have had a problem," he said. "It snowed heavy that night. I went back the following day and the thing was froze like a brick. If you kill a goat high and have to leave the meat, due to the elevation and wind chill, the meat will freeze solid in a night."

While that mountain goat meat was served at the family dinner table in the winter that followed, Yannone was quick to point out it would never pass as yearling deer or elk. "Goat meat is good tasting but goat meat is very tough," he said. "You can beat on it and hammer on it and it's really tough stuff. You're not out primarily for the meat, you're out primarily for the trophy, the horns and the hide and the mount. It's nice to skin the whole goat out and you'll have years of usage of the skin. It depends on your economic ability but that's one thing people should remember if they can't afford to have the head mounted. I had the whole skin with the hooves on it tanned for less than half the price of what it would have cost to have the head mounted."

But hunters should remember that while the trophy is nice, mountain goat hunting is no time for heroics that could get them in trouble. The harsh realities of the terrain the goats live in make a hunting trip for them a time for care and planning, especially if they go after them late in the season.

"If you're hunting and stalking and doing things properly, you probably should do it in the morning," Yannone said. "You shouldn't make a late evening shot. If you don't make a good shot, it gets down in the rocks and if it snows that night, you're done. Shooting in the morning gives you ample time for stalking and tracking. In the evenings, hunters should spot and come back the following morning.

"Anyone who has a permit in the high mountain ranges can anticipate snows to come anywhere about September 15. It can be dangerous. It's always good to have somebody with you when you're hunting mountain goats or bighorn sheep for a lot of reasons.

"You should always go cautious because things can happen quickly in the high country."

Moose

Metzie McCormick has been packing a gun in hunting season ever since she was big enough to handle one. She's been hunting more than five decades in all, can claim to have taken each of the ten big game species that Montana has to offer and has hunted in many parts of the Treasure State.

But there's one statistic that would stand out to the hunter of today. Among the big game trophies she has taken over the years, she can point with pride to three moose, a legal tally that's almost unheard of in this day and age when tags are so hard to come by. And, for good measure, she helped her friend, Joe Murphy, take three more moose as well.

"They're creatures of habit," the Butte native and current resident of the Bitterroot Valley said. "They use about the same type of terrain at the same time every year. After I got this kind of area down, it was duck soup to get a moose.

"Early in the year, they're down in the lowlands and then after the regular season opens and the hunters get to shooting, they go over the mountain. The moose like jackpine thickets and they go into the high country looking for them about the time the hunting season starts.

"They're sort of cagey, too. They get a little smarter. I sometimes think they read," she laughed. "About the day the hunting season opens, they know everything."

That high country nature of moose is something of a trademark for the species here compared to other parts of Montana where wet or moist habitats are used more heavily. "In this area, they tend to be a little higher than in other areas," said John Firebaugh, regional wildlife manager for Fish, Wildlife and Parks in Missoula. "They're kind of spread out more in the fall. You find them on the drier, timbered ridges. They don't go back into the creek bottom and river bottom areas until there's snow. And they can get by in quite a bit of snow. They can get along in three or four feet of snow without a lot of trouble. They put up with some pretty tough conditions sometimes."

Locating moose in those thick stands of lodgepole pine during the hunting season can be difficult, especially if there's no tracking snow to help a hunter along. Firebaugh found that out when he finally drew a tag of his own several years ago. "I got a cow, finally, on the last afternoon of the season. I hunted ten or eleven days and kept track of it and figured I walked about ninety-five miles," he said. "I worked at the Darby Check Station and people were telling me about all the moose they were seeing just driving down the roads. It was frustrating. But it was one of those years where there wasn't much snow. I finally got some snow and cut some fresh tracks and got the cow moose by tracking it. It was the last day of the season and I couldn't be too choosy."

McCormick agreed that moose could be tough to find in the lodgepole. "They'll go in the real thick stuff. It doesn't matter how many windfalls or how high they are, either, because their legs are so long. They'd go in there and just stand and never move," she said. But snow or moist earth gives the hunter an advantage. "It's nice to have a horse, then you can get on a trail and go through a drainage and look for tracks. You know a moose track when you see one," McCormick said. "They take a longer step than

Early in the fall, moose are down in the lowlands but tend to spread out during the season. Michael Sample photo.

an elk. They've got pretty good-sized feet. And they've got pronounced dew claws on all four feet. On snow or mud, it's real easy to tell."

The tendency to move into the high stands of lodgepoles during the hunting season causes other problems, too. For one thing, that type of habitat is usually associated with deer and elk, not moose, and it contributes to illegal kills.

"We get quite a bit of illegal harvest," Firebaugh said. "Some years, we know of as many or more illegally-taken moose as legally-taken moose. In some areas, we've had to cut back on the legal take because of it.

"I think there are some cases of mistaken identity where the individual who is hunting is not familiar with the area and thinks the only thing there is elk and deer. They see an animal move in the thick timber and just shoot. At other times, it's probably illegally taken for the meat. Occasionally a guy is caught, but it's not easy to catch them. We put some signs up in some areas to let people know there were moose there to take care of the mistaken identity kills, but there isn't much more we can do. We have gone more restrictive on moose because of the balance between the legal and particularly the illegal harvest."

That only contributes to the Montana truism that while finding a moose may be difficult at some times, finding a moose tag is difficult at all times.

"There's a lot of demand," Firebaugh said. "It's running something like two percent of the people who apply in this region get a tag. I got in on it with the old preference system where you could build up preference by being unsuccesful in the draw over a period of years."

But that preference system became too cumbersome to administer and was phased out and it's a lucky individual indeed who gets his application thrown into the hat with all others and comes out with a moose tag these days. When someone does get lucky in the special permit drawings, it's usually pretty easy to tell. "They always print up a list by hunting district and send it to the regional offices first and there are a lot of hunters who come in to look at that list," Firebaugh said. "You hear the cheers every now and then, with a lot of moans and groans in between."

Upland Birds and Waterfowl

Jack Tanner never claimed to be a great bird hunter. He never said he was a crack shot, either. But growing up in the Bitterroot Valley in the 1960s, he took his share of pheasants and ducks anyway.

"Back when I was between twelve and eighteen, it wasn't all that difficult to get a pheasant or two," said Tanner, of Corvallis. "Dad raised dogs, German shorthair pointers, and he had one super pointer, a three-legged dog named Old Duke. After he hunted in front of me about three times, he had the system down. He pointed it, flushed the pheasant and then he'd lie down so I could shoot. He knew I wasn't a real good shot with a shotgun and I guess he didn't want to get peppered in the butt. When the pheasants were only about two feet off the ground, the dog would get pretty upset."

But despite his claims to lack of prowess, the hunting was good in those days and Tanner figured between his take and that of his dad, the family of five would eat pheasant about once a week during the season and were often looking for people to take ducks off their hands.

"We duck hunted a lot. We'd potshot in little ponds and side streams in the Bitterroot," he said. "When I was in high school, two friends and I would sneak down to the river bottom and potshot ducks after football practice. It was mostly mallards and anything else that happened to fly in front of our guns."

But things have changed in the Bitterroot and other parts of Tall Timber Country. While it never was a super place for the bird hunter, the few opportunities available have diminished in the face of subdivisions, posted signs and the simple fact that for some species, the habitat just isn't there.

"A western Montana hunter goes through withdrawal if he wants to hunt birds. Then he learns to hunt elk and everything is okay," explained Bill Thomas, information officer for Fish, Wildlife and Parks in Missoula. "We have a few pheasants on private property in the Bitterroot Valley. There is some very limited waterfowl hunting. And some people are interested in mountain grouse. But we don't boast very much about our bird hunting."

While hunters here, like elsewhere in Montana, are interested in pheasants, the habitat for them is extremely limited. In the Bitterroot, intensive farming has claimed some of the pheasants of years gone by, others have been hurt by the housing boom of the last twenty years, and posted signs have taken care of hunters getting to the rest. "The sportsmen's club has worked very hard to improve the habitat by working with private landowners. And it is showing some results, but it's still nothing like east of the Divide," Thomas said.

The hard-core upland bird hunters in this part of Montana turn to mountain grouse species instead, with blue grouse as their primary focus of attention. "Most people are interested in blue grouse but we do have some ruffed grouse fanatics that basically come from the Midwest. They can never get enough of the ruffed grouse hunting," Thomas said.

"Most people road hunt the blues, or at least take a road to the top and then

Blue grouse are the most popular target for hard-core upland bird hunters. Michael Sample photo.

hunt the ridges. The open grassy hillsides are where the birds seem to be during the early grouse seasons," he added. "Ruffed grouse are basically in the creek bottoms and they hunt them either driving or walking. It's not as difficult to walk, terrain-wise, as to get to the top of some places to get the blue grouse."

On the Clark Fork side of Tall Timber Country, pheasant opportunities also are poor in comparison to mountain grouse, especially in the years since the last pheasant stocking program in the state was terminated. But here too, there are few upland bird hunters. Wood cutters may pack a shotgun along when they head into the mountains to lay in a supply of fuel for their winter fires, but few go out of their way to hunt grouse. As a result, there is only small interest in them during the years of good hatches and almost no interest when the hatches are poor.

"There are a lot of Hungarian partridge here," said Lyn Nielsen, wildlife biologist with Fish, Wildlife and Parks at Deer Lodge. "But most western Montana bird hunters aren't Hun hunters. There are a lot of Huns here, coveys everywhere in the good years but almost no one hunting them. They are virtually untapped in this valley."

In the Clark Fork instead, the shotgun hunters have turned their attention to waterfowl. "When I go looking for wood in the fall, I take a shotgun along for grouse but mostly when I want to hunt, I walk the creeks for ducks," said Jack Kelly, of Anaconda. "We have a lot of warm-water creeks in this area that don't freeze over. They're all full of watercress and they're real good for jump shooting."

Some of the reason for interest in waterfowl here can be attributed to the 4,500-acre Warm Springs Wildlife Management Area, leased from the Anaconda Co., which provides public hunting areas which other parts of Tall Timber Country just don't have.

Most waterfowl hunters are looking for geese, but find ducks are far more plentiful. Frank Martin photo.

"It's just about all mallards in this area," Kelly said. "They'll sit in little bunches on the creek or sit on the ponds at night and you can catch the flights in the morning and evening. Nasty weather helps. It keeps them low. But I've got an old 97 Winchester with a big long barrel and I can really reach out there."

Waterfowl hunting is also available in the Bitterroot Valley but it's very much a matter of who you know and how long you've known them.

"There's quite a bit of waterfowl hunting that goes on," said Bob Hoy, game warden for Fish, Wildlife and Parks at Stevensville. "But it's all on private property and you have to have the permission of the landowner and that's the toughest part to get. If you don't know the landowner beforehand, you're probably not going to get on."

For the fortunate hunters that do have an in someplace, the Bitterroot offers some good gunning for ducks with a chance at geese as well. "The most popular way to duck hunt is to sit someplace and wait for something that comes along," said Hoy. "It's not the creeks so much here, it's the river and sloughs of the old river channel. It's mostly mallards but there's a mixture of a little of everything. The goose hunting is a little tougher. They're more wary. I suspect that most people are actually after geese but take the ducks incidentally."

The first few days of the season are considered to be the best for waterfowl hunting in the Bitterroot, when local birds are available. After that, it's the whims of the weather that will determine how much of a chance hunters have at the migrants as they move through.

But, once again, upland bird hunting and waterfowl hunting in Tall Timber Country is pretty much where you find it and a passion for the few. In terms of numbers, there are far more hunters who will pick up a rifle or bow to chase deer and elk and keep their fingers crossed all summer long in hopes of getting lucky in the draw for the trophy species. It's big game country, for the most part, and that suits the folks who hunt here just fine.

Wilderness Country

Stop any hunter on the street in a distant state and ask him to close his eyes for a moment. Tell him to imagine a hunting trip to Montana and have him describe what he sees in his mind's eye.

It's a sure bet he'll smile and the image he tells about will be bright and clear of snow-dusted mountains, backcountry camps, pack strings leaving the trailhead, and steep mountain slopes teeming with elk, deer, bighorn sheep, and mountain goats. Delve into his dreams a little more and you'll hear of secret wishes to see a grizzly bear in the wild—at a distance, of course—and to taste the cold, crisp waters of a high country spring.

These hunting dreams and spectacular visions of Montana embrace everything we call Wilderness Country, the diverse mountain forests and breath-taking valleys of northwestern Montana. It's been called the best of what's left of this land which was first visited by the mountain men and fur trappers more than a century ago. While civilization came here long ago, Wilderness Country still holds some of the more romantic place names that hunters have grown to revere in the years since then.

The Rocky Mountain Front, where the mountains seem to grow right out of the broad face of the prairie, conjures up images of heavy-horned sheep and broad-antlered mule deer driven to the mountains' edge by the first snows of winter.

There's the Bob Marshall Wilderness and its reputation for big bull elk and grizzly bears. Pack strings still head down its trails and legends are born every year in the hunting camps of autumn.

The Kootenai National Forest of far northwestern Montana offers incomparable black bear hunting and some of the better moose hunting to be found in the state.

60

And in the high country of the Cabinets, Mission Mountains, and Swan Range, a hunter lucky enough to draw a tag can greet the clouds as he looks for mountain goats on the rugged cliffs and feels the first chill of winter.

That doesn't take into account the excellent white-tailed deer opportunities to be found throughout the region.

Wilderness Country also can boast of the last limited opportunity to hunt for grizzly bear in the lower 48 states. And it holds mountain lions in sufficent numbers to hold a season each year for houndsmen and those who simply yearn to follow a track in the winter woods.

In contrast to many parts of Montana, most of Wilderness Country is public land where the difficulty of getting permission to hunt is replaced by problems of how to get back into these vast tracts to hunt. The hunter's best friend on the U.S. Forest Service lands is often the logging road which either allows him to drive directly to his hunting area or to reach the trailhead where he'll strap on his backpack or mount his horse to continue the journey. But these roads and the logging that spawn them can also be a curse because they seem to promote road hunting, cut into secure habitat for species like elk and moose, and limit wintering habitat for others like white-tailed deer.

Wilderness Country also offers a different look at Montana than any other part of the state. While the Big Sky above is just as clear, blue, and broad, a hunter heading westward through the mountains from the Rocky Mountain Front toward the Idaho border will find the timber gets more dense, the clearings less frequent, and the brush undergrowth more pronounced as the precipitation influence of the Pacific Northwest increasingly comes into play. It is, in fact, the closest thing to real rain forest that Montana can claim as its own.

The high peaks, dense timber and backcountry nature of Wilderness Country provide some unique problems for the hunters who go there. But those who take the time to solve them and keep coming back over the years will be rewarded with variety that few other parts of the Treasure State can match.

Not to mention the fact they can enjoy a rich wildlife heritage and take part in a hunting experience that those in other parts of the country can only dream about.

Elk

The sun was little more than a glow on the western horizon and darkness was starting to flood the eastern heavens when the symphony began. In some distant meadow, a big bull elk was tuning up the evening's concerto and because of his music, the wilderness was just a bit wilder.

It was the rutting time of September, far back in the Bob Marshall Wilderness, and this lone bull's shrill, throaty bugle marked the beginning of a show that every hunter should witness not once, but many times in his lifetime. Soon other bulls joined him in song and the coyotes howled along until it seemed like the whole world, which had been so quiet just a few minutes before, was alive and vibrant with wildlife.

Advertising their lust for the cows and telling other bulls just how tough they really were, the big bulls answered one another with their bugles and

Persistence is the key to locating a bull elk in the rut to answer your challenge. Mark Henckel photo.

roars. And when two bulls felt the competition was just too near, they might move in on one other and decide the issue right there in an antler-rattling fight.

My hunting day was over and the smell of steaks cooking over an open fire and a bubbling pot of coffee reminded me that those bulls would still be waiting tomorrow for an early-morning assault with a bugle. But I stood there for a time anyway and let my senses revel in the wondrous smells of freshly-fallen aspen leaves, the feel of a crisp autumn evening, and the heavenly sounds of those bugling bulls, secure in the knowledge that the civilized world was twenty miles away back at the trailhead and that the ringing phone would survive without me for another week.

Hunting bugling bulls in the rutting time of late September and early October certainly isn't limited to Wilderness Country, but there are few other places where a hunter can get such a primal feeling from it. It belongs here in the land of pack strings of horses and mules, high mountain camps, and hunters who venture far from the beaten path.

Elk hunting in the Bob Marshall-Great Bear-Lincoln-Scapegoat Wilderness complex is a classic hunting experience but not one that the average hunter can just go and do on a weekend. It is an equal opportunity hunt, however, in that Wilderness Country offers three of the four hunting districts in the state where rifle hunting begins Sept. 15. Most hunters who venture into the wilderness to take advantage of it are either nonresidents willing to pay an outfitter to get them there or residents who feel that the beauties of the country in autumn make it worth feeding a pack string the rest of the year and buying tack and equipment of their own to make the trip. Of course, that pack string doesn't have to be a big one.

Ron Granneman, of Fort Smith, got a lot of mileage out of just two or three horses and took fifteen bulls in fifteen years with his bow and arrow, including eight that made the Pope and Young Record Book. Hunting Wilderness Country and other parts of Montana, his success is a tribute to persistence and understanding of the animals he went after. But that isn't the only reason he hunted there.

"There's a success side and there's a satisfaction side. They're separate, but important. I hunt not only to kill a big bull but to derive the most pleasure from a hunt," Granneman said. "I want to get back away from roads and away from people. I like a long hunt. I don't like to come back. I like setting up a good camp in an area where there's few or no other hunters."

Once he finds such an area, either by consulting the map for large tracts of roadless land or by following leads from other hunters, he plans to be there during the bugling time. The rest of his secret is simple.

"I operate under the theory that there's a bull bugling someplace. Although they may not be bugling here, from opening day to the end of the season, there are bulls bugling someplace in Montana and all I have to do is find them," he said. "I put my boots on and go into drainage after drainage after drainage looking for the areas where they are bugling. Sometimes on foot, sometimes on horseback, I'll cover twelve to fifteen miles in a day."

Granneman said the amount of bugling will vary quite a bit from drainage to drainage. "The more bulls you have in a drainage, the more they're going to bugle on an average because they are going to incite themselves. Everywhere else, there's no bugling going on but in that drainage, they can be going gangbusters."

He will bugle often in his travels in hopes of getting a reply from a bull or finding that particular hot drainage. "I bugle every fifteen to twenty minutes with a long-range bugle and a grunt tube. The whole key to elk hunting at that time is bugling. If a bull answers right away, that means that he has a good chance of coming to me. If it's thirty seconds or a couple of minutes, I try to determine if he's coming to me or not and I may go to him," he said. "Then I bugle once every five minutes or so and try to imitate him, make the sounds they make. Sometimes they come, sometimes they shut up and you may never see or hear them again."

The key is to not get discouraged as the days pass, even if the bulls seem

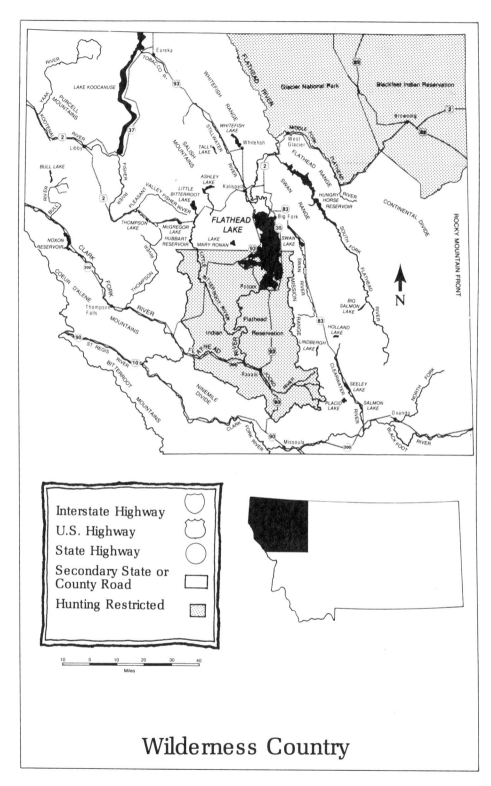

Interstate Highway

U.S. Highway

State Highway

Secondary State or
County Road

Hunting Restricted

Wilderness Country

reluctant to play the game. Persistence is the key, along with the knowledge that if a hunter keeps doing the right things long enough, his luck will change. "I reached a low almost every year I hunted," Granneman admitted. "After ten days or two weeks, I figured I'd had it. I'd tell myself that this would be the year I wouldn't get one. But I stuck with it and it turned around."

And when things turn, they can do so quickly. In 1979, Granneman shot his second-largest bull in such a rapid-fire fashion that most hunters would still be shaking from the episode. "I bugled and he came to me up the hill on a dead run to six yards. It was a six-point, my second biggest," he said. "I have absolutely no fear of elk. I've never heard of anyone being hurt. But I did wonder if I'd get run over by that one. Usually as soon as they see you and especially if they smell you, they're gone. They may doubt their eyes, but they never doubt their nose." The bull later scored 336 2/8 to put it high on the list of elk taken in Montana with a bow and arrow.

While Granneman's advice comes from a bowhunter, it is valid for any hunter no matter what his weapon is during the rut. Though rifle hunters have the equipment to reach far beyond the fifty-yard range that most bowmen feel is their limit, they, too, should be prepared for close encounters in the thick timber of Wilderness Country.

Those early-season rifle hunts which put a gunner within reach of bugling bulls can be highly successful as well, and bulls run larger than in many other parts of Montana. "Hunting success is about twice as high as the unguided hunting outside the wilderness," said Jim Cross, wildlife manager for Fish, Wildlife and Parks in Kalispell. "If we're getting about nine percent outside the wilderness, it's about eighteen percent in the wilderness.

"Generally speaking, we don't have as much hunting pressure in that area and we have an older age structure in that elk population. We have more bulls that have the older age and the antlers to go with it," he said. "It's old enough that we still have enough prime age animals that are five, six, and seven years old so they get full antler development. Usually you don't get a nice six-pointer until they're four or five years old and they'll retain it until they're eight or nine and then they start to drop off. They lose the ability to digest food and take the proteins that are necessary for good antler development."

Not that elk hunting outside the designated wilderness areas isn't good or that elk there are necessarily small. In truth, elk numbers are good enough throughout the region that opening the first week of the season to either-sex hunting has been the rule in the past, followed by a bulls-only hunt. "It hinges in large part on the fact we have a lot of National Forest land and pretty good security for the elk," Cross said.

Timber management outside the wilderness areas, and finding the right mix of roads open and roads closed to vehicles, is the key to keeping those elk populations in good shape. While there should be some access for hunters into those areas, too much access can be detrimental to the species. "Jointly, we designate roads with the Forest Service that should be closed. We have enough roads to get the hunters into an area but not so many the hunters can get right in there and shoot them up too badly. It's closing roads to benefit the elk," he said.

Pack strings big and small head into the wilderness each fall in search of big game. Mark Henckel photo.

Hunters should remember, too, that the nature of northwestern Montana's forests changes the further a hunter heads west. The eastern edge of Wilderness Country has more parks and meadows mixed in with the big tracts of timber, but the openings shrink in size the closer one gets to the Idaho border.

While those mountains on Montana's western border provide excellent elk habitat, they can pose problems for hunters because of their thick timber and dense brush understory.

"That kind of habitat does allow for quite a bit of security so deer and elk can stay in areas where they might otherwise be pushed out of due to hunting pressure," said Shawn Riley, wildlife biologist for Fish, Wildlife and Parks at Thompson Falls. "But it's a situation where you can look across a canyon and see a deer or elk far away but your chances of getting a deer or elk in front of you is slim. You've really got to take things slow and sometimes you'll get face-to-face with elk at real short distances.

"The mountains are also really steep," he added. "It's a lot more rugged than any other parts of Montana I've been in. It's real thick vegetation and very little open parklands. Our biggest openings consist of brushfields left over from early forest fires. A lot of guys have problems with it coming from outside the area. And, it's easy to get lost in.

"The best way to hunt elk here is to keep your eyes on brushfields in the morning and evening and hunt the timber real slow during the middle of the day."

Dan Moore, an archer from Kalispell, explained just how bad the brush can be and how shifting winds can be tricky in the western mountains for the elk hunter.

"I've called bulls within ten yards and couldn't get a shot at them it was so thick. And the wind changes. I had three bulls coming in at one time and all three got within fifty yards and winded me and they came in from three different directions," Moore said. "There are some superb elk, some monster bulls. The problem is that it's so brushy, unless you bugle. If you bugle, there's no problem with hunting elk here. If you're just going to try to stalk, this is impossible country."

In hunting most parts of Wilderness Country, an outfitter or a friend with knowledge of the area you plan to hunt can be invaluable. They can't guarantee you'll go home with a nice bull but they can put you in good elk country right away and eliminate the years of looking it sometimes takes to find these spots. If you plan to head into the designated wilderness, there's also no substitute for having someone along who has been there before and has the equipment to make the hunting trip a joy instead of a misery.

Hunting camp tests the skills of cooking ability before an appreciative audience. Mark Henckel photo.

Wilderness Country offers some of the better elk hunting to be found in Montana in some of its wilder places. It has big bulls filling the air with the bugles of September and clinging to steep, snowy slopes when Thanksgiving rolls around and the hunting days grow short.

Not to mention the fact that it's a great place to get away from the world, hike well off the beaten path, and get so far into the backcountry that a telephone will seem like a contraption that belongs to a different place and time.

Whitetails and Mule Deer

Whitetails are the deer of choice for hunters throughout much of Wilderness Country. Big-bodied whitetails. Tough whitetails. And whitetails in habitat where hunters in other parts of Montana might be tempted to look for mule deer.

That doesn't mean there aren't mule deer worth going after in this part of Montana. It just means that mule deer hunters tend to be either specialists or opportunists here. Whitetails are always available in a variety of habitats.

"The strict association between whitetails and river habitat isn't as distinct in northwestern Montana as it is in eastern Montana," said John Mundinger, wildlife biologist for Fish, Wildlife and Parks in Helena. "We've got a lot of water up here. It's a combination of the river habitat and the associated mature coniferous forests. The Swan is an excellent example. You've got the main river flowing down the valley but you've also got all the tributaries flowing into it which provide habitat over a large area."

Those mature stands of mixed ponderosa pine, lodgepole pine, Douglas fir, and western larch provide hunters with a different problem than they face in hunting whitetails in other parts of Montana. Elsewhere, whitetails are often restricted by the brush in creek bottoms or small patches of cover which tend to concentrate them.

The tall forest habitat of northwestern Montana provides some other survival advantages in addition to boundless escape cover. "During the winter, the mature forest reduces wind, reduces the amount of snow that reaches the ground and reduces the extremes in temperature. It doesn't get as warm during the heat of the day but it doesn't get as cold during the night, either," he said.

While that kind of cover may be kind to the deer, it definitely is not kind to the deer hunter who has to cope with the brushy undergrowth, restricted vision, and wary whitetails which inhabit it.

"I think it's hard to hunt whitetails in the Northwest. We've got deer in pretty good densities but the heavy coniferous cover puts the deer at a distinct advantage over the hunter," said Mundinger. "It's noisy country to walk unless you've got snow cover and the deer are usually aware of you long before you're aware of them."

Nevertheless, moving slowly through the woods, so-called still hunting, is the most popular hunting preference here. But it takes a real pro at the game to get nice bucks on a regular basis. "I sat on the Swan Check Station for nine years," Mundinger said. "There are a few people who hunt

Whitetails make up seventy-five percent of the deer harvest in northwestern Montana. Frank Martin photo.

that Swan and kill five to six deer in their party every year. The majority of them are very adept still hunters. The people who are consistently successful find well-used game trails and work down them very slowly and carefully.

"There are a few tree stands but I think they're used more by archers than rifle hunters. As for deer drives, the Midwestern-type deer drives, it doesn't seem to work very well. It doesn't seem to be consistent. We're not used to hunting in big hunting parties in Montana."

For bagging a big buck, a hunter can improve his odds by waiting until late in the season when the rut often makes the mature bucks think more about survival of the species than survival of themselves. "Sitting on the check station, you'd see a fair number of young bucks killed early in the season and a fair increase in the number of mature bucks after the fifteenth of November. They're more active then, a little less wary."

Hunters who bring home a mature whitetail from Wilderness Country can expect to put away a good amount of venison in the freezer as well. Whitetails are bigger here than in most other parts of Montana, with the possible exception of the prairie whitetails of northeastern Montana.

"It's not at all unusual to get mature bucks that will hog-dress over two hundred pounds. The biggest I weighed was 243," Mundinger said. "My yearling bucks are fifteen pounds heavier than the Lewistown area and the does are ten pounds heavier. The average yearling here will hog dress about a hundred twenty pounds.

"The reason is we're dealing with a different subspecies of deer up there. The one we have in eastern Montana is with the subspecies in eastern Montana and the western Dakotas. This one is in northwestern Montana and into southern Canada. In western Montana, the average whitetails would also be five to ten pounds heavier than the corresponding mule deer by age class. The extremes are probably the same but for the average deer, the whitetail is bigger."

With that kind of size and availability, it's little wonder that Mike Aderhold, Region One information officer for Fish, Wildlife and Parks in Kalispell, confirmed that, "Just one out of every four deer taken is a mule deer in this region. The harvest has been running that way, from twenty-five to twenty-nine percent mule deer, for the past ten years."

Mule deer are available throughout Wilderness Country, however, for those willing to work for them. And in some areas, particularly along the Rocky Mountain Front, they still are the primary species that deer hunters go after.

"The good mule deer hunting is harder to get to. The people have a lot better access to the whitetails than the mule deer. The tops of the Swan Range, Mission Mountains, and Cabinet Mountains have some very nice mule deer bucks but very little pressure on them," Mundinger said. "That's because you're talking about steep hikes of five to six miles to get in to them and there aren't many people willing to do that. And those that do are a little different."

The same situation exists on the Rocky Mountain Front side of Wilderness Country, according to Gary Olson, wildlife biologist with Fish, Wildlife and Parks in Conrad, and Helga Ihsle Pac, of Bozeman, who conducted a study on mule deer in the area. In Wilderness Country, most hunters simply wait and hope for late autumn snows to move the deer within reach of their rifles.

"The guys that hunt good bucks earlier are going in for a week at a time and they're hunting very high for them," Olson said. "A lot of times, you'll see them clear up with the goats. If you have a lot of time and a horse, you're in business. It's several miles back in and very rugged country.

"But probably eighty to ninety percent of our mule deer that winter on the Rocky Mountain Front are migratory and about five years out of six or seven, you'll see a few scattered storms late in the season that will move the deer out."

The migrations the deer make to reach their wintering areas can be lengthy indeed, according to Pac, and the time they leave their summering

Mule deer are far back in the mountains on the high ridges during most of the hunting season. Michael Sample photo.

areas varies a great deal as well. "The mule deer are in three groups — the resident herd, an east of the Continental Divide herd, and a west of the Divide herd," she said. "As for the furthest one, I had a radio-collared buck that went thirty airline miles into the Flathead drainage. Most of them would be less than that but most of the deer that summered between there and the Front would winter on the Front. There just isn't much wintering area on the Flathead side of the Divide."

The deer that have to travel the furthest to reach the wintering areas leave the earliest to get there, often before hunters would expect them to because of deep snow depths. "The first heavy fall snowstorm would move those deer back over," Pac said. "It wasn't amount of snow, but the first heavy snowfall. For the other deer, east of the Divide, that snowstorm wouldn't bother them that much. It would be the later storms that moved them."

What hunters are looking for is a series of those heavy snows early in the fall to get the deer moving and concentrate them on the Front before the season ends. In such a year, the hunting for big mule deer can be outstanding and the harvest will be heavy.

"It depends on the weather one hundred percent," Olson said. "In a normal year when we don't have hard storms, those animals will stay up on the Continental Divide. You'll see herds of bucks high on the peaks of the mountains on both sides of the Divide. They stay there until they're forced out of it."

But in one recent year, the weather frowned on the deer and the hunters smiled. "They were out on the winter range early," Olson said. "I went up with five other guys on the tenth of November and we each had four-point bucks by noon. I got one myself that scored 180. We normally have several big bucks in the thirty-inch class that come out of there in years like that. Four-point bucks were a dime a dozen up there that year. But I would hope we wouldn't see that for another three or four years so we can get some big ones again."

In addition to having the benefit of bucks within reach during the stormy years, hunters also have plenty of them to choose from, he said. "We have a pretty high ratio of bucks to does. It varies by area, but in one area it's forty bucks per one hundred does. In other areas subjected to heavy hunter harvest, it runs from sixteen to twenty-five bucks per hundred does which is still high."

With the migrations in mind, hunters would be well-advised to wait until the final weeks of the season before heading out for mule deer in Wilderness Country and hope to catch them on the wintering areas. "November is the best," Olson agreed. "They're either staging to come out or they're out."

But Wilderness Country does offer you the choice. Hunt big whitetails down low throughout the season, hit the high country for mule deer early, or wait until the final weeks for the migration to bring them to the wintering areas. Or, if you want to do it all, you can do that, too, for Wilderness Country offers a full season of deer hunting for big-antlered and big-bodied deer no matter how your hunting schedule works out.

Bighorn Sheep

After eighteen years of waiting to draw a bighorn sheep hunting permit, Bill McRae wasn't going to rush things. He wasn't going to draw down on the first three-quarter curl, legal ram he saw. And he really didn't want to wait until the rut to take one the easy way, either.

Bighorn sheep hunting is something to be savored in Wilderness Country or anywhere else in Montana. Few knew that better than McRae, an outdoor writer and photographer from Fairfield.

"It took me eighteen years to get my first permit," he said. "I've taken thousands of pictures of bighorns. Big rams. Huge rams. But it took a long time to get that permit to hunt them."

McRae decided to go after sheep early in the season to get the most out of his opportunity and to avoid the early onset of winter in the high country which can cause a hunter problems. And he decided to be picky about which ram he shot, too.

"You've got to look at a lot of sheep to get a good sheep," he said of his tactics. "The big thing on sheep is finding them first. You need to have a good pair of binoculars with high resolution glass, preferably a nine or ten-power or a good spotting scope. It helps if you have seen hundreds of sheep. You know what you're looking for. Then, when you think you're in good sheep range, just sit down and glass and glass and glass."

McRae glassed plenty before he finally found the ram he wanted.

"After walking about a hundred miles, literally, and hunting about twenty days, I finally located a bunch of big rams, spooked them once and made a shot at about four hundred yards which is a little farther than a guy should shoot at anything. But I had a lot of time and knew my rifle well," he said.

The ram McRae took later scored 180 5/8 to earn him his place in the Boone and Crockett Club Record Book. It's the only chance he's ever had to hunt bighorns though his wife, Mary, has also drawn a tag and taken a ram that scored about 170. But McRae is still trying, filling out his special permit application each year in hopes of getting one more crack at them in the future with a bow and arrow.

Hunters should be choosy when picking out what could be their ram of a lifetime. Michael Sample photo.

"My goal is to take one with a bow. I have a good ram already," he said. If the luck of the draw is with him, he also knows what his plan of attack will be and the advice he is willing to offer anyone else who heads into sheep country. "They're considerably easier to hunt during the rut but you're going against the weather. Weather can be real bad in sheep country at that time. My advice to anyone hunting sheep is to spend as much time as they can from the beginning of the season until they get their ram."

Wilderness Country offers several areas where bighorn sheep hunting is available and that kind of advice can pay off. Among them are the hunting districts on the Rocky Mountain Front, the Clark Fork near Thompson Falls and in the Kootenai River country near Libby. Each area has produced some fine rams over the years but they have their differences, too.

"In this country, they seem to have a tighter curl," said John McCarthy, wildlife biologist for Fish, Wildlife and Parks at Augusta. "You might get just about a full curl and its horns will only run thirty-four inches long. You go other places, Rock Creek or Thompson Falls, and at thirty-four inches, they're three-quarters curl."

Shawn Riley, wildlife biologist for Fish, Wildlife and Parks at Thompson Falls, said sheep in his area mature earlier but are relatively short-lived. "Rams that are four years old here are comparable to a six or seven-year-old in the Gardiner or Stillwater country. What we've seen is that these rams tend not to live as long as those on the Stillwater and the Sun. They put on a lot of growth, do a lot of breeding, produce higher lamb crops, have a lot of social fighting, yet are shorter-lived critters. They burn themselves out.

"In the Kootenai, there is a little more timber, a little less quality forage and a little tougher winters so they don't have the growth," he continued. "We've had some record book rams come out of the Kootenai, though. They're certainly there, too."

In most parts of Montana, bighorn sheep hunting is considered to be the easiest during the latter part of the season when they move onto the winter ranges. But there are things to be said for those who get out there during the more pleasant days of September when the season begins.

"Most of the hunting seasons begin September 15 and they're on the summer ranges then," McCarthy said of the fall patterns of sheep in his area. "It's fairly high, getting into your alpine stuff. There are lots of rocks, plenty of escape cover around. Maybe some wet areas, a few springs in the area or some boggy areas. On those summer ranges, you're talking about a backcountry type of hunt. You can look over a lot of animals.

"There's a gradual movement off the summer ranges and they get onto the winter ranges about November 1. They generally move regardless of snow. They begin the rut about the first of November and it's a traditional thing with them. Those ewes will move down early and the rams will follow the ewes onto the winter range. We've got some migrations that might be as far as fifteen airline miles."

No matter whether it's summer or winter range that you plan to hunt them on, taking your time is a must. "You look over a lot of animals. They move around a lot so if you're in a good area, you can see a lot of them. You should have yourself a good spotting scope and a lot of time," McCarthy said.

In defense of the winter range hunts, it should be pointed out that it's an excellent time to get on big rams, especially if they tended to spook easily or were in unstalkable situations earlier in the season. "If you're willing to wait and take a chance on the weather, when they drop down on the winter ranges, you stand a good chance to get a good animal," he said. "The winter ranges are down low. They're pretty accessible. And those rams are a little crazy then. They're easier to approach and they'll get to chasing those ewes around and they pay less attention to the things going on around them."

The Thompson Falls area also provides good access during the rut in the rocks along the Clark Fork River face. "It's easily accessible because there are roads along the base of the winter range," Riley said. "If you want the high, alpine hunt, you can get that in the early season. Late in the season, the rams move down on the river front and they're easily hunted by car. You can see as many as thirty rams a day in your car. But seeing a ram and getting one are two different things. It's steep country."

Not to mention the fact that sheep with a good vantage point have keen eyesight when it comes to spotting danger or anything else in their mountain homes.

"Sheep eyesight is equivalent to an eight-power binocular," McRae said. "They're on a par with antelope. I wouldn't say they're better. I'm sure they have a pretty good nose, too, but their main defense is their eyesight."

As for getting a record book ram in your sights, however, hunters should remember that the most important factors are to have the time it takes to find one, to cover enough ground to find them and to recognize one when you see him. To do that, you either have to see hundreds of rams like McRae has or do some homework before you take to the field.

"It's probably experience as much as anything," McCarthy said. "There are enough mounted heads around that if a guy is starting out, he can look at enough heads to get some idea. They've got to be up in the forty-inch bracket and have a pretty good base to make the book. We pull about one forty-incher out of here a year."

That means tall odds and plenty of time and effort to bring home a genuine trophy head. But no taller odds than drawing a bighorn sheep permit in the first place. And no more time or effort than a hunter should expect to put in when his bighorn sheep opportunity in Wilderness Country could be a once in a lifetime hunt.

Mountain Goats

It isn't just the mountain goats that lure hunters to the high peaks of Wilderness Country. It's the high peaks themselves and the rugged, austere beauty of the places these goats call home.

"I just like to hunt in the high country," admitted Jack Whitney, of Bigfork. "They're an interesting animal to study. I've spent an awful lot of time at it. I've probably climbed a thousand rock miles going after them with a bow. I know every goat trail where I hunt and practically every goat." In the process, Whitney also put five mountain goats in the Pope and Young Record Book over a span of eleven years.

While goats are not generally considered to be the wariest of animals, it's the country they're found in that makes them a difficult target. These animals are specialists in the niche they've carved out for themselves in life. They have learned to survive on the rugged cliffs and rocky ridges. They can take the early onset of winter that rages through the high country and still scratch out a living. And they can certainly go in places where hunters fear to tread.

"They're a tough animal," Whitney said. "You have to be ready for some lousy weather and tough conditions if you're going to hunt them. I've been up there in many a blizzard where you couldn't see fifteen feet in front of you and you couldn't see your tracks fifteen feet behind you because they were covered by snow. But I got so I liked the snow better. You can stalk them and see where they've been. When your eye gets trained to them, you can pick a goat out of snow like it's black and white."

But goat hunting can have its frustrations, especially for the bowhunter who needs to get in close for a shot. That holds true even if you know where the goat is you're after. "It takes a lot of patience. I stalk them. I come in from above and watch the wind. But when the sun hits their area, the wind can change and sometimes you've got just minutes to make a parallel stalk to them," Whitney said. "I hunted one goat for several years. I could write a whole book on him alone. They'll stay in a locale and there was this world record goat in the Swan and I tried for him for several years.

"One time, I got right above him and I was going down on him in about eighteen inches of wet snow and I fell. I threw my bow and the string came off and I'm twenty thumbs trying to get the string back on. Another time, I got up on him and a coyote came between us and he spooked. Another time, I got on him and my friend across the canyon shot another goat and I had to go help him. Another time, I knew he was bedded down

Nanny survival determines whether mountain goat herds will thrive or perish in their harsh homeland. Michael Sample photo.

close but I still had my arrow in the quiver—it's just safer carrying them there. I didn't take three steps and he was fifteen yards or less and looking right at me.''

That goat was later taken by a rifle hunter and points out the fact that mountain goats are very much creatures of habit closely tied to the same areas year after year. That can be a boon for the mountain goat hunter lucky enough to draw a tag but it can also be a death sentence for the goat herd which gets hit too hard by those hunters.

"Goats are so tremendously traditional," said Gayle Joslin, a wildlife biologist with Fish, Wildlife and Parks based out of Helena who has studied mountain goats in the Cabinet Mountains and on the Rocky Mountain Front. "People learn to say there's always a goat here and they're usually right. In some areas, the goats were almost decimated because of it. They won't go wandering off like a moose or deer.''

Because of their ties to tradition, Joslin and other wildlife biologists stress that hunters should harvest the mature billies, rather than the nannies which are the herd leaders. "The female is pivotal because she's using the prime spots in the habitat. If a prime nanny is lost, she is then filled in behind by lesser females that don't know the habitat as well," she said.

In the herd, the mature nannies are at the top of the social structure. But in addition to that, they are the ones who are relied on to know where the best feeding and bedding areas are, how to move from one cliff area to another safely, when to start migrations in spring and fall, and where the escape routes are for the herd. In short, they carry the knowledge and tradition of the herd that has been responsible for its survival in such a rugged habitat. If hunters begin shooting off the mature nannies, the whole herd can be lost.

"They're dumb," Joslin said. "They cannot adapt to anything new and different. If they did, they wouldn't be specialists in the terrain they live in."

"We try to encourage hunters to look for a male goat," said Jerry Brown, wildlife biologist for Fish, Wildlife and Parks at Libby. "Females, especially females with kids, are fairly critical because they have the best chance of keeping the population up. They also select some of the best winter range and they teach the kids to select the best winter range. The young learn from them. A female kid will learn its home range from its mother while the young males tend to move off."

The problem is that both billies and nannies look very much alike. They both have the white, shaggy coats and black horns. The notion that a lone goat is always a billy doesn't always hold true, either.

"There are certain subtle traits that can be used to tell them apart," Joslin said. "Look for urination postures—females squat like horses and males stretch. You've got to sit there and wait to see it, but it might save you in the long run. The male will be stockier, more massive in the front shoulders. He tends to have more exaggerated pantaloons. The face and beard are longer. The male's horns tend to curve back in a uniform arch while the females curve in the upper third of the horn. The circumference of the base of the horn is much greater on the males—you're going to see more black. The females' horns will be thinner overall. The females' horns will give the illusion of length because of the thinness, but when you're looking for a nice trophy, that circumference of the billy's looks nice on the wall. The males also dig these rutting pits, pawing the ground until a depression is created, then urinating in the pit and laying in the moist dirt. The males get all dirty, but this does clean up and when the taxidermist gets done with it, it will have a clean white coat."

Judging horn size on mountain goats takes some time and a good pair of binoculars or a spotting scope. One of the keys, however, is to use the ears to judge them. "A kid's horns are just little nubbins two or three inches long. A yearling's horns vary but generally aren't more than four inches long, the same length as the ear. The length of the ear will vary from about three-and-a-half inches to five inches for an adult. You're talking about real trophy horns on the East Front when they're eight to ten inches long, about twice as long as the ear," Joslin said.

The biggest problem that mountain goat hunters often face is the weather in the high country. Snowstorms can be expected in September and October while the valleys below are still basking in warm autumn. "In the fall, it's a rugged type of hunt," Brown said. "Most people hunt them fairly early in the hunting season because weather conditions can run them out of there."

But the weather can be critical in other ways, too. It can affect where the goats will be. "A lot of times early in the season before the snow, the goats are a lot lower than people sometimes think they are. Some of them move down quite a ways into some brushy country in fall. As it gets a little later, they start moving up. Then you might start looking on winter range areas late in the season," Brown said. "They come down off the divides into the side canyons and select some bluffy country and little benches. Those are generally situated out the canyons a little ways.

"I like to get on one ridge and glass across to other ridges. The warmer it is, the more they tend toward north exposures. The colder it is, the more they tend toward south exposures. You get on a vantage point, spend a lot of time glassing and try to spot some and determine if there's a billy in the bunch. You need to spend a lot of time with your binoculars," he said.

When a hunter spots the billy he wants, he should try to move in position for a shot from above while paying attention to wind currents that could alert the goat to his presence. "They've got a good sense of smell and excellent eyesight," Joslin said. "Often, you can make lots of noise. They live in a noisy country with rocks falling all around them."

But hunters should be aware that bagging a billy isn't really the high point of hunting for them. It's all the things that go into goat hunting that makes drawing a tag so special.

"The thing about hunting for the goat is not in the killing of the animal," Joslin said. "It's in their terrain, being with them in the rugged country in which they are found."

Moose

Hunting for moose in Wilderness Country can be as easy or as difficult as you care to make it. It can be a high-quality hunt or a low-quality hunt. And you can take a big bull or just whatever happens to be standing in the road.

Road hunting, in fact, is by far the most popular way to hunt moose in the northwestern corner of Montana, which has been blessed with plenty of moose and plenty of old logging roads. "They drive around a lot," said Jerry Brown, wildlife biologist with Fish, Wildlife and Parks at Libby. "A lot of people won't shoot a moose unless it's on the road or on the uphill side."

Their tendency to be near the roads is due to the fact they're closely tied to the old timber cutting units which open up good habitat for them. But even without the cutting units, this corner of Montana is prime country. "It's related to the vegetation," said Jim Cross, wildlife manager for Fish, Wildlife and Parks in Kalispell. "We've got a fair amount of moisture. We get good growth in the forest. It's an environment in which moose can do well."

The logging has just enhanced the situation for the moose and moose hunters, creating breaks in the forest and providing access through a system of logging roads. "A lot of the logging up here has created some situations that have been conducive to moose," Brown said. "Old cutting units that are fifteen to twenty years old create some of the best moose habitat. The brand new cuts, five or ten years old, the moose don't use as much."

Because of their ties to roads and timber cutting units, moose have gotten a reputation of always being easy once you get past the monumental difficulty of obtaining a moose tag, one of the toughest draws to make in the special permit system. But moose hunting doesn't have to be directly tied to the gas gauge on your car.

"People think they're really dumb, but to get out in the woods and really hunt them, you've got your hands full," Brown said. "They've got excellent hearing and they hear just about everything that goes on. You start moving around in the brush and they keep track of you. A moose is a big animal, but he can hide himself very well."

Old timber cutting units are good habitat for moose while newer units aren't used as much. Michael Sample photo.

To get a good bull moose, it takes time and a willingness to work the cutting units until you locate him. "The thing about them is that a lot of big bulls just hold in an area and don't move around a lot," said Terry Crooks, a hunter from Libby. "If you do a lot of glassing, you might see them in the morning or evening.

"It's easy to get a moose, but if you want a nice bull, it's going to take some time. I know, in most years, you hear rumors up here about where the big bulls have been found. But then when you've got the tag, they just vaporize."

Another method for locating moose is to listen for them. That system led Brown to his moose, an old bull, some years ago which he took with a bow and arrow. "If you're hunting during the rut, you can listen for them. They'll do a lot of grunting and groaning and you can hear them and move in on them," he said. "My bull was rutting and grunting and we worked in on him for an hour. We lost him once or twice before I got him."

There also seems to be an elevation shift which takes place during the fall as the animals react to their changing environment. "It seems like when the season first opens, they're down in low elevations and moist areas," said Cross. "They use these areas until we get a good frost, then they'll leave these areas and move upslope. They'll sometimes move up to five thousand or six thousand feet and it can be more difficult to hunt them. Then, fairly late in the fall or early in the winter, when the snow gets deep, they have a tendency to move downslope again."

But it can take an awful lot of snow to move a moose, and hunters who wait for that to happen may find their tags go unfilled. "They can cope with four to five feet of snow," Cross said. "Think of the length of the legs on the moose. They can walk through three feet of snow without having it touch their brisket."

Having to go up the mountain for them causes other problems as well. Rather than loading the animal whole, like the road hunters are often able to do, it will require quartering and packing. While that's not a difficult task, loads are created that a hunter isn't necessarily going to relish carrying for long distances. "There's probably somewhere in the neighborhood of four hundred to five hundred pounds of meat, field-dressed with the legs, head and hide off," Cross said. "There's no problem with quartering. You're still talking about packing a little over one hundred pounds per quarter and that's not excessive for short distances."

The packing is well worth it, once the moose has been put away in the freezer. "As far as eating, they're spectacular. It's hard to believe how good they are to eat," said Crooks.

Because of that fact, few tags go unfilled in northwestern Montana. Whether by road hunting or getting back off the roads to make it a little more sporting, hunters aren't going to let the draw of a lifetime pass them by.

"We've been averaging between eighty-eight and ninety-five percent success on our moose permits, region-wide," Cross said. "Once you get the permit and have the time to get out a little bit, it's almost a cinch."

Black Bear

Travel westward through the mountains of Wilderness Country and you'll notice some changes. The open parks and meadows will start shrinking in size and eventually all but disappear. The forest will grow more dense in nature as the influence of Pacific Northwest rainfall becomes more apparent. And, if you've got a trained eye to look for sign, you'll notice that the frequency of black bears is increasing rapidly.

Northwestern Montana undoubtedly offers the best black bear hunting to be found in the Treasure State, accounting for about half the bears taken in the state each year. Not that black bears aren't found throughout Wilderness Country and in other parts of Montana as well. This part of the state just has the best habitat for them and also the best access system into that bear habitat with its old logging roads.

In a good area, hunters can see ten to fifteen black bears in a day's time with the help of binoculars. Frank Martin photo.

"It's because of the precipitation," said Jerry Brown, wildlife biologist with Fish, Wildlife and Parks at Libby. "When you have a lot of moisture, you have a lot of variety in plants and a lot of fruit-producing plants. There are a lot of huckleberries in this part of the state. We grow things like mountain ash, bear berry, service berry, and Oregon grape, and they'll use any of that as it's available. It's also densely forested. We get a lot of the Pacific Coast type of vegetation that's not likely to occur in other parts of Montana. We've got a lot of cover, shrubs, and timber for bears."

Keith Aune, a wildlife biologist for Fish, Wildlife and Parks who works the Rocky Mountain Front side of Wilderness Country out of Choteau, said his area has bears, too, but not nearly as many. "We've got a good, solid density of bears, but it doesn't compare quite as strong as west of the Divide or the Cabinets where they've got extremely high densities. We're running a good strong bear for every four to six square miles. West of the Divide, you're talking about one bear per two square miles to four square miles."

In terms of taking advantage of the bears, the northwest also comes out on top simply because the hunters can get to them more easily. "A lot of it has to do with accessibility," Aune said. "A lot of black bear hunters are hunting where they can drive a lot of miles of road. The logging roads that extend through most of that country allow them to go through a lot of area in a weekend. On the East Front, you've got to walk or go horseback. It cuts down on the amount of area you can cover."

Both spring and fall hunting has been available for black bears in the past and in each season, the patterns have been predictable enough that hunters usually don't have too much trouble locating bears.

"In the spring, they're feeding on the southern slopes on the green-up," said Chuck Gibbs, a bear hunter and photographer from Libby. "In the fall, it's more of a process of searching out the high huckleberry patches. You get up on a good ridge and do a lot of glassing. If you're in a good area, you should see ten to fifteen black bears in a good day's time. They have quite a pattern they follow each year and year after year you'll see the same bears in the same areas at the same time."

While road hunting has been the norm in years past, it has been drawing some fire in recent years. "People drive the roads and that's been a real bone of contention up here. A lot of people don't like it, they don't think it's hunting. I don't like it," Brown said. "There are some roads that are being closed. They open them up for logging and then they close them. But you can walk those roads and the bears don't tend to get spooked off because there are no vehicles using them."

Another concern has been hunters mistaking grizzly bears for black bears and shooting them. With grizzlies accorded the status of a threatened species, a war of words has raged over whether the black bear season should be severely limited in grizzly range or even opened at all. While the incidents have been few, some argue that losing even one grizzly, especially a sow, to a hunter's bullet is too many.

"There is the opportunity to mistakenly identify the bears. My feeling is that ten percent of the black bear population could be misidentified as a grizzly or vice versa," Aune said. "The key is to spend a little time watching them and looking for the features to tell them apart."

Among the differences between the bears are the large shoulder hump of the grizzly; its dished in face and longer snout compared to the rounder, shorter features of the black bear; the claws of the grizzly which are very long, more blunt, and usually shiny and ivory-colored compared to the short, curved, dark claws of the black bear; and the appearance of a ruff around the neck of the larger grizzlies compared to the smoother lines of the black.

The color of the bears is one of the least-distinguished characteristics. "We've worked it out over the years on black bears and it's coming out about sixty to sixty-five percent of them are black and thirty to thirty-five percent brown from chocolate to light cinnamon," Brown said.

"Don't go by color," Aune warned. "There undoubtedly will be some cases of mistaken identity but it will never grow to the magnitude that some people feel here is. If it looks like a grizzly to you, don't shoot it."

Upland Birds and Waterfowl

Shotgun hunters are a relatively rare commodity in Wilderness Country. Not that there aren't birds to hunt or that absolutely no one is out hunting them, but opportunities here pale when compared to the wealth of big game hunting available.

"In general, the economics of bird hunting have changed over the past ten years," said Mike Aderhold, regional information officer for Fish, Wildlife and Parks at Kalispell. "Most people take a shotgun along when

Spruce grouse live in a lodgepole pine and huckleberry habitat in the mountains. Michael Sample photo.

they go looking for firewood, but to go out all day with a dog and look around for birds, it's really fallen off. You used to be able to get a tank of gas for two or three dollars and drive around all day and look for the pockets of birds.''

Wilderness Country does hold good populations of ruffed, blue and spruce grouse along with some pheasant and waterfowl hunting in the Flathead Valley.

"The valley bottoms are good areas for waterfowl and pheasants," Aderhold said. "For spruce grouse, it's generally the lodgepole pine and huckleberry habitat. For blue grouse, it's dry ponderosa pine, older pine stands, and the ridges. For ruffed grouse, it's the wetter Doug fir, wet meadow type of country. Generally, it goes that the ruffed grouse are at the lowest elevations, blue grouse in the foothills and spruce grouse higher up.''

But most grouse tend to be taken by opportunists who are out in the forests doing something else. Either it's a big game hunter who decides to take one home as a bonus or a wood cutter who sees the chance to add some meat to his take of fuel. "There never have been a lot of them that go out straight for grouse, but there are a few die-hards," said Dick Weckwerth, former wildlife manager for Fish, Wildlife and Parks at Kalispell. "Some hunt with dogs while others just road hunt."

The take of grouse rises and falls with the cycles of the grouse but the ruffs and blues seem to be the preferred species with the hunters. "I would say the ruffed grouse are the best eating, the blue second and the spruce grouse third," Weckwerth said. "Especially if you get an older bird, the spruce grouse are pretty dark-meated and sometimes they're pretty strong. The young ones are all right.''

In the latter stages of the season, it's mostly mallards for the waterfowl hunter. Mark Henckel photo.

Pheasant hunting is limited by the available cover and considering the area runs as high as eighty-five percent forest, the opportunities aren't great. "Most of the pheasant hunting is in the Flathead Valley from just north of Kalispell south toward Ronan and St. Ignatius," Weckwerth said. "Cover is a little bit lacking. Down in the Ninepipes area, we've got good cover and there are pockets here and there throughout the lower valley which are good pheasant hunting."

Waterfowl hunting is also relatively limited in Wilderness Country but when the flights come in, there is some interest. The hotbed of waterfowl activity in this part of the state is centered around Flathead Lake and the federal and state areas at Ninepipes, near Ronan.

"They hunt parts of Flathead Lake and some of the smaller lakes around the Flathead Valley down by Ninepipes and Ronan," Weckwerth said. "I'd say most of it is decoy hunting."

Don Shepard, who manages Ninepipes Wildlife Management Area for the state, has hunted the area since the 1940s and said the area has changed quite a bit over the years. "I grew up south of Ronan, not too far from Ninepipes," he said. "At one time, it was more farms and when I was a kid, we had a lot more ducks and geese coming through here. We still get geese in here and mallards, pintails, redheads nest here and canvasbacks move through. There are other types of ducks as well."

Early in the season, there is a wide variety of waterfowl moving through and hunters take advantage of it. In the latter stages of the season, it's mostly mallard shooting wherever there's open water to be found.

"It usually is a good opening with the local birds. There'll be a little bit of a lag until you get the flights coming through," Weckwerth said. "Then, if it doesn't freeze up right away, we'll have some good shooting on mallards until it finally does freeze up."

While the upland bird and waterfowl opportunities in Wilderness Country are among its humblest offerings, they, too, show just how bountiful this part of Montana can be. The upland birds and waterfowl are there for the people who want to take advantage of it. Just as the elk are there, the whitetails, mule deer, bighorn sheep, mountain goats, moose and black bear. No matter what your target, Wilderness Country is rich, rich hunting country indeed.

High Plains Country

A land of wheat fields, river breaks, and isolated mountain ranges, High Plains Country holds the last vestiges of the open prairie along the northern tier of the United States. This is the final look at the so-called flatlands of eastern Montana before encountering the rugged face of the Rockies where they rise from the croplands in all their splendor.

While many hunters look westward to the mountain wildernesses and their hunting for bighorn sheep, elk, bear, and mountain goats, High Plains Country is some exquisite hunting country in its own right, guarded fiercely by the locals and often coveted by hunters from west of the Continental Divide who pour over the passes each fall to take advantage of the deer and bird hunting opportunities that can be found here.

High Plains Country, while lumped as part of the flatlands, actually offers a mixture of terrain as varied as the unbroken fields of wheat in the rich Golden Triangle, the smooth and steady flow of the wild and scenic Missouri River, rugged river breaks, and the forested ridges of mountain ranges like the Bearpaws, Highwoods, Judiths, Belts, and the north end of the Snowies. All but a small portion of this big broad land is privately owned and access is definitely a matter of knocking on doors and asking permission. But for those who will take the time to become a true friend of the landowner, the rewards can be rich.

High Plains Country offers the northwestern edge of Montana's "Deer Factory" where, in times of plenty, mule deer provide multiple-tag opportunities that can put a lot of venison in the freezer for the winter.

It has an excellent and under-hunted whitetail population in the creek bottoms throughout the region and in the mountain foothills where aspen stands and agricultural bottoms combine to create prime habitat.

High Plains Country also has impressive flights of big tundra swans, snow geese, and ducks which hunters intercept as they head toward their wintering grounds in California and beyond.

And shotgunners will also find good flocks of sharptails, excellent pheasant habitat, and one of Montana's better areas for Hungarian partridge. For the mountain hunters who will seek them, there are also some ruffed grouse tucked amid the aspens and blue grouse on the ridges.

High Plains Country offers other hunting opportunities as well, but these are of less importance when compared to other parts of the state. There are antelope scattered throughout the area where stands of tall sagebrush provide winter range, but good concentrations of pronghorns are relatively few compared to the country further south and east. Elk can also be found in the mountain ranges that fringe the area, including the Little Belts, Big Belts, and smaller mountain ranges that form the southern and western edges of High Plains Country, and in the Sweet Grass Hills to the north. But, as a region, hunting for elk is more limited than areas further west and south and can be available by special permit only.

In its deer, waterfowl, and upland bird hunting, however, this part of Montana ranks among the best that the Big Sky Country has to offer. It's privately-owned ground well worth getting to know on a more intimate basis, and a part of the Treasure State of which local hunters are justifiably proud.

Mule Deer

Dave Randall doesn't mess around when it comes to filling his deer tags every year. He's got the mule deer hunting world by the tail and he knows it.

"I'd never consider shooting anything less than a five-by-five," the Great Falls taxidermist said. "I shoot a twenty-eight or thirty-incher every year."

That kind of talk would be easily dismissed as just another tall hunting tale in many parts of mule deer range, but it's entirely possible when hunting High Plains Country. The river breaks and brushy draws that lead down to the major waterways of this part of the state provide some of the better hunting for muleys that Montana has to offer.

Not that Randall's big five-points are to be found everywhere, though they're certainly out there. The strength of this country, rather, is in its bountiful deer numbers which provide opportunities to fill multiple tags in years of plenty and offer excellent habitat for mule deer reproduction.

"I got out one day this year and got my buck," Randall said, offering an example of just how bountiful this area can be. "I passed about forty-five bucks that day before I saw the one I wanted. I just watched him go to bed at about noon and never saw another one bigger so I went back about sundown, he was still in his bed and I shot him."

The buck would later score about 170 according to Boone and Crockett Club measuring standards. Not a Boone and Crockett buck, but definitely a trophy by many hunters' standards. "There's a lot of respectable bucks out here," Randall said.

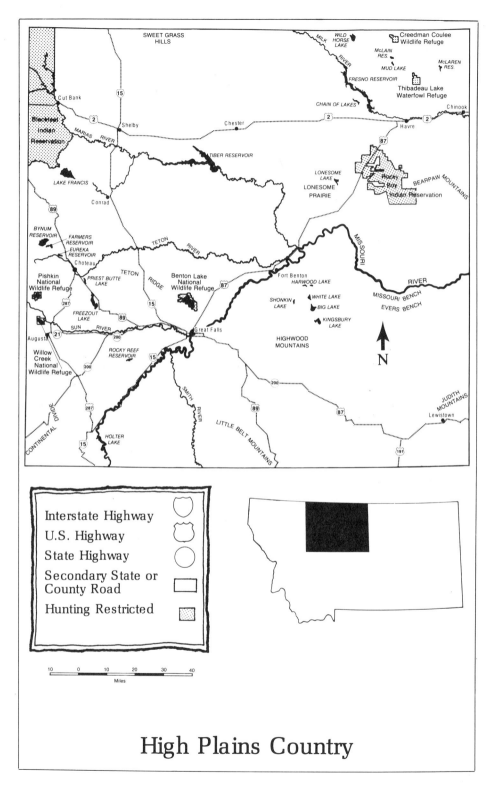

High Plains Country

Prairie areas, especially those between Great Falls, Lewistown, and Havre, provide the big drawing card for mule deer hunting, according to Harley Yeager, information officer for the Department of Fish, Wildlife and Parks at Great Falls.

"We get scads of hunters from Missoula and Kalispell into those areas," he said. "We have such good deer hunting over here compared to there. The populations over here are so much better. And they want to come over and hunt those easily-hunted mule deer and get away from the whitetail hunting over there."

The bulk of High Plains Country's mule deer hunting would have to be classified as the prairie variety and methods here tend to be much the same as in other prairie areas of eastern Montana. Hunting from a vehicle is popular but certainly not the best way to get big bucks.

"I like to get out and walk the coulees, I think you have a much better chance to get a big one that way," Randall said. "I just ease along and stay out of sight as much as posible. This country is full of those coulees and once you catch one down in there, there's no way they can get away."

But even if a stalk fails and the buck finds an escape route, there are certain to be other opportunities just around the bend. Put in other words, deer are virtually everywhere when you get into the right prairie country, compared to the mountains where deer can be much tougher to find.

"Any of the breaks at all, whether you're talking about the breaks of the Teton, Marias, Missouri, or another drainage, it's excellent mule deer country," Yeager said.

Mule deer spread out into the agricultural prairie areas as well, especially in times of bountiful deer herds. But while these areas may provide good food sources, they lack the secure habitat to protect them from

Prairie areas are generally more productive, per square mile, than the mountains for mule deer. Michael Sample photo.

hunters and leave them vulnerable to the ravages of cold and snow when a severe winter hits the High Plains.

"These prairie areas are generally more productive and per square mile, you've got more deer," said Kerry Constan, wildlife biologist with Fish, Wildlife and Parks in Great Falls. "You've got more miles of habitat, per se, compared to the mountains. And it's more of an open type of hunting. You just pick an area and spot long distances and then sneak on it before it disappears on you."

While that mule deer hunting can be easy on the prairie in times of plenty, the boom and bust nature of our prairie herds dictate there are other times when hunting isn't so easy. Back in the 1930s, for example, the combination of drought conditions, more primitive understanding of wildlife populations, and a natural downward spiral of mule deer numbers created a situation where animals were exceedingly scarce.

"People with hundreds of deer on their ranch now will tell you that back in the '30s when they saw a deer track on their ranch, they'd go to town and tell people about it," Constan said. "The agricultural practices have changed since then and I wouldn't foresee anything like that again unless we'd get something like a national or global type of drought like another giant Dust Bowl."

But populations can vary a great deal from year to year here, just as in other parts of eastern Montana. Whether it's due to drought conditions or a more mysterious, possibly cyclical fall like the one that hit all of the state during the mid-1970s, it will force hunters to change their tactics.

During those hard times, hunters will have to look at areas of more secure habitat including the roughest breaks, timbered areas, or the isolated mountain ranges.

"Instead of being found just everywhere, they show up in the best areas," Constan said. "When they're coming back, they fill up all the better habitat first before they start filling in the marginal stuff."

For that reason, mountain ranges like the Bearpaws, Judiths, Snowies, and Belts may offer some of the more reliable mule deer hunting, if not the most spectacular peak populations, High Plains Country has to offer. Because of their security, they can also hold some of the bigger bucks.

Great Falls taxidermist Mark Smart generally relies on these mountain areas for his mule deer hunting in most years, regardless of the population trend at the time.

"I like to get out and walk, walk the ridges, and glass a lot," he said. "You have to get up where the road hunters aren't and then you stand a better chance of getting a good buck.

"I like to get on a vantage point and then glass them early in the morning when the big bucks are out moving. I've taken nice bucks that way and my brother has shot a few a little nicer than I have."

Smart sometimes uses a horse to get back where the road hunters can't reach and, at times, will stick with a big buck once he knows it's in the area.

"I shot a real tall buck once that way. He was taller than he was wide," Smart said. "I spotted him a couple of times and took a shot at him once but missed. I just kept on working the same area where he was and finally I caught him up on a high ridge.

"I spooked him out below me. First about six or seven does filed out but

I kept waiting, maybe a good five minutes. Finally he came sneaking out through the timber. He was a pretty sneaky old buck but I had seen him before and I knew I wanted him."

That buck had five points on each side of a heavy rack that measured just twenty-two inches wide but was twenty-three inches high.

Just as in mule deer areas elsewhere, the rut of late November gives hunters here a definite advantage because the big bucks tend to be more active and less wary at that time.

"The key to mule deer and whitetail both is to hunt them late when they're in the rut," Constan agreed. "As soon as they've got other things on their mind, they make lots and lots of mistakes."

But hunters who plan to take to the field in High Plains Country should remember that there's a definite distinction between big deer and record book deer. Though this part of Montana does indeed have big deer, that doesn't mean there are record book deer just waiting to be shot.

"As far as a Boone and Crockett head, there are very few of those. In Montana, the most difficult one to get in the trophy book is the typical mule deer buck," said Yeager. "I've been scoring for eighteen years and I haven't scored a typical mule deer buck that made it yet. Some nontypical have made it, but not very many."

And hunters should remember, too, that High Plains Country, with few exceptions, is privately-owned country.

"There are a lot of ranches open to hunting, but you've got to get the permit from them first," Randall said.

That's good advice for big game hunters here and in most parts of eastern Montana. And it's also the law.

White-tailed Deer

The day is down to its final hour as the sun casts long shadows on the barley field before you. You shiver a bit, for the evening breeze is sliding down the hillside toward the valley below, but there's no time to think about the cold now.

The evening's procession has already begun into the cut-over barley, and a doe and two fawns are out there just as they were the evening before. Soon other does and fawns emerge from the timber and feed out into the shadows. Small bucks will follow and hold their jousting matches of pushing and shoving with spindly antlers as they try to show off for the ladies and work off steam they don't understand in these weeks just prior to the rut.

If you're lucky, when the shadows turn purple and the end of shooting time draws near, the big boys will appear and your three hours of sitting will pay off with a heavy-antlered whitetail. But even if that big buck doesn't show, the performance of those whitetails in High Plains Country would be hard to match anywhere else in Montana.

There are parts of this country that are literally crawling with whitetails and hunting them can be as easy as taking a stand at the edge of a wheat, barley, or alfalfa field.

But that's not the traditional Montana way and whitetails are not the traditional deer of this part of the Treasure State. As Wayne Arnst, outdoor writer for the Great Falls Tribune, so aptly puts it, "Montana hunters are keyed into mule deer hunting but there are an awful lot of whitetails. There are probably some pretty good old whitetail bucks around, too, but the average whitetail buck seems to be smarter than the average whitetail buck hunter."

Whitetails simply take a different approach than many Montana hunters are used to. You usually can't walk the ridges and spot them, then move in close for a shot. You can't drive the edges of the coulees and expect to get them. And if you do spot them, you can't expect them to stand there and wait while you draw a bead on them.

Not that whitetails have any more innate intelligence than mule deer, it's just that their habits, lifestyle and defense systems are different. To get whitetails, a hunter has to prey on their weaknesses just as those with long-shooting rifles take advantage of a mule deer's tendency to stand there at two hundred yards and let you take a shot. Though whitetails tend to be more jumpy and will run at the first sign of danger, they are definitely creatures of habit and stand hunting can pay off with bigger dividends than a mule deer hunter could ever get with the same technique.

To find whitetail areas in High Plains Country, a hunter should look to agricultural ground in the creek bottoms or to the mountain foothills where good stands of aspen are mixed among the pines.

"Some of the most oustanding whitetail habitat is agricultural areas with brushy creek bottoms and river bottoms. Most of your major river bottoms provide outstanding reservoirs of whitetails," said Kerry Constan, wildlife biologist with Fish, Wildlife and Parks in Great Falls. "The Lewistown country also holds good populations of whitetails in the Snowy Mountains and other mountains around there."

But, once again, don't be fooled by bountiful numbers. If you don't hunt them right, white-tailed deer will seem scarcer than reindeer. You just can't apply mule deer hunting techniques to whitetails and expect to score consistently on them.

"I've been hunting whitetail bucks exclusively for years," Constan said. "They are so much more of a wary animal than a mule deer, it's unbelievable. They're just tougher.

"This fall I hunted several areas where there's both mule deer and whitetails. I'd hunt from stands and about two and a half hours before dark, mule deer were out feeding. The first whitetail poked his nose out at 4:00 and most of them didn't poke their nose out until after dark."

Hunting from stands is probably the most effective method of taking deer in these areas, and doing some preliminary scouting will help to put venison in the freezer. The amount of scouting done will largely depend on how nice a whitetail you want to hang your tag on and how much time you have available to you.

Frank Martin, of Lewistown, has been hunting the area for years with both a gun and a bow and believes in starting his scouting activities early, before the season begins.

"I go out and get up on a big bluff and glass for deer," he said. "I get there right at evening with a big spotting scope and look in the grain fields and alfalfa fields. When you see those spots come out in the distance, you can tell where they are. Then I go back and look at those places to find a place where a bunch of runways come out at one spot. Then I put up my tree stand there."

Hunting from a tree stand is effective for both archery and gun hunters looking for a whitetail. Bill McRae photo.

The deer seem to follow the same patterns with the big bucks coming out last, often pushing legal shooting time before they break out into the open.

"Sometimes, the fawns come out racing around just like kids. Then the doe will peek out. Sometimes there will be twenty deer out in the open before the first buck shows up. I've seen four or five little bucks show up and then you can see, back in the brush, the tips of the antlers of the big buck. He might not come out at all. I've even seen them bed down back in there until after dark," he said.

The problem can often be judging the size of the deer from a distance, especially before the bucks' antlers shed their velvet.

"When they're in the velvet, they're pretty hard to see. But you can tell the young bucks even if you can't see the antlers because they'll be pushing each other. Generally, it's the little bucks that do that," Martin said. "But as soon as the antlers are polished, you can spot those bucks pretty well."

After he spots the buck he wants to work on and figures out which trees will afford him a good shot under different wind conditions, he lets the area rest for several days before the beginning of the season. Then, he will begin his nightly visitations until the buck makes a mistake or plans on an early dinner.

Hunting from tree stands in this deer-rich country also gives a hunter some rare opportunities to witness the wildlife world. Because you're above the wildlife, the wind isn't as likely to carry your scent to them and unless you hunt an area where tree stands are common and animals have learned about them, they rarely look up to detect danger.

"One time, I was in the tree for about forty-five minutes when a badger came along. When he hit my footprints, he froze and turned his head and looked all around. Boy, he knew I was there. But finally he eased off and walked away," Martin said. "Another time, I'd been in the tree for a half-hour and a big doe came under the tree and froze like a dog on point. I dropped a small twig on her back. She never even flinched. Finally, she settled down and she sneaked out. She was a smart old gal.

"You see foxes, ruffed grouse. I sat in a blind once and heard three ruffed grouse drumming in October. I pinpointed where each one was and went out there the next day with my dog and got all three of them," he said.

While trees offer one method of hunting from stands, they are certainly not the only way to do it. For those (like me) who have an aversion to spindly branches beneath them and the prospects of sudden collisions with the ground below, hunting from a ground blind works almost as well. To do it right, the best way is to get a piece of camouflage cloth to prop up in front of you and shield your movements. Then, find a tree on the edge of the fields to lean against. And, finally, make sure there is a solid background of brush behind you to break your outline. The hazards are that the wind is more likely to blow your scent to the deer and you may have to set up further away and take longer shots to avoid detection.

Constan takes advantage of a good compromise between the airborne tree-stander and the down-to-earth denizen of a ground blind.

"I like sitting on a haystack. It's the best way in the world to hunt," he said. "I do a lot of my hunting where I spot them in the morning and see where they go back in the brush. Then I come back at night when they come out to feed or vice-versa. The main advantage of the haystack is that it gives you some height. It's a nice vantage point. You get some flat country and you can't see very far but there's usually a haystack somewhere in agricultural country.

"You can sit there and sometimes snuggle down into it if the wind's blowing and it's cold. You can even put up a bale and use it as a shooting stand," Constan said.

In these whitetail strongholds, deer can also be taken by organizing drives when enough hunters are available to push through patches of cover. Even still hunting is possible, though a hunter will have to move much slower, do much more looking around, and have far more patience than would ever be required when hunting mule deer.

Times of plenty will also find white-tailed deer spreading out from these strongholds.

"It used to be that mule deer and whitetails were pretty well separated but over the past dozen years or so, we're getting more and more of a mix on them," Arnst said. "Whitetails are going further up in the hills."

Hunting pressure can also force whitetails, especially the bigger bucks, to forsake their river bottom homes and move into country that a hunter wouldn't usually associate with their species.

"In your larger river bottoms like the Missouri, they'll go up the side draws and up onto the prairie and lay down in the grass. There isn't much cover up there, but no one bothers them," Constan said.

Harley Yeager, information officer for Fish, Wildlife and Parks in Great Falls, said these movements can sometimes be extensive. "Whitetails have pulled right up into the areas you wouldn't think of as whitetail habitat at all," he said. "You go up in those upland areas and expect to see mule deer and find whitetails there. I saw that time and time again during the last hunting season when hunters went down and worked on those bottoms. Sometimes those deer would move out two or three miles."

Hunters should be aware, however, that whitetails here don't run nearly as big as the mule deer or even as big as their kin further east.

"They're not big like those in the grain country of the Dakotas," Martin said. "They'll run thirty to forty pounds less in average weight. A two hundred-pound whitetail in this country is really rare. Most of the bucks I've shot will run around a hundred forty pounds. A four-point whitetail in this part of the country will run a hundred thirty to a hundred forty pounds field-dressed."

But what High Plains Country whitetails lack in size, they certainly make up for in numbers. And hunting here for them can be excellent no matter what method you use, as long as you remember one thing. They're not mule deer, never will be mule deer, and you just can't hunt them the same way and expect to score.

Waterfowl

Whistling wings riding the north wind out of Canada are very much a part of High Plains Country each fall. Big tundra swans, major flights of snow geese, and grain-fed mallards bound for their wintering grounds in California make this part of Montana a regular stop on their migration path.

With wheat and barley fields for food, big reservoirs and marshes for resting areas, and long windy autumns for open water conditions, High Plains Country smiles on waterfowl and waterfowl hunters alike.

While ducks and geese can be found over the entire region, no areas attract as much attention as Benton Lake National Wildlife Refuge, near Great Falls, and Freezeout Lake, near Fairfield. These are the traditional gunning grounds for hunters in this part of Montana and annually provide a significant portion of the state waterfowl harvest as well.

"We probably have fifteen or sixteen different species of ducks and we know we have two or three subspecies of Canada geese. There are quite a number of snow geese and its subspecies of blue geese. We see an occasional white-fronted goose in with the snows and blues and we get the little Ross' goose. And there are the swans," said Bob Pearson, refuge manager at Benton Lake, in describing the variety of waterfowl that frequent this part of Montana.

With those kinds of waterfowl possibilities, however, the area is hardly a secret. Hunters flock in from throughout Montana, especially nearby Great Falls, and waterfowlers looking for solitude would be well-advised to look elsewhere.

"We would have well over a thousand hunters on Freezeout on opening day and they'd be averaging three to four birds per hunter. After opening day, the hunting pressure would fall off to thirty to fifty hunters during the peak migration periods," said Dale Witt, who was stationed at Freezeout Lake for twenty-two years before being transferred by Fish, Wildlife and Parks to department headquarters in Helena several years ago.

Pearson echoed Witt's view on his area. "Our biggest day as far as number of hunters is opening weekend. It's kind of a madhouse situation and I don't recommend people coming for that. There are maybe too many hunters," he said.

The reason they come, of course, is big populations of ducks and geese. And, surprisingly, they take their share of them despite the heavy gunning.

Bryce West, of Simms, for example, was a regular at Benton Lake during waterfowl season when he lived in nearby Great Falls and he still remembers the scene there during those peak pressure times. "The guys would be eighty to one hundred yards away from one another and war would be declared," he said. "But there still were enough birds coming in. There are thousands of them and you'll get your share of shooting."

Hunting pressure will slack off some after that opening day barrage and success will drop off, too, during the bluebird days that often make up the early part of the season. "If you've got warm, still days, the birds don't respond very well. Hunters have to beat the bushes to get things up and flying," Pearson said.

For many hunters, the season will end there as the start of big game season takes them to other fields of operation. But the best waterfowl hunting season is still to come, especially with the flights of snow geese and with the swans which are hunted on a special permit regulation and limited harvest basis.

"There are upwards of 200,000 to 300,000 snow geese that come through the area," said Witt. "I have seen that many at one time in spring. That is really a spectacular sight. There's probably close to 50,000 swans that come through there. I've seen as many as 10,000 to 15,000 there at one time."

But snow goose hunting has changed over the years and isn't quite as reliable or as long-lived as it was in the past. "Snow geese are moving out of Canada maybe a month later than they used to, which has impacted the hunting at Freezeout quite a bit. The peaks are about the same but the extent of when they're here is a lot shorter," said Don Childress, statewide waterfowl coordinator for Fish, Wildlife and Parks.

"They used to be in by the 10th of October and now they don't come in until after the 1st of November unless weather moves them," Witt added.

That difference, most likely caused by changing agricultural practices north of the border, doesn't make snow goose hunting as available to

Snow goose hunting has changed since 1966, when the birds flocked by the hundreds of thousands around Freezout Lake. Roger Fliger photo.

hunters here. But there are still plenty of goose hunters who take advantage of the geese when they do come in.

"What most hunters are watching for is some of that severe weather that would freeze up Canada or heavy snow that would cover up their food supply," Witt said. Then, when they arrive in Montana, hunters will go after them in several ways.

"We do have a variety of hunting situations. A lot of the novice hunters will hunt shoreline areas," said Pearson of Benton Lake. "We do have some areas designated for hunters with retrievers only. Your more seasoned, skilled hunters will usually have a boat and decoys and a retriever but some of our hunters haven't used a shotgun before. We get quite a cross-section of hunters."

While boats aren't necessary for Freezeout, either, Childress said they have their value, especially for hunters who want to find a hunting spot of their own. "There are a number of areas you can hunt without a boat," he said. "But a boat does give you a few more options, especially on a weekend in getting away from other hunters."

Goose hunting on the big flocks that move into this part of Montana breaks down into several methods. Some hunters use field shooting techniques, following the flocks from their watery resting areas and spotting where they feed, then setting up for them the following day. Others use floating decoys on Freezeout, Benton Lake, or other wetland areas the geese are using for resting areas. Still other hunters simply pass shoot at them as they go about their daily flight routines.

"Most use snow goose decoys and it's very similar to Canada goose hunting although the snow goose flocks themselves are usually larger in number. The most successful hunters in the field use larger and larger spreads of decoys, up to a hundred or so. Some guys put out sticks with rags on them and they'll lay right out in them with white clothes on," Witt said. "As the geese become more wary, the ones with the larger setups will be more successful at having the flocks come and give them a look."

The snow geese can range a long ways, depending on hunting pressure, to the wheat and barley fields that make up their feeding areas. Canada geese, which make up a much smaller proportion of the hunting opportunities here compared to other parts of Montana, tend to stay closer to the waters.

"At Freezeout, snow geese will go twenty to thirty miles at times to feed, depending on the pressure," Childress said. "Canada geese are staying closer, about five miles as a general rule."

The big duck flights also absorb their share of pressure in High Plains Country and wintry weather up north brings tremendous numbers of them within range of Montana hunters' guns. "The big duck is still the mallard," Witt said. "It's the most predominant in the bag. It's the most predominant on the water. And scaup and canvasback, you'll get them every year."

The best hunting at Freezeout and Benton Lake comes when heavy weather is brewing and the flights are on the move.

"It isn't so much rain and snow. If you've got the wind, you can do pretty good," Childress said. "Birds are restless. They are looking for other places to sit down. And that's one thing about this country, you generally do get a lot of wind."

West recalled some of those windy days spent hunting with his son-in-law, Hugh Smith of Great Falls. The weather made the trips memorable enough, but the tricky pass shooting of ducks and geese riding that cold wind was unlike any other gunning experience a waterfowl hunter could imagine.

"It's terrible windy and can be colder than the dickens out there," West said. "You'd have to get down in the weeds just to get out of that wind. And that pass shooting is where you really learn how to shoot.

"I've seen Hugh hit a teal with a strong tailwind and he nailed that thing. But it went a quarter of a mile before it hit the ground. He said he led him about thirty feet. Hugh, he's a duck hunter. He's a good shotgunner."

West said that the windy days when flights were coming in would also bring an endless variety of waterfowl to the hunting grounds. "There's every kind of duck you can think of, redheads, canvasbacks, teal, mallard, widgeon, snow geese, and the Canada geese," he said. "I shot a redhead once that was coming right at me and he hit me in the chest and damn near knocked me down. As far as I'm concerned, these are fabulous places to hunt."

Freezeout and Benton Lake don't have a corner on the good waterfowl hunting in this part of Montana, of course. There are other large reservoirs on the flight path of the fall migrations and rivers like the Missouri, Sun, Marias, Milk, and Teton which hold birds until freeze-up sends them further south for the winter.

"You've got other reservoir types of situations which do hold quite a few geese in the fall. There's quite a bit of goose hunting on them and I think it's picked up over the past few years," Childress said. "It's kind of a well-kept secret in a way"

While these secluded spots can offer a more pristine place to hunt waterfowl and are well-kept secrets in High Plains Country, the fact the big flights of ducks and geese use this part of Montana as a major thoroughfare on their migration paths each spring and fall is no secret at all. The haunting sound of whistling wings as they set into decoys and the rattling song of wind ripping through the marsh grass are music to the ears of waterfowl hunters no matter where they find them in High Plains Country.

"It's not just the numbers of waterfowl but the variety that everyone can see, that's one of the things that everyone enjoys," Childress said. "And the marsh situation gives them some classic waterfowl opportunities. That's why we get alot of people coming back. It's a nice place to go hunting."

Upland Birds

Grazing patterns and wheat fields are the key ingredients the upland bird hunter should be watching for in High Plains Country. There are a wealth of Hungarian partridge, sharp-tailed grouse, and pheasants in this part of Montana if the hunter can just match the right ingredients to the bird he's seeking.

In the vast wheat fields that stretch north of Great Falls toward the Canadian border, it's the Hungarian partridge that's likely to offer the sporting target a hunter is after. In the brushy creek and river bottoms, there are fast-footed pheasants. And for sharptails, some grain fields, berry bushes, or the mountain foothills are good spots to walk.

"This region provides a significant portion of the upland game bird hunting in the state," said Harley Yeager, information officer for Fish, Wildlife and Parks in Great Falls.

"We have fierce competition for the good bird hunting spots," added Frank Feist, a wildlife biologist working out of the same office. "The most important thing up in this area is to get into the good habitat. That requires the permission of the landowners."

In terms of statewide significance, Hungarian partridge probably provide the most important upland bird resource in this part of Montana. This sheds light mainly on land use practices here and the rugged little bird's tolerance for intensive agriculture.

"They can tolerate more intensive farming than our other game species, including big game," said John Weigand, a Fish, Wildlife and Parks research biologist working out of Bozeman who did a major study on Hungarian partridge in the Golden Triangle north of Great Falls. "They can tolerate up to ninety-five percent of an area in grain as long as the other five or seven percent offers a noncrop situation with some cover.

"There are some desert areas where the guy has an area fenced off for his house, grain bins, and machinery, and plows right up to that fence. Then they're out of luck. But much of this country falls into the limits of what they can take."

As long as there's some ungrazed or lightly-grazed grassland mixed in among the wheat fields, a hunter is in luck. "What you're looking for is where the grainfields butt up against some noncrop situation," he said. "They're a bird of the edge."

Some of the better spots are old, abandoned homesteads and shelter belts, but any grassy cover will suffice. And once a hunter finds birds, he should remember the spot where he jumped them.

"When jumped, you'll see them fly up to a quarter of a mile. Normally, the flights are two hundred yards or less," Weigand said. "Their home range is generally within a quarter of a square mile. They're hatched, they live, and they die within a quarter of a square mile, just a hundred sixty acres."

That close-to-home nature can be put to good use by a hunter if he takes the time to keep records on his activities.

"There was a fellow up in Conrad who was a Hun hunter and he shot one of my banded birds. He said the way he hunted them was like quail in California. He would plot the location of every covey he saw, regardless of the time of year, and he would establish routes in hunting season where he could touch base with ten coveys in a day. He would generally find them in that quarter of a square mile, shoot two or three birds and then go on to the next covey. He told me he shot about a hundred fifty birds in a year."

With an annual mortality rate of seventy-five percent and the ability to average fifteen young in a brood, Huns can stand considerable hunting pressure. In fact, Weigand said, "The Huns could stand significantly more hunting pressure than they're getting."

It's also interesting to note that despite their small size and the severity of the winters that blow through High Plains Country, they are an amazingly hardy bird.

"Huns can dig through a foot of snow to get to feed and they'll use snow to burrow in," Weigand said. "But if it gets much deeper than a foot or if the snow is hard, that's a detriment to them. If it crusts over or you get a rain and it freezes, that's detrimental. But because Montana east of the Continental Divide has such a semi-arid climate, you don't often encounter that type of thing."

One final word of advice on Huns is that a dog is helpful, but not required, when hunting this little speedster. "You do not need a dog necessarily to find them, but they're handy in retrieving them," Weigand said. "They won't run like a pheasant but if you drop them in rough country, they might be tough to find."

Pheasants in this part of the state are another story. Long patches of heavy cover and the pheasant's ability to run through it at high speed ahead of the hunter make a good dog a valuable commodity indeed.

This most-highly prized of Montana game birds inhabits all the bottom-lands of High Plains Country wherever there's some sort of brush or thick tall grass for cover.

"The most important thing is the degree of use by livestock. If you can find an area that is very lightly grazed or not grazed, it's amost a cinch you'll have pheasants," said Rich Johnson, of Lewistown, who estimates he hunts upland birds more than forty times a year. "Woody vegetation of some type is good, too. What that does is give them some protection from avian predators in the winter months. I also think alfalfa is important but they can eat a variety of agricultural crops."

It's almost impossible to find bottomland cover that's too thick for

Areas with brush or tall grass for cover are the places a hunter should look for pheasants. Michael Sample photo.

pheasants themselves, but those long stretches of heavy cover can cause plenty of problems for pheasant hunters. Birds can run ahead of hunters for miles on these creek bottoms and never feel the need to fly. To combat that tendency, Johnson has devised a few plans of operation that have put ringnecks in the bag.

"After the first two weeks of the season, the birds get pretty wild and they'll run on you. If you start working up a bottom and they hear you, they're gone," Johnson said. "What you really need to do is have somebody block them off a third of a mile or a half mile ahead of you.

"If you're hunting by yourself, you loop on them. You hunt them in one direction for a while and then go a half mile or a third of a mile ahead and then go back on them. They'll be reluctant to go the other way because you were there before. They'll either fly or they might go up in the sagebrush or up in the side coulees and you can work them there," he said.

Either of those tactics work better with a dog, however. "Hunting pheasants here without a dog is tough. In my judgement, the best dog would be a springer spaniel for pheasants but I like to hunt them with a pointing dog."

In his annual journeys for birds, Johnson will also take his German shorthair pointer into the hills for sharptails. High Plains Country offers some good opportunities for this prairie flyer. But contrary to pheasants, finding available food sources for them seems to be more critical than identifying cover areas. That food can come from a variety of sources depending on the year and relative abundance.

"Grain is a little more important for sharptails than pheasants. The

Hunting for the hunting spot can be the most important part in bagging sharp-tailed grouse. Frank Martin photo.

berry bushes are important with buffaloberry and Russian olive as the key species," Johnson said. "I like to hunt in grasslands where there are little coulees coming in. They're in the buckbrush and the berry bushes in those coulees, particularly early in the season."

Mountain foothills, especially where grain fields are interspersed with grassy slopes, are another excellent place to look for sharptails. And sharptails also invade the edges of pheasant cover, especially late in the season, when grouse may fly into the bottomlands to pick up an easy meal of grain or fruit.

But for all these species in High Plains Country, hunting for the hunting spot can be far more important than hunting for the birds. Because so much of the land is privately-owned and close to population centers like

Great Falls, Lewistown, and Havre, there's no substitute for being an active proponent of landowner-sportsman relations.

Among those who go out of their way to thank farmers and ranchers for hunting privileges is Feist, who makes it a year-round activity.

"I think if hunters expect to get on a piece of private ground often and really get serious about bird hunting, you have to do that," he said. "I do it by trying to remember the people at Christmas time. Or, if I'm in that neck of the woods, stopping by and chatting. Not just when it's time to go hunting, but at other times, too.

"My wife is a potter and often, I give them a little bit of her pottery. If a guy likes to drink a bit, a fifth or something of that nature is good," Feist said.

"If you don't do those things and the landowner doesn't know you that well, he may let you on once or twice a year. He may not let you on a lot. Most bird hunters don't go four or six times a year, but avid bird hunters go as often as they can. And I think the landowners remember and appreciate what you do for them."

Breaks Country

Few regions of the Treasure State can conjure up such rich images as those of the country surrounding the Missouri Breaks of northcentral Montana.

Big flocks of sharp-tailed grouse boil up out of a buffaloberry draw. Pope and Young bull elk work down a juniper-strewn coulee toward Fort Peck Reservoir. Majestic mule deer bucks gather their harems and defend them against intruders on a pinnacle ridge. And goose music drifts southward from the wheat country of Canada on the cold winds of late autumn.

This is some of the wildest country in Montana, yet somehow it's often forgotten amid the talk of such designated wildernesses as the Bob Marshall, Lincoln-Scapegoat, and Absaroka-Beartooth. It's also some of the richest hunting country in terms of wildlife, though it doesn't share the variety that other parts of the Treasure State may boast.

But there are blessings in buffers and distance that Breaks Country has to offer a hunter. Far removed from the major population centers of Montana, it also has the advantage of other hunting country surrounding it to shortstop nonresident hunters who travel to the Treasure State.

As a result, it still holds the solitude that many older resident hunters grew up with twenty and thirty years ago and which the out-of-state hunters dreamed about when they first envisioned what hunting here would be like.

There are some drawing cards to Breaks Country that do attract some heavy attention, of course. Most notable among them is the archery hunting for elk in the Missouri Breaks and mule deer opportunities during the rifle season in the rugged cuts scattered throughout this region.

There is also some top-notch antelope hunting throughout the region, including some areas in the Jordan and Cohagen country which offer as good a chance at a Boone and Crockett buck as can be found anywhere in Montana.

But duck and goose hunting based out of Bowdoin National Wildlife Refuge is also worthy of note along with upland bird hunting for pheasants, sharp-tailed grouse, and sage grouse.

White-tailed deer are less of a factor here than in other parts of Montana but good populations exist on the Milk, Missouri and Musselshell river bottoms and those of their smaller tributaries. Scattered populations of Hungarian partridge can also provide some excitement for upland bird hunters. And there are opportunities to hunt the big flocks of migratory sandhill cranes which are available at few other places in Montana or anywhere else.

Breaks Country also has the benefit of some large blocks of public land where hunters can roam without permission. The biggest single chunk among them is the million acres of land that forms the Charles M. Russell National Wildlife Refuge which straddles Fort Peck Reservoir and the Missouri River. Large tracts of U.S. Bureau of Land Management-controlled land can also be found north of the CMR and in the rugged breaks north of Malta and Glasgow, with smaller parcels in Petroleum and Garfield Counties to the south.

But hunters coming here from other parts of Montana and elsewhere should also note that Breaks Country is not an area blessed with many paved highways. Most of the hunting country can be found off of gravel and gumbo clay roads which are firm and solid beneath a pickup's wheels when it's dry, but slippery, sloppy, and, at times, virtually impassable when it's wet.

Yet it's well worth the price to eat a little dust heading down the backroads of Breaks Country in fall. The hunting can often be wilder than anywhere else in Montana and offers the serenity and solitude beneath the Big Sky that most think can be found only in the mountains.

Elk

At one time, elk were a common sight in eastern Montana, living side by side with the buffalo, antelope, and deer. But hunting and land use practices of the white man eliminated them from that portion of their historical range.

It forced elk to forsake their prairie homes everywhere, except the Missouri Breaks. In the steep hills and pine and juniper stands on both sides of the Missouri River and Fort Peck Reservoir, elk still thrive after being reintroduced there by the white men who once drove their kin westward into the mountains.

From a strictly wildlife point of view, seeing elk grazing out on the prairie again would be enough in itself to make the Breaks elk herd a unique and wonderful sight. And as such, they are a point of pride to most everyone in northeastern Montana. But from a bowhunter's point of view, they mean something more, for the Breaks offer an opportunity to see and hunt for elk unlike any other in Montana. With the open ground nature of the Breaks, an abundant elk herd, and vast acreages of public land, it's unique in every way.

While there's limited hunting on a permit basis for rifle shooters, the real action in the Missouri Breaks begins in September when the area acts like a magnet for bowmen from throughout Montana and the world as they take advantage of the archery season there.

"We get hunters nationwide that come for elk archery alone," said Ralph Fries, manager of the million-acre Charles M. Russell National Wildlife Refuge. "In one year, in just the month of May, we answered 513 inquiries concerning opportunities on the refuge."

Each year, about ten percent of the licensed bowhunters in Montana can be expected to spend some of their time walking the ridges and coulees of the Breaks. Success doesn't run that much higher than anywhere else in the state, but unlike many other areas, there are few archers who come out of this country without tales of elk seen, elk encountered, or elk missed.

According to Harvey Nyberg, wildlife biologist for the Department of Fish, Wildlife and Parks at Malta, the herd is managed for a minimum of fifteen hundred animals during the winter. It's also managed to provide big bull opportunities.

"Each year, there are several Pope and Young elk that come out of there. We manage that Breaks herd for fifteen to twenty bulls per hundred cows and there is a good diverse age structure," he said.

But while the elk are there, many bowmen just don't hunt the Breaks correctly to take advantage of them. For one thing, the bugling tactics used elsewhere during the rut of September and early October just don't seem to apply here. For another, the elk's habits are different because they live in a hotter, more wide-open environment than that of the mountains.

Buck Damone, of Lewistown, and Steve Schindler, of Glasgow, are two bowhunters who have hunted the Breaks regularly for years and have adapted their techniques to the territory on the east and west ends of the Breaks.

"In the western half, there is more timber so the elk are a little less visible. In the eastern part, the elk are more visible, but they're only visible for the first few hours in the morning or the last hours before evening," Schindler said.

Schindler, who primarily hunts the eastern Breaks, said his routine is to get up early and be out on the various points and ridges where he can get a good view of a lot of country. "The elk will be down in the green creek bottoms feeding and they'll be feeding into the wind. You either try to get ahead of them or off to the side of them and you intercept them on their travel route," he said.

In some of his hunting, it's just a matter of putting to use the knowledge he has gained in previous years. "We watched elk for nine years in a row that would feed in this creek bottom. There's a yellow patch of grass halfway between where they'd be feeding and their bedding area and there's juniper bushes nearby where a guy can hide and shallow gouges in the ground. Sometimes, we could get them within ten feet of us but through the season, they might change their path a little bit and be out of range."

Schindler said seeing elk during the bowhunting season on the eastern end of the Breaks is no problem. Because the country is so wide open and elk are so large, they are often visible for miles. "You can see a lot of them but they're using so many of their senses, they're awful hard to get close to," he said.

Bowhunting for elk in the Breaks takes a different approach than those commonly used in other parts of Montana.
Mark Henckel photo.

"These elk over here are a combination of four animals. They've got eyesight like an antelope, a nose like a white-tailed deer, often they'll bed where an old mule deer buck will and they're as unpredictable as elk. You can get within sixty to seventy yards of them no problem, but getting to within thirty yards where a guy can make a killing shot is pretty hard to do."

Working to the bowman's advantage on the eastern end of the Breaks, however, is the wind. When he sets up a stalk or plans a way to intercept a moving herd of elk, the wind direction tends to be influenced by the big body of water nearby. "Along Fort Peck Lake, the wind will come off the lake for the first three or four hours in the morning. After that, when the ground warms up, the thermals will go toward the lake," Schindler said.

107

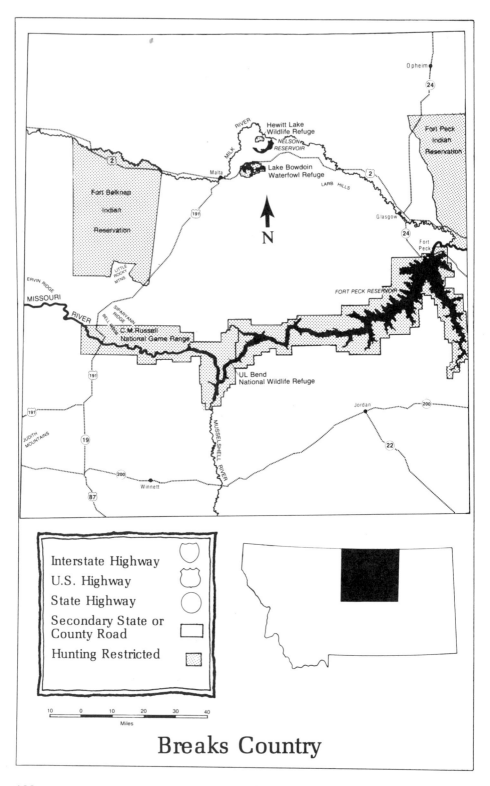

Breaks Country

Interstate Highway
U.S. Highway
State Highway
Secondary State or County Road
Hunting Restricted

10 0 10 20 30 40
Miles

Hunting more on the western end of the Breaks, Damone uses slightly different strategies to hunt big bulls. His area holds more timber and juniper and also has the thick willow bottoms and islands of the Missouri River. But it also tends to get more hunters.

"On the willow bottoms, all the elk and all the people congregate. Lots of people, lots of elk," he said. "People see elk, they get a lot of shots, and have a lot of close encounters but it's a happenchance type of thing. It's so thick you just have to hope you can see them."

Some hunters have solved the thick willows problem with tree stands but in many areas, there just aren't trees large enough to hold them. And elsewhere, more than a few hunters have erected their tree stands in the dark only to look around at first light and spot a dozen other hunter-filled tree stands within view.

"To me, it's not a very pleasing place to hunt if you're a bowhunter. I like your regular Breaks type of hunting where you key in on their bedding, watering and feeding areas," Damone said. "If I could give one key to that, it's to pattern the elk. They're easy to pattern if they haven't been pushed. But you still don't just go down there in a day and do this."

He patterns his elk with preseason scouting and using the knowledge gained in hunting seasons past. Over the years, Damone has found that elk will move from a mile to three miles from their beds to find stock ponds and reservoirs for watering and feeding areas where green vegetation is still available.

"With those three pieces of information, you can hunt the water holes, you can get them going into the bedding area early and get them when they're coming out. My favorite is the bedding area coming out," he said.

These bedding areas are almost always on north-facing slopes of the coulees with thick pines overhead and a dense understory of juniper bushes. Because they're so thick, the chances of walking up on a herd of elk during the daylight is relatively slim. There are just too many elk eyes to see you. So Damone relies on timing instead.

"So many people hunt the Breaks wrong," he said. "Between 10 a.m. and 4:30 p.m., the Breaks shouldn't be hunted. Don't mess with them in the heat of the day. Go back to camp. Do something else. Because once you go into those bedding areas during the day, you're going to spook the elk out and you'll have to start all over. If nobody bugs them, they're not going to leave."

Damone said it is possible to hunt the bedding areas but only if it's done right. "If you're going to hunt bedding areas with the elk coming in, you're going to have to get there before daylight. Or find a spot to hide where they're coming out in the evening."

Damone said challenging a bull with a bugle is another error when trying to hunt the Breaks. While it may work well in the mountains of western Montana, it's just a waste of time and effort here. "They bugle a lot less than in the mountains. If I can hear one, I use it to locate them but I never bugle down in the Breaks."

He does use other elk sounds, however, and they helped him get a Pope and Young bull with eight points on one side of a wide rack and seven points on the other.

"I use a diaphragm call and make cow talk, chuckles and grunts. If you want to get a bull, just slip in among the cows and chuckle and grunt the

Elk are a very visible animal in the wide-open country of the Missouri Breaks. Michael Sample photo.

way a bull does to make a cow stand for breeding. That big bull came roaring in from two hundred yards to about fifty yards and just shredded a juniper. At about forty-five yards, he turned broadside and I had my shot."

The reason for the lack of bugling is the number of big bulls, the fact that the Breaks are basically a closed population and the heat of the prairie environment which sends elk back to their cool bedding areas earlier in the day than one would expect in the mountains. "The pecking order has been handled before the rut," Damone said. "In all the time I've put in up there, I've only seen three good fights and I think it was a bull coming through from some other part of the Breaks."

Both Damone and Schindler rely on having a part of the country to themselves for their methods to work. And, in an area as big as the Breaks, that's possible throughout the season if you go far enough from the beaten path. But pressure is increasing and hunters are getting more resourceful in finding these areas to the point that even boats on the Missouri and Fort Peck Reservoir are being used to transport hunters to the further reaches of the elk range.

How far will the elk go when pushed? Nyberg, who has the benefit of Fish, Wildlife and Parks' tracking studies to back him up, said it's not uncommon for them to travel for miles or even leave the Breaks entirely.

"They usually head out of the timbered breaks out into the dry and treeless coulees as far as fifteen miles from the Missouri River," he said. "If you're hunting on the north side, it's conceivable they'll be pushed clear across the Missouri and Fort Peck Reservoir to the south side. On the south side, they'll push them to the north side."

110

He said the willow bottoms also are a haven for elk when pressed because they are so thick that the elk have all the advantages to elude hunters without being seen.

"Once archery season starts, the thing that determines the distribution of elk is the hunting pressure," he said.

As Damone put it, "The way to be successful is to find a place where there aren't hunters. Then you can make it a quality hunt for them and for yourself."

Mule Deer

More than a decade ago, it was a friend at work who first piqued my interest about mule deer hunting in the Missouri Breaks. The late Gene Meyer, a printer at the Billings Gazette, was recalling the halcyon days of the 1950s and '60s when the rugged breaks along the Missouri were alive with deer.

"It was the most amazing place to hunt you ever saw," Meyer told me then. "Every hunter who went up there came back with a big mule deer. If you wanted a five-point, you waited until you saw one. If you wanted a four-point, you'd shoot one of those. And anyone who came out of the Missouri Breaks with less than a four or five-point wanted to shoot something smaller."

Those are some mighty big claims, but fact was as big as fancy in the deer-rich Breaks of those days. And things really haven't changed that much except that the mule deer of Breaks Country are understood a little better these days.

The steep ridges, timbered coulees, and rough cuts of the breaks along the Missouri and Fort Peck Reservoir, and other less well-known rugged country north of Malta and Glasgow, are still havens for mule deer bucks and an attraction for mule deer hunters during the rifle season every fall. But trophy mule deer bucks aren't that easy to come by these days. It's not that Breaks Country doesn't have its share of nice bucks, however.

"There are few big bucks in terms of real trophies, relatively few of them have ever come out of there. Yet we always have lots of good, mature mule deer bucks in there," said Dick Mackie, professor of fish and wildlife management at Montana State University, who began studies on mule deer in the Missouri Breaks in the early 1960s. "You rarely find bucks over seven to eight years old but there's a good distribution of them up to that age. The racks tend to be higher, rather than wide and a twenty-eight to thirty-inch spread could be about tops."

There are several ways a hunter can increase his chances of getting onto one of these bigger bucks. One of them is to cover enough country early in the season to find them. Another is to key in on the more secure habitats beyond where the average hunters will go. Or, a hunter can wait the deer out, holding onto his tags until the final week of the season when the rut will lure the big ones out of their hiding places and make them more vulnerable.

During the early part of the season, one of the more effective methods is to be on the lookout for buck areas. And the Breaks are riddled with them, though you won't find a buck area by just studying a map or even locate them by just looking over the countryside.

Mule deer bucks can be found in the same spots year after year, spreading out from those hiding places only during the rut. Michael Sample photo.

"There are some areas that have been consistent buck habitats for twenty-five years. I can go in there year after year and find good adult bucks. And there are a lot of other places where I've never found them except in the rut," Mackie said. "These areas look pretty much like everything else except that you'll find two to five good, mature bucks using a particular drainage every year. There were about twenty-five such areas on that hundred square-mile study area that I could identify. If you know where they are, you've got a good area to key in on for hunting."

That kind of strategy puts a premium on getting to know an area and going back to it every fall. And, according to Ken Hamlin, a biologist for the Department of Fish, Wildlife and Parks who has carried on with Mackie's work in the Breaks, that's exactly what some hunters have done.

"The hunters that seem to be consistently successful are the ones that don't run to the latest hot spot. They've hunted in there for a number of years and are used to hunting particular coulees and know the deer's escape routes there," Hamlin said. "A lot of these buck areas seem to be on the fringe of what appears to me to be not good habitat, but you'll get three or four big bucks hanging out there. If you've found one of these buck areas, hunting early in the season will give you an advantage."

Home ranges for the deer of the Missouri Breaks run up to ten square miles but often the deer will inhabit just a small part of that during the early season. During the rut, however, they may use all of it in their travels.

To find the buck areas, Mackie strongly advises using a vehicle to travel the trails and backroads and stopping often to glass. "It is good country for road hunting. Drive, glass and watch. You cover a lot of terrain and the deer are fairly well distributed across it. Road hunting is probably the most effective way of hunting it," he said.

While travel has been restricted by road closures on the Charles M. Russell National Wildlife Refuge, there are still many trails open there as well as on Bureau of Land Management acreages which border the refuge and in the other breaks areas of this part of the state.

In talking about the breaks north of Glasgow, biologist Bruce Campbell said the tactic works well there, too. "If you're buck hunting, driving out on those rims and doing a lot of glassing is the best way because you can just cover more ground that way. The big buck hunters head into those breaks areas."

According to Mackie, the trail and road system also helps the breaks areas absorb a lot of hunting pressure. "The roads and trails tend to spread out the hunters fairly well. The hunters tend to cover it all but no area tends to get too much pressure. And that hunting pressure in general has little effect on the deer population. Hunters spread out their take pretty well," he said, adding that this is the way it has worked in the Breaks for the past twenty-five years. "That's basically always been a road hunting type of terrain and it still predominantly is.

"There are places where we drive out, glass, then walk out ridges. Often, we'll make circles down through draws we know hold numbers of deer consistently," he said. "But we do that in places where we know the deer are. If not, you could walk a lot of places where there aren't any deer."

During the breeding season of late November, things change a bit in Breaks Country. The bucks spread out from the summer and early fall hiding places and roam the rough hills and coulees in search of does in heat. The big bucks might turn up anywhere. For the hunter who doesn't have much time to put in at getting a nice buck, yet has the patience to wait until the last week of the season to fill his tag, this is the best time of all.

"If you've got a short time to hunt, wait for the rut," said Matt Golik, a Malta native who still travels back to Phillips County from Wolf Point when he wants to hunt big bucks. "You have to wait until the bad weather and wait until the late season. That's generally what I do."

To get the biggest bucks, Golik said it's best to find the areas where other hunters just don't get back in to. "To see trophies anymore, you've got to get out and go to the game preserve or the country you can't drive in. My biggest buck was a thirty-four-inch spread but I've shot quite a few around the twenty-eight to thirty-inch range and a couple over thirty inches. To do that, I just get into the best country that I figure nobody else gets in to."

He said that despite the great number of trails, there is still some country left to the hunter who wants to walk. "There's such an expanse of country and a lot of it is really, really rough. I like to get out there early in the morning and spot."

By spotting them with binoculars first, Golik can get an idea of the size of the buck he'll be heading after and whether or not he will be able to make a successful stalk on him.

"I usually wait until they bed depending on how many other hunters are out and how anxious I am. If you let them bed and if you're any amount of a stalker at all, you should be able to get within a couple hundred yards of any deer. If you get a real cagey one, though, you might have to take that four hundred-yard poke across the canyon.

"And up in this country, they don't get big and old by being dumb," Golik said.

The morning approach works best, he added, because he can catch the deer while they're still active. "The evening is all right, too, but you usually don't see the bigger bucks in the evening. When they're up and about, it's usually after dark when you can't get them."

The late season may also force the Breaks deer to change their positions in their home range. It's almost like the mountain migrations of deer driven from the high country by snow, but lacks the heavy traditions and the wholesale changes in deer distribution.

"A lot of them have almost a migratory habit like the mountain deer, but it's much shorter," Hamlin said. "In summer and fall, they might be anywhere in their home range. In winter, they'll be on one end of it. There are some deer that have a five to six-mile movement in tougher winters.

"While that may not be far, it may mean the difference to a hunter who has some deer located every year but comes back one year and finds they just aren't there."

Still, there's no doubt that in Breaks Country, getting to know the area you plan to hunt in and the deer you can expect to find there will pay dividends over time. Once you find the areas the big bucks hide in during the early season, it's likely you can go back to those areas year after year and get your mule deer buck. But Breaks Country offers opportunities for the first-timer as well just because it's possible to cover so much country so quickly and get the feel of what deer are living there.

It's great mule deer country and an area that every Montana hunter owes himself the chance to hunt at least once in a lifetime.

"It's reasonably far from human population centers," Mackie said. "It is good, secure habitat even though it's highly accessible. Road access is good except for the gumbo roads which are literally impassable when it's wet. And generally, the further you get away from the highway, the more you can get away from it all."

Antelope

Some of the bigger bucks in the state, the most untouched country, and the chance to hunt pronghorns on a one-on-one basis are among the reasons why Breaks Country is such an attraction for antelope hunters every year.

Antelope can be found in every corner of this part of Montana, but the heartland for the big bucks is in the Jordan area south of Fort Peck Reservoir.

As Duane Pyrah, biologist for the Department of Fish, Wildlife and Parks at Lewistown, put it, "From our check stations, most of the big bucks we get come from east of the Musselshell. I don't know if it's better habitat. The winter is about the same. But they live longer and there's less hunting pressure out there. The males east of the Musselshell are definitely older."

It's that combination of older age, food supply, and the severity of the previous winter which blends with genetics to make a big buck. But the biggest key to this area's success is secure habitat and in many parts of Montana, the habitat just isn't secure enough to allow an antelope to reach old age.

114

The ease of access and hunting pressure often determines how big the antelope bucks will grow. Michael Sample photo.

"A lot of this area is big enough there are not a lot of roads, even the two-track trails," said Bernie Hildebrand, biologist for the department at Jordan. "It's rough enough that they can't drive it and there are big expanses of sagebrush that haven't been broken up. We've even got some of the native prairie in certain spots."

In that big country, an antelope has the room to roam without bumping into a pickup-load of hunters. And, in truth, that's how most Montanans hunt, driving the roads until they see an antelope and then trying to get close enough for a shot.

"There's a fair amount of road hunting up here but the hunters are catching on more. They used to go out to spot an antelope and pop over the hill in their vehicle and every antelope could see them. It's best to walk over that hill and don't show the vehicle and don't skyline yourself. From watching them, that's the most common mistake hunters make—skylining themselves."

Hildebrand said hunters would be better off to practice some stealth and rely more on their stalking skills if they're really after the big bucks. But that doesn't mean a hunter has to be out there on opening day.

"I, myself, usually find my antelope on opening day but I don't hunt them then. There's just too many other people moving antelope on you during the opening week. If the bunch hasn't been harassed, I know the general area. If they've been harassed, you've got to hunt a bigger area, but you know the part of the country they're in," Hildebrand said. "Just glass them and find the group first, then you can usually find them again and sneak in."

There are other benefits, as well as missing the opening week rush of hunters, to waiting until later in the season to hunt. For one thing, it's much easier to judge size among bucks. "When somebody tells you that a lone antelope is a fourteen-inch buck, that's not true. It can't be done," he said. "Big antelope are just too hard to judge without another buck to compare them to. And when somebody tells you about a seventeen-inch buck up here, that is a line of bull. They must be talking about Wyoming."

While Montana has its share of big bucks and puts some pronghorns into the Boone and Crockett record book every year, it usually isn't because the horns were all that tall. But because measurements are made on other things like circumference and length of the prong, the Treasure State provides a share of genuine trophies each year.

"I don't think we've broken seventeen inches up here yet. We have come out with some sixteens. But a trophy is in the eye of the beholder and I don't think any guy should be ashamed with anything over fourteen inches. And there are fourteen-inchers which have made the book," he said. "If you were shooting for the book, I would look for how massive the horns are and how big that prong is. Everybody else is looking for length."

It often takes until later in the season to judge that properly, however. Not until the antelope begin gathering in their wintering herds can the comparison be made with any degree of accuracy.

"Wait until the groups get bigger," Hildebrand said. "You might get fifty or a hundred antelope in a bunch. Then, when you sneak up on a group, you can compare the bucks and pick out the big one. And look them over close. A lot of those horns are broken, they've been busted up in the rut. Tips have broken, the prongs have been busted up. But that takes some good glasses and some good sneaking to get in there close enough to see it."

There are big bucks scattered throughout other parts of the Breaks Country, too, but lower densities and easier access to them often means that most bucks won't reach trophy size. "Anywhere we've got a lot of hunting pressure, they're not going to survive very long," Pyrah said.

Part of the reason is that the bucks are still tied to breeding territories they have been defending during the rut of August and September. "I think we're talking about two or three square miles as being about as big an area as they could defend. They're like other males, they're tied to that territory. Hunting them when they breed or just after they breed, it makes them more vulnerable because of that," Pyrah said.

Those close ties end as the season progresses, especially when the first blasts of winter begin working their way southward through the Breaks Country. The herds will begin bunching up into bigger bands and could even move out of an area completely if forced to by bad weather.

This phenomenon occurs quite commonly in the northern tier of Montana counties where antelope actually move south out of Canada to escape the rigors of winter there.

"During the latter part of our antelope season, it would be conceivable for our hunters to be harvesting Canadian antelope," said Harvey Nyberg, biologist for Fish, Wildlife and Parks at Malta. "In really severe winters, they can get as far south as Malta, Chinook, Harlem, and Glasgow. I'm sure most of them go back but we see some distributional shifts in our population surveys after a tough winter."

Pyrah said these periodic infusions into the northern antelope herds aren't something traditional, but rather more of an aimless movement toward better winter range. "Down in Wyoming and in Idaho, they have migrations where the young ones learn the route from the older ones. These survival migrations just take them in a direction that they hope they can find something to survive."

On this northern fringe of antelope habitat in Montana, there are some trophy-class bucks but hunters should be aware that pronghorn densities aren't as high as the Jordan country and areas further south. "Our densities run to three or four antelope per square mile in some areas up here while south across the Missouri River it may go as high as ten and down around Billings it may go up to fifteen where the habitat is better," Nyberg said.

"But we do have some areas with significant permits and a good antelope herd. We figure it at about three hunter days per permit we issue and every year, we have some in that fifteen to sixteen-inch horn area taken out."

That's an antelope big enough to interest most hunters in doing some walking, glassing, and sneaking for him in any corner of Breaks County. And rest assured, that's not just the best way to get him, but possibly the only way as well.

Waterfowl

The sound of goose music is a common and beautiful melody during the weeks of September and October along the Hi-Line area of Breaks Country. Not just the scattered formations of a few birds moving through, but Canada geese by the thousands.

Spilling southward out of Canada to the wheatfields and reservoirs of the Malta area or riding the first blasts of winter out of the North, their honking flights are sweet music to the ears of hunters who take after them every fall.

Though it's not what it used to be, according to Charles "Pete" Stewart, of Malta, it's still not bad today. And fall still finds Stewart chasing his beloved geese every fall, just as he first did in 1940 and continued to do for thirty years with his hunting partner, Charles Adam, who died a few seasons back.

"I still like to hunt geese, there's no kidding about it," Stewart said. "Charlie and I had a lot of fun."

In the old days, it was pretty much all field hunting for them and the field hunting was good. "My partner and I—he even thought like a goose—we'd find a spot where they were feeding in the fields and watch them for a couple of mornings to make sure they were coming in to the same spot. Then we'd set up our silhouette decoys so when the geese came in against the wind they could see them, and wait for the birds to come."

In that fashion, many a goose fell to the No. 2 and 4 pellets which the partners threw up at them from their shotguns.

Many geese still fall that way, but competition from other hunters has grown keener in recent years. The big flocks of Canadas attracted increasing attention and drew more and more hunters to the Hi-line.

"This Hi-line is a pretty good goose area. The combination of glaciated terrain and the wheat-growing provides all the habitat needs these migrating geese desire," said Gene Sipe, refuge manager of the Bowdoin National Wildlife Refuge at Malta.

"The numbers right here on the refuge aren't spectacular. If we get a one-time peak of a couple-three thousand birds, that's about it. But there's no one localized site that gets a great buildup. They're scattered all along the Hi-line, on potholes here, reservoirs there."

Those waters provide the resting and roosting areas for the geese while the stubble fields provide the food for the morning and evening feeding flights. The classic method of hunting the geese is the field method which relies on Stewart's recipe of scouting, digging shallow pits to lie in, and putting out either silhouette decoys or shells to lure in the birds.

"What we always did in field hunting was use silhouettes. We never used more than a dozen," Stewart said. "If you get out there the first day when they haven't been shot, you can bring them in easy with a dozen decoys. After a while, I wonder if it wouldn't be best to hunt without decoys. They seem to associate those decoys with being shot at."

It's a fact here as elsewhere that as geese get more wary, it takes a bigger spread of decoys to pull them in. And geese in recent years have been getting more wary with the increasing pressure.

But Stewart said there are other ways to get the job done with geese. One of them is hunting them over water while another is to spot them on the small reservoirs and work up on them for a shot.

That final method can often produce bonus birds on a deer or antelope hunt and Stewart rarely fails to take a shotgun along with him when hunting for big game.

"When the geese get spooked off the bigger bodies of water, they'll get out on these little dryland reservoirs. You can spot geese on them from up on a knoll when you're hunting deer, then go down and work up to them and shoot with no decoys or anything," he said. "It isn't quite as much fun as the other ways of hunting them, but it is successful."

Hunting islands at Bowdoin is another productive method but requires the use of a small boat and floating goose decoys. "You can use those floating decoys without any spotting. It's a case of catching them when they fly by," he said. "When you see them, you don't want to overcall. But

Scouting to learn where to set up your decoys is the most valuable ingredient in goose hunting success. Mark Henckel photo.

when they get close enough to hear, just give them a honk or two and shut up."

Bowdoin also offers some good duck hunting during the fall migration, according to Sipe. "We can expect anywhere from 60,000 to 75,000 birds for a peak on ducks with probably gadwall, widgeon, and shoveller as the most predominant species. We do get good numbers of teal early. We also have some fair numbers of mallards in some years and there's representative numbers of scaup, canvasback, and redhead."

The Hi-line also offers an impressive migration flight of sandhill cranes but hunting for them is a little less predictable than for other species. "Sandhill cranes are really wary birds," Sipe said. "They roost standing in water from twelve to sixteen inches deep and because of that and because the depth of most of our reservoirs is deeper than that, either they fly right over us high or they set down in the grain fields for a couple of hours and feed and then get back up.

"People hunt them, but they don't shoot very many of them. Most guys get a permit and hunt them incidentally to geese. Then if a bunch comes into the goose decoys they can shoot them."

Sandhills do offer some variety, however, to an already rich waterfowl hunting area. The various species of ducks add some spice. And though Stewart may have been lucky enough to hunt the great days of the past, there is still some good goose hunting to be had in the fields of the Hi-Line when their music fills the air.

Upland Birds

When hunters get their first taste of the upland bird opportunities of Breaks Country, it can be a little overwhelming.

There was the time when my brother, Bob, journeyed to the Missouri Breaks and had just an hour of hunting left in the day when he started off with a springer spaniel at his side and a full box of shotgun shells in his pocket. By the time the sun set, enough sharptails had chuckled their way out of the buffaloberry coulees of the Breaks that he was borrowing shells and saying "Wow!"

There was the time my father, Art, headed west for a hunt in the Breaks and I had one of my rare good days behind the butt of a shotgun. When a healthy flock of sage grouse took wing, I managed to knock down my limit with a triple and my setter beneath them must have figured it was raining birds. My dad screamed "Whoa!"

Odd occurrences and reactions? Hardly. Upland bird hunting for grouse in Breaks Country is like that and the pheasant hunting along the mainstem and tributaries of the Milk, Musselshell, and Missouri rivers isn't too shabby, either.

"The bird hunting is tremendous up here," said Harvey Nyberg, biologist for the Department of Fish, Wildlife and Parks at Malta. "We have real good hunting for pheasants, sharptails and sage hens. But the cycle seems to have gone through bird hunting for most of the people."

There are enough other hunting opportunities to keep them occupied, like bowhunting the Missouri Breaks for elk, hitting the rough country for mule deer, and the open range for antelope during the rifle season or heading for the stubble fields to hunt geese.

What they're missing is some classic covers for the various upland bird species. In the northeastern reaches of Breaks Country, it's the buffaloberry coulees which provide such hot action during the years when the fruit hangs rich and full. To the south, there are the sagebrush hills of the Winnett, Grass Range, and Jordan areas which provide excellent sage grouse habitat. And the small creeks and big rivers have enough streamside fields to hide more than their fair share of pheasants.

Unfortunately, most of the grouse hunting done here is of the roadside variety, which hardly does the birds justice.

"Driving the roads is the most popular way. It's not the most effective way. The people that are the most successful are the ones with dogs," said Bob Watts, biologist for Fish, Wildlife and Parks at Lewistown. Those hunters are much more likely to consistently hit the areas where birds can be found.

The only exception is for sage grouse early in the season in the dry years when the roadside borrow pits get a boost from the runoff from the road itself and tend to stay greener. "Sage grouse will be eating forbs and feeding in the alfalfa fields and on dandelions in September. They'll be bunched up where it's green when it's dry," Watts said. "For the bulk of the hunting season, though, they're in the sagebrush. This is one of the few areas in the state where there's large expanses of sagebrush left."

Sharptails are a different matter. Their food habits tend more toward the fruits of the plants, whether it's grain, snowberry, rosehips, chokecherry, or buffaloberry. In good grasshopper years, there will also be a high percentage of insects in their diets.

120

A good bird dog will help a sage grouse hunter more than all the gasoline burned road hunting for them. Frank Martin photo.

"People that drive the roads are much less successful on sharptails," Watts said. For them, it's best to walk the edges of grainfields or the buffaloberry coulees or to find them on the ridgetops resting at midday.

"The buffaloberry coulees are the classic sharptail habitat north of the Missouri," said Nyberg. "Coulees where they end in grain fields are another good bet."

Pheasants present a different problem and a different approach has evolved to hunt them. While the birds themselves and their valley bottom food habits are pretty much the same as elsewhere in Montana, the covers aren't as broken up with fencerows and fields.

Few hunters take advantage of the sharp-tailed grouse that Breaks Country has to offer. Mark Henckel photo.

"They usually have a large amount of habitat available to them and they run like a son-of-a-gun," Nyberg said. "The farming practiced up here isn't as intensive in the more heavily developed areas. Most of our creek bottoms don't have grain crops in them, they have hay, so the cover in the fields is continuous, too."

As a result, the trend has been toward larger groups of hunters who try to corner the birds to make them flush.

"Most of the people up here hunt by pushing the birds toward the center from two different directions and then having some good shooting in the middle. They go as many as twelve at a time with six in each group and spread out for a half-mile or mile working a river bend or a stretch of ditch," Nyberg said.

"People who hunt in two different directions usually do much better than we do with dogs. They must look at us as being eccentric, but not harmful."

Breaks Country also has Hungarian partridge to offer, but their populations aren't as dense here on a regular basis as in areas where wheat is more of a staple crop.

"Huns typically are in grain areas," Watts said. "They do the best in grain areas. It's marginal habitat for them out in areas like at Winnett but in some years, those marginal habitats can build up some good numbers of birds."

With much of Breaks Country privately-owned, hunters should be aware that they should ask permission for access. But for bird hunters with their relatively short-range weapons, that usually isn't much of a problem.

The beauty of hunting Breaks Country for birds, however, isn't just the number of birds the area holds or the ease of access, but the fact that there are few people who hunt them here.

After the opening weekend rush, it's possible for serious bird hunters to go the rest of the season without bumping into another shotgun-toting hunter. With plenty of birds to shoot at and plenty of acres to shoot them in, it's no wonder that those first-time bird hunters in Breaks Country usually want to become regulars.

And somehow, some way, they find an excuse to get back to hunt Breaks Country for upland birds again.

Farm Country

Montana hunting has always been typecast as a thing of glamor, spectacle, and high places. Snow-dusted peaks, pack strings heading up the trail, and long stalks for mountain goats are examples. Big bull elk bugling in high mountain meadows provides another common portrayal. Or, how about wide-racked mule deer bucks, with winter at their backs, following mountain migrations to the low country.

Those are some vivid images and wonderful wildlife experiences, but they don't tell the whole story about hunting in the Treasure State. Lost in the splendor is some of the down-home opportunities that northeastern Montana has to offer. Believe me, it can offer some spectacles of its own and some rewards that are tough to come by anywhere else.

This often-forgotten corner of Montana is Farm Country, a place which takes the Treasure State from the open range and sagebrush pastures to the more settled croplands near the North Dakota border. It's not often heralded by publicists as glamorous hunting country and isn't the type of place you'll read about in outfitters' brochures.

But it's one of the few areas of Montana where a diligent hunter can find a white-tailed buck that tips the scales at two hundred pounds dressed and look over a hundred deer in a day. It offers some of the more unspoiled pheasant and sharp-tailed grouse hunting in the state and has sage grouse and Hungarian partridge as well. And there are pockets of native grass and sage where mule deer and antelope abound.

For the naturalists, it's a place where endangered whooping cranes cross on their annual migrations and an area where goose hunters get the first crack at honkers coming over the border from Canada. It's also the only part of the state that can rival North Dakota in terms of duck production.

Farm Country takes in the lower reaches of the Yellowstone River, too, and some of the higher densities of whitetails to be found in Montana.

There's the Fort Peck Indian Reservation which has fine upland bird hunting for non-Indians who carry tribal licenses in their wallets along with their state permits.

Farm Country is not wild country in terms of mountain wilderness, but there are some vast tracts of roadless ground and big farms separating small towns. People population is generally sparse and their roots in the area run deep.

Much of this part of Montana is simply rolling hills and flat benches where dryland wheat and other small grains provide the basis for an agricultural economy.

With few exceptions, it's privately-owned hunting country where obtaining permission before you shoot is as much a part of the trip as packing a gun in the first place. But it's a friendly part of Montana, too, far removed from the cities and bustle of big cities, where hospitality to old friends and newcomers alike is simply a way of life.

Farm Country is hunting country, but not the type of hunting country you're likely to hear about unless you were lucky enough to be born here or to discover, later in life, this often-forgotten corner of Montana.

White-tailed Deer

Farm Country whitetails are unlike any other the Treasure State has to offer. And, the country they live in is unlike any other white-tailed deer habitat as well.

To see it for the first time, a hunter wouldn't think anything, save for a few sharptails and Hungarian partridge, would be able to exist in the wide-open country that comprises much of northeastern Montana. It's dryland wheat strips punctuated by a few sloughs, some scattered shelter belts, and a few stock reservoirs and creek beds. In the winter, its weather is among the coldest and windiest the Treasure State has to endure, while the summer heat can bake the earth hard and brown and send heat waves shimmering above the wheat.

That's a far cry from the brushy bottoms of the Yellowstone River which is more typical of the whitetail habitat in Montana.

But Ralph Fries, of Lewistown, can tell you that the wide-open wheat country certainly doesn't lack for deer. "One opening morning, hunting on a federal Waterfowl Production Area, each one of the family picked a certain spot to sit. I was on my favorite hill. When it got light enough to see, I had twenty-eight deer in the sweet clover field in front of me. It was just a matter of picking out the one I wanted," he said. "And my wife, Vonnie, shot a buck from this certain rockpile four years in a row."

There are some that would argue that northeastern Montana deer are a different breed and live a different lifestyle than their brethren on the bottoms.

"People call them a prairie whitetail. I think it's a little different race of white-tailed deer," said Steve Martin, of Medicine Lake. "There's very little in the way of typical white-tailed deer habitat up here. But they've evolved some tactics to help them survive."

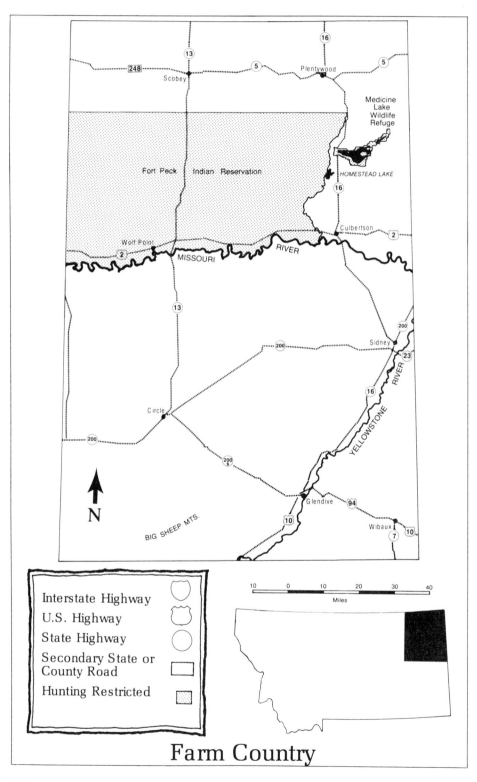

Farm Country

In the country north and east of the Fort Peck Indian Reservation, the deer have adapted to their open-ground habitat using every wrinkle in the landscape and every bit of available cover. It's much the same in the newly-pioneered whitetail areas of the Circle country where the deer seem to be moving in from the east.

"There's a lot more farming around here than there used to be and they're moving into the new farmlands," said Ron Stoneberg, biologist with the Department of Fish, Wildlife and Parks at Circle. "Their needs are the same here as elsewhere. They need the food and cover. They're getting beautiful food in these grain fields with spilled grain and forbs. For cover, they will use stock ponds with trees around them. They'll center on that. The grassy waterways, you can walk those and jump them.

"But a lot of times, they'll be a long way from cover. Their cover is their line of sight. They're using the rolling topography to hide themselves. They'll be in a hollow out in the wheat fields where you can't see them. They'll use whatever is available."

Whitetail bucks use whatever cover is available to them in the wide-open spaces of Farm Country. Frank Martin photo

That kind of adaptability puts whitetails into many different situations and forces hunters to sort out their options if they hope to hunt northeastern Montana successfully.

Some of the hunting spots are obvious, especially in the early part of the season. Patches of brush, where available, are certain to hold deer. Bullrushes and cattails around sloughs will hide them. Basically, any place that isn't cultivated has a chance to hold deer.

"A lot of the stuff they're in is less than thirty inches high. They'll lay down in it and that's all they need. It's the kind of places you'd expect to find sharp-tailed grouse," Martin said.

The bigger bucks get even more sneaky in their choice of bedding area as the season progresses. "You'd be surprised where an old whitetail buck will hide," said Fries. "As the season progresses, they bed down in less and less-heavy cover. On the first day, you're not going to find one lying in a rockpile in the summer fallow, but as the season progresses, they know people aren't going to look there.

"The does and fawns tend to stick to the traditional cover but the bucks tend to select those small isolated patches. And sometimes they can stick real tight to it. It startles you sometimes when you almost step on a big buck and you don't realize how you couldn't have seen him."

But whitetails in Farm Country also use their mobility as a defense against hunters. In typical river bottom habitat, deer don't have to go far to elude their pursuers. Up here, they do. "If you try to approach them, they can run for miles," Stoneberg said.

Hunting tactics vary in Farm Country depending on the availability of cover, conditions and the time of the season. "The way some locals hunt them is to get in their trucks and go like hell. They'll drive the edges of all the coulees or out in the stubblefields until they jump them. But that's not what I'd recommend," Stoneberg said. "I find you have much higher success if you walk for them. There are roads most places and you can drop a guy off and have him walk a piece of cover. It's almost like jump shooting."

Hunting from stands is another good technique if you can find an area where the deer are moving through, either when they're pushed by hunters or on their daily travels between feeding and bedding areas.

"You could put a tree stand on a fencepost but that's about the only way you could use a tree stand up here," Martin said. "But you can get in areas where you know there are good numbers of deer and big bucks and sit for them.

"I spent ten hours on my stand the first day and I saw probably a hundred eighty deer that day. I could have killed a half-dozen nice bucks and missed one that another hunter got later that had a twenty-four-inch spread and dressed out over two hundred pounds."

Martin got his deer later that season, but ended up relying on another popular and highly effective method to get him. "I did a lot of glassing with a spotting scope on the backroads, glassing areas to find deer that were bedded. I put a stalk on him and got within a hundred yards and killed him in his bed," Martin said. The deer was a good Montana four-point with antlers that had a spread of eighteen inches and were a foot high. The three and a half year-old dressed out at 175 pounds.

If there are several hunters in the party, drives also work well for getting up deer. Fries said his daily routine was to sit on stand for the first couple of hours in the morning and then to organize drives with Vonnie and their hunting age children, Jerry and Diane.

"I don't like too big a group from the safety factor, but there's no upper limit if everybody is safe," he said. "We'd put a couple on post and send some drivers through the field of tall grass or marshes. It's all waist high and less, but that's where they'll hide."

Though most of Farm Country is privately-owned, that kind of cover can be found in the public hunting area of Medicine Lake National Wildlife Refuge and on the forty federally-owned Waterfowl Production Areas that dot the northeast corner of the state. There has also been a walk-in area designated on the privately-owned six-section Sand Hills area near the refuge.

All these areas attract deer both before the season and when they are pushed, but hunters shouldn't feel limited to them. Landowners are generally accommodating to hunters who ask permission to hunt and any patch of cover is capable of holding deer. It's simply up to the hunter to check them out by walking them or glassing with a good pair of binoculars or spotting scope.

In two-deer seasons with the whole family hunting, the only difficulty Fries found on his prairie whitetail trips was getting all the deer back home again that his family had shot. "A lot of the guys I hunt with kidded me that I was the only guy who'd go deer hunting with a boat and trailer. I didn't have a pickup and the only way I could carry them was to load them in the boat for the trip home. They'd say, 'Here comes the guy from North Dakota, he didn't know enough that you use a boat for fishing. He goes deer hunting on dry land with it,'" Fries said.

Just to set the record straight: though he worked in North Dakota for a time, Fries' ancestry dates back to Minnesota and perhaps that's one of the reasons why the prairie whitetails suit him so well. When you're jumping deer in this wide-open country, the norm is to see the buck running and putting yardage between himself and the hunter quickly.

"To me, it's a real thrill to shoot at a moving target like that," Fries said. "I grew up hunting fox in Minnesota, with high-powered rifles, that were being chased with foxhounds. I'm used to running targets and I enjoy that kind of hunting."

According to Doug Clark, who grew up in the Froid area and still farms there, hunters should be prepared to take those long shots in Farm Country. "You should have a gun that shoots a long ways flat," he said. "The shots probably average about 250 to 300 yards. It wouldn't be less than that."

Big body size and good antler growth at an early age are another hallmark of these prairie whitetails and the main reason for that, Clark feels, is nutrition.

"They graze alfalfa and small grains, wheat and barley. In the winter, they're feeding on my hay," he said. "There are a lot of nice four and five-points, even yearlings with small four-points. We don't see many spikes or forkhorns up here."

That doesn't mean there are Boone and Crockett or Pope and Young whitetails to be had everywhere. Those rare trophies are hard to come by here, just like anywhere else, but body size and antler growth still outstrip the whitetails from most other parts of the state.

While the bulk of the whitetail hunting opportunities in Farm Country come on the prairies, there are some river bottom deer worth mentioning, too. The lower Yellowstone River, for example, has excellent whitetail numbers.

"We've got densities of seventy to eighty deer per square mile on the river bottom. I don't know of anyplace else in eastern Montana with deer densities that high," said Gary Dusek, biologist with Fish, Wildlife and Parks at Glendive. "They have everything they need in terms of cover and high-quality food."

In the dense brush of the river bottom, hunters usually use stands or stage drives to get their deer. "They find an area where there's quite a bit of evidence of going to and from it on their way to feeding. It's important to establish their daily movement patterns," he said.

Many of the deer drives on the river are done in conjunction with a boat. Several hunters are dropped off at the head of an island and one or more of the others float the boat down to the other end and take a stand. The drivers then push the deer toward those on stand. With that method, all the hunters end up at the boat and can quickly float to another island downstream to do it again.

"The deer on the Yellowstone grow fairly good antlers for the age classes that are there but the hunters are fairly efficient at cropping the bucks down so you don't get many over four years old," Dusek said. "You might have to hunt a long time to get a Boone and Crockett buck but they commonly shoot Pope and Young trophies down there."

Bowhunting, in fact, is a popular pastime on the Yellowstone bottoms in the Glendive and Sidney areas. "Bowhunting, for a lot of these guys, is something they can do in an evening. They can go out and sit on a stand for a couple of hours after work and stand a good chance of getting a deer if they put in a little time at it," he said.

Though the Yellowstone's cover is secure, Dusek said he has noticed that hunting pressure does tend to move the deer around. "They'll move in the path of least resistance. When there's hunting pressure on one segment of river bottom, there will be some movement to areas that aren't getting hunted at that time. You do have a constant movement of deer all season long," Dusek said.

One other benefit to opting for the river bottom deer is that year-in, year-out, their populations are more dependable. Because their cover is more weather-proof, the whitetails here are more likely to survive the really tough winters. When the blizzards roar across the prairie and the temperatures drop far below zero for long periods of time, the prairie whitetail population can suffer some severe setbacks.

But either place you go, the venison from those whitetails will be among the best that has ever graced your table. As Stoneberg put it, "They're fat and they're delicious. Those grain-fattened whitetails are hard to beat."

Mule Deer and Antelope

Mule deer and antelope are often victims of progress in Farm Country. With the plowing of the prairie, their niche becomes ever smaller in this part of Montana.

Not that there aren't mule deer and antelope in northeastern Montana.

Mule deer need the native prairie, which is shrinking here as more ground is being opened up for agriculture. Michael Sample photo.

There are still pockets of them scattered throughout the region, but their existence here has become more precarious in this century and their importance pales when compared to white-tailed deer.

"They've got to have more native prairie than the whitetail. The whitetail is like the red fox. He can live almost anywhere," said Harold Wentland, regional wildlife manager for the Department of Fish, Wildlife and Parks at Glasgow. "The native prairie or where the native prairie and farmland are intermingled fifty-fifty, that's where you're going to have them."

There are still significant numbers of mule deer and antelope in the southeastern corner of Farm Country. In fact, the rugged breaks north of Terry are considered excellent mule deer habitat. And antelope, given the benefit of several mild winters in a row, will expand easily into the more heavily farmed areas.

"We're at the northern edge of the antelope range. During good years, they will get up into Saskatchewan and will thrive in northern McCone County and north of the Missouri River," said Ron Stoneberg, biologist for Fish, Wildlife and Parks at Circle. "But a couple of hard winters and you're going to lose a bunch of them. A bad winter and they're just going to stack up against the roads and the fences. They'll start driving south and if they come up against a fence or road or something they can't get past, they're going to stop and possibly die. Antelope are not as well adapted to these northern climates as deer."

Mule deer are hardier, but still need the diversity of the prairie and the security of areas like the finger draws on the Redwater River-Big Dry Arm Divide to really prosper.

Hunting methods for mule deer and antelope are similar and, like in other parts of eastern Montana, vehicles are used heavily by local hunters.

"I see people driving the trails and trying to see antelope they want," Wentland said. "I don't think it's that much running them down with a pickup. But there's so much country between trails. It's big country and they don't want to take off until they see something. You can say the same thing about mule deer."

Stoneberg defended the hunter afoot, however, and said that being without a vehicle can be a help in hunting an area if you already know it holds pronghorns. "You can stalk them, watch where they are. They'll circle around," he said. "You play with them and work them. They're not going to leave the country. They'll come back and look at you.

"Some hunters will find where antelope pass through areas and wait for the other hunters to push them around. They'll watch and see where the antelope go and then let the antelope come to them."

The key is persistence and following up the antelope and deer you see. "If you keep after them, pretty soon you'll get a shot. You can always find them, but they're not always in range. It's open country," Stoneberg said.

One hunting method growing in popularity in northeastern Montana in recent years is bowhunting for antelope during the special archery season of September and early October. That time of year coincides with the breeding season and bucks become territorial and protective of their bands of does.

"We have monkeyed around with silhouettes for a couple of years. We cut quarter-inch plywood and paint the features of a buck antelope on it," said Steve Schindler, of Glasgow.

"We have had some success with it. We had some antelope come in but they usually catch you totally off guard. You flash that silhouette at them at about three hundred yards and the next thing you know, the buck is ten feet away and you're not ready for him," he said.

An antelope silhouette can provide some excitement and close encounters for the bowhunter in September. Michael Sample photo.

The bucks will come in to run off the intruder and hopefully provide a good, close-range bowshot. The key is to be there at the peak of the rut, usually in early September, and to get in position undetected by the buck or the rest of the herd. "If you catch them off guard, they usually come in right away. Sometimes they'll dilly-dally around but generally that means they know something is up."

Stalking and sneaking are other methods that bowhunters use to get within range of antelope, along with staking out a water hole. "They water the same place every day," Schindler said. "I don't know how many times a day they water but the middle of the day is about the best. They'll generally water between 11 a.m. and 1 p.m."

Mule deer hunting is almost all done by stalking, for bow and gun hunters alike. Because of their nature to stand their ground until they positively identify the source of danger, they are extremely vulnerable to a careful stalk by a rifle hunter who only needs to get within a couple hundred yards.

Bowhunters need more refined stalking techniques but can get within range if the topography and wind direction smiles on them.

While much of Farm Country can't be considered prime range for mule deer and antelope, opportunities for them do exist here for hunters who can recognize the right kind of habitat. And for big game hunters who travel here primarily to hunt whitetails, they can provide both another tag to fill and another experience to remember from Farm Country.

Waterfowl

It doesn't take much of a hunting mathematician to know that the sum of adding wheat and water is waterfowl. Farm Country hunters have been relying on that simple formula for years to get in on some fine goose shooting in the northeastern corner of Montana.

The hotbed of this goose activity is in the wheat fields surrounding Medicine Lake National Wildlife Refuge, and few hunters have taken better advantage of it than Larry "Tuts" Portra, of nearby Froid.

"I've been hunting them for over forty years. I like goose hunting better than anything. It's mostly trying to outsmart them," Portra said.

While it's no great compliment, I suppose, to say Portra is smarter than the average goose, he has shown uncommon proficiency when it comes to putting geese on the ground. "In the 1950s and '60s, we had awful good goose hunting up here. There have been years when I've shot over one hundred geese legally in the fall," he said.

The most popular method is field shooting and, like field shooting everywhere, this takes some equipment, knowledge of their habits, and the patience to put in the time scouting their movements.

"It's mostly field shooting with decoys and scouting up here. You do a lot of spotting and checking and let them feed several times in the same area. On about the third morning, you set up," he said. "You either dig pits or use a natural blind. The pits work the best but they're a lot of work. You dig the pit about three feet deep so you can sit down in it. They're by far the better pit."

While there are some practical limits to the number of decoys a hunter can carry, the more the merrier when it comes to bringing in geese.

In recent years, geese haven't stayed in the area as long as they did in times past. Michael Sample photo.

"When we first started, none of us had many decoys. But now we usually set up from seventy-five to a hundred full-bodied decoys," Portra said.

The simple matter of equipment, the work of digging pits, and local interest in geese make hunting groups in Farm Country larger than in some other areas. But fewer hunters are really more desirable.

"Two or three is ideal, but usually you don't get by with just this many people," he said. "My wife, Debby, hunts with me all the time and there's my hunting partner, Dave Skillingberg, of Homestead. We usually end up with five or six in the group.

"We dress in camouflage clothing and use those camouflage nets. But with people who aren't used to hunting geese, you always get movers in the bunch. Geese can see the face real well on a person. It really shines out. So you can't be moving when geese come in. They're real spooky. Most of the geese that get here have been shot at two or three weeks in Canada before they get here. They're decoy smart."

Much of the hunting in the Medicine Lake area is for Canada geese but there is also a good flight of white-fronts or "specs" that comes through. Portra admits he prefers the specs when it comes to eating, but they present more difficulty in hunting.

"I like to hunt the specs the best. But they're not dependable like honkers. They don't decoy as good and they're not habit feeders like the honkers," he said.

The geese tend to home in on Medicine Lake Refuge for resting and spending the night, but fan out to surrounding wheat and barley fields for their feeding. "I've shot geese coming off of there thirty miles away, but just over the fence to three or four miles is usually where they go," Portra said.

With increased hunting pressure in recent years, the geese don't seem to stay as long in the area as they have in the past, when shooting was possible clear up to Thanksgiving. Some of the reason for that is that the area has become more popular for out-of-state hunters, primarily from North Dakota and Minnesota, who have added to the number of guns pointed at geese here.

In addition to the migratory flocks of Canadas and white-fronts, there is some goose production on Medicine Lake itself, according to Gene Stroops, manager of the 31,000-acre refuge.

"We produce somewhere between seven hundred and eight hundred geese a year. That's our local production of the Great Basin Canada Goose, a subspecies of the giant Canada goose," he said.

There are also some impressive flights of ducks that use the refuge and the forty federal Waterfowl Production Areas scattered across the far northeastern counties.

"We've got all the species of puddle ducks—mallards, pintail, gadwall, widgeon, teal, shoveller," he said. "We seem to have an awful lot of shoveller that move in here, 100,000 shoveller at one time. The lesser scaup is the number one diver. On occasion, we get quite a few migrant ruddy ducks. Some years, they would record 25,000 to 30,000 ruddy ducks and there are redheads and canvasbacks."

But hunting pressure for these ducks is extremely light compared to other parts of Montana.

"The few shotgun hunters around are mostly goose hunters and the few duck hunters are mallard hunters. If they can't hunt mallards, they'd rather not hunt ducks at all," Stroops said. "We probably had less than twenty-five duck hunters on the public hunting area of the refuge on the opening weekend. Most of the people that are hunting for mallards shoot them out in the fields."

If duck hunting is a nearly untapped source of recreation, doing it with decoys is even more obscure. The bulk of the duck hunting is by pass shooting, finding a flight path between sloughs or over a particular part of the refuge. But because of the diversity of ducks that move through the area, busting loose at high-flying ducks can have its dangers. Some years ago, there was a story of visiting dignitaries who came to the refuge from far away to check out its facilities and were eager to do some shooting at low-value puddle ducks as they passed between two Waterfowl Production Areas further north.

The point system for ducks was in effect and one-hundred points was the daily limit for the Central Flyway. Unfortunately, the first duck through the pass was crumpled by one of the visitors who saw his hunting day end quickly when that redhead fell. It was, after all, a 100-point limit all by itself at the time.

There is also some hunting for little brown crane to be had in northeastern Montana, but not on the refuge. "Sheridan County is designated as critical habitat for the endangered whooping crane. Some of those radio-collared whoopers coming out of the north country have used the refuge in the past in both spring and fall," Stroops said. "But little brown crane hunting is permitted off the refuge."

Just as waterfowl hunting elsewhere depends on good water conditions, Farm Country lives and dies with its rainfall and snowmelt.

Northeastern Montana is a major waterfowl production area for many species, like these newly-hatched gadwall. Mark Henckel photo

In the drought years, often the geese just fly over the area to areas further south with better water conditions. Duck production in the sloughs and potholes of the glaciated hills in the northern counties is down. And hunting is generally poorer than average.

But when the water is plentiful and production booms, Farm Country can offer some of the better goose hunting to be had in Montana and perhaps the most secluded duck hunting to be found anywhere in the United States.

Upland Birds

In Farm Country, it pays to be kind to your bird dog. Give Fido that extra ration of food in late summer. What the heck, buy that box of doggie treats. And if he's determined to sleep on your spouse's favorite chair, then your spouse will just have to sit somewhere else.

There's every reason to be kind to good old Fido, because investments in that dog will reap big dividends when the bird seasons arrive.

Farm Country is the kind of place where a dog can be invaluable in hunting up pheasants and sharptails, two commodities that this corner of the state has in abundance. There are sage grouse and Hungarian partridge, too, but they're not as reliable as those roosters and chuckle chickens.

"Overall, I would say the bird hunting is generally excellent here," said Gregg Pauley, an avid bird hunter from Fort Peck. "They're not just everywhere, though."

The key is to find the right habitat for the particular bird species the hunter is after.

"The best sharptail hunting is anyplace you can find water and cover along a grainfield," said Matt Golik, a shotgunner from Wolf Point. "The easiest hunting is in the stubble in the early part of the season. During the late part, the birds in the stubble are awfully spooky. You end up spooking them out of the stubble and hunting them in the creek bottoms.

"You don't need a dog to do it, but it sure makes life a lot more pleasant," he said.

Sharptails are spread out all over Farm Country from the Sand Hills Area near Medicine Lake to the buffaloberry draws of northern McCone County and the farmed areas near Glendive. They're all the same species of bird, but tactics do vary some from place to place.

"You're looking at the ones tuned in to crops and the ones that are natural, the ones tuned into other feed like the berries," Pauley said. "For the ones tuned in to the crops, look in the coulees that border the cropland. Grouse like high areas, too, like the major ridges. Croplands in those areas will always hold grouse.

"The best way to hunt sharptails is to get up early in the morning and listen for the grouse to get a fix on them. They get up on the edge of the coulee or the side of the hill and you can hear them. They sort of cackle and you can figure out what part of the coulee they're in. Certain areas of a coulee will hold them while other areas won't."

Pheasants also require the proper mixture of food, water and cover but the emphasis here is on thick cover. "The pheasants are the least cyclic of all the birds here. And when we have the good years, the pheasant hunting is the best around," Pauley said. "Take any of the creek bottoms that have

A dog can make hunting a lot easier for the shotgunner looking for sharptails. Mark Henckel photo.

water in them on a year-round basis and you have a good place to start looking.

"Dogs are an absolute necessity because the cover is so thick. Unless you have an army, which is one way to approach it, and then you can surround them."

The pheasant cover tends to be large unbroken patches of low brush and grass which gives the birds a distinct advantage when it comes down to eluding their pursuers. "These birds are runners up here, they don't fly unless they absolutely have to," Pauley said. "Fly is the last resort. So one way to do it is to go in with your dog and hunt them like whitetails. Don't say a word all day and just let the dog work them up."

The giant Fort Peck Indian Reservation is one good place to hunt pheasants and sharptails but hunters need a tribal conservation license and tribal bird license in addition to their state licenses. Reservation permits can be obtained from tribal police or offices at Wolf Point and Poplar and the investment in them can be well worth the extra dollars out of the wallet.

"The reservation is good because the grazing and agriculture isn't so intensive and there's enough cover left for the birds," Pauley said.

The lower Yellowstone River bottoms also offer good pheasant hunting, along with the lower Missouri and its islands, and creek, spring and marsh areas throughout the region.

Hungarian partridge are a boom-and-bust bird in Farm Country, flourishing in times of mild winters and where enough cover can be found amid the grain fields to give them protection from the elements. "They're a cycle bird but you can find them in good numbers some years. Any old

Food, water, and heavy cover are the recipe for producing pheasants in northeastern Montana. Mark Henckel photo.

building with a shelter belt is always a good place to look for them. That's what we call a Hun Hotel," Pauley said.

Huns also key in on many of the same areas as the cropland sharptails and it's possible to get in on good flocks of both species on the same hunt.

Large tracts of sagebrush for winter food and cover are the main requirement that limit sage grouse numbers in northeastern Montana. There still are some big patches of sage in the southern portions of Farm Country that provide hunting for this species but with more ground being plowed for grain production, the future for sage grouse isn't bright.

Despite the opportunities for upland birds in Farm Country, hunting pressure is generally light and, because of that, access to private land is relatively easy to obtain.

"Generally speaking, most of the people are pretty good. If you stop and ask, they might tell you not to hunt a certain section because there are cows in it, but they will let you hunt their land," Golik said.

"Hunting up here is like it was ten or fifteen years ago. There are quite a few out-of-staters but birds don't provide the big impact that draws them like elsewhere. You find the water, cover, and feed, you'll find the birds," he added. "

"The species you find will depend on the terrain, but you'll definitely find birds."

Cattle Country

Once upon a time, there was a resident of the western Montana mountains who happened to drive eastward across the open range toward the North Dakota border. And when he returned home, he told three hideous lies. "It's all so flat. There are no trees out there. And, it's devoid of all wildlife."

Unfortunately, the hideous lies have become the folklore of western Montanans as they thumb their noses toward Cattle Country. In their hearts, they actually believe that it's flat, that there are no trees and, just because they don't see elk and moose standing out among the sagebrush, that this part of Montana is wildlife-poor. Nothing could be further from the truth.

Cattle Country is an incredibly diverse part of Montana which, in addition to the millions of acres of open range, has good stands of ponderosa pine on national forest land as well as deep cuts, sweeping wind-blown hills, and rugged breaks. As for its wildlife, consider the fact that in the 1984 season, a hunter who filled every deer and antelope tag available to him could have stacked six deer and two antelope in his freezer.

There are some things besides snow-capped peaks that Cattle Country doesn't offer. There are no moose, elk, mountain goats, or mountain grouse. But there are mule deer, white-tailed deer, antelope, an isolated herd of bighorn sheep, turkeys, pheasants, sage grouse, sharp-tailed grouse, Hungarian partridge, and a booming business in waterfowl.

For the hunters who seek these species, Cattle Country offers other rewards. It offers a solitary hunting experience for everyone, which can be enjoyed in the mountains only by those equipped well enough so that horses can carry them far back amid the high peaks. Here, that solitude is for every hunter who is willing to drive the dusty trails into the hills.

Though there are some large tracts of national forest land in the Ashland and Ekalaka areas, and BLM parcels are scattered throughout the region, Cattle Country remains a land largely owned by the ranchers and farmers.

Access, especially access in some parts of its southern and southeastern reaches, is not to be had by all. Every ranch gate is not thrown open to the public and a hunter is much more likely to run into trespass fees here than anywhere else in Montana. The term *landowner tolerance* was also born here and surfaces again each time a hunting season opens. Put in simple terms, it means that a landowner will only tolerate so many hunters in the course of a day, week, or season before he gets fed up and closes the farm or ranch to hunting. But the equation is a changeable one and the answer differs from one place to another and from one year to the next. Suffice it to say that the more deer and antelope there are in Cattle Country, the more hunters will be given access. It boils down to the simple question of which one is more of a bother, the game animals munching on a field of alfalfa or tearing up a haystack, or the hunters who pound at their door every morning or, even worse, don't pound at their door every morning and trespass instead.

But don't get the wrong impression of the year-round residents of Cattle Country. They are among the warmest, most hospitable, unselfish, and down-to-earth people to be found in Montana. It's just that during hunting season, these people of a quiet landscape tend to get outnumbered by truckload after carload after truckload of orange-clad people packing guns. In most parts of Cattle Country, in most seasons, gaining access is simply a matter of the common courtesy of asking permission to hunt, remembering to close gates when you go through them and not forgetting to say thank you when you leave.

That's not too much to ask for excellent hunting for mule deer, whitetails, and antelope and maybe a few grouse or ducks in the bag as well. Believe me, it's a bargain for which a hunter will be paid many times over amid the trees, sweeping hills, and rich wildlife of Cattle Country.

Mule Deer

Mule deer are a common feature of the landscape in Cattle Country these days. Hunters expect to see them. In fact, they expect to see a lot of them when they travel to southeastern Montana.

But it wasn't always that way and even hunters who take aim today at this part of the Treasure State should be prepared for varying populations of mule deer from year to year.

"I was born here on the ranch in 1907 and I was twelve years old before I ever saw a deer," said Norris Cole, who still lives on the family place between Forsyth and Sanders. "The homesteaders came in and, as I grew up, the deer and antelope disappeared. In this area, every half-section or section had a homestead on it and that's what those people had to live on. If the deer left one section, they ran into somebody on another section."

That was simply more pressure than the mule deer could stand and their numbers plummeted throughout eastern Montana. It's a testament to the

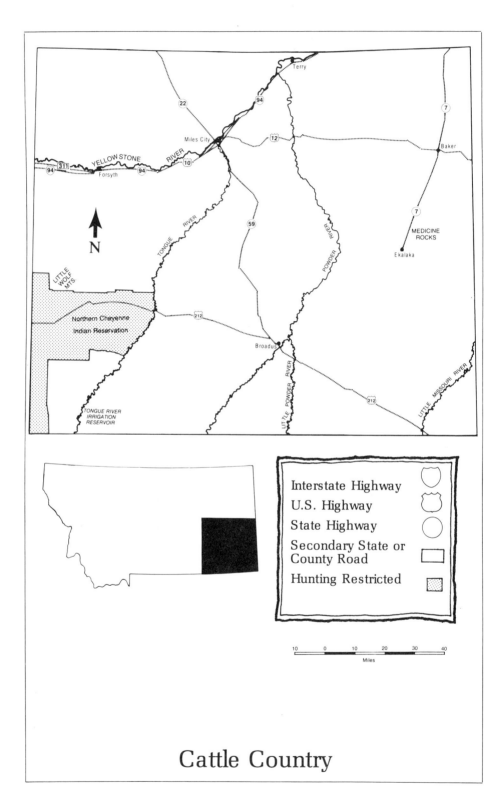

Cattle Country

species, however, that when the pressure eased, the mule deer came back. "As the homesteaders left, through the '20s and '30s with the drought and all, then the deer started increasing."

It certainly wasn't an instant recovery, however. Knocked back that far in numbers, the recovery took place over several decades. "Even in the 1930s and early '40s, it was a real novelty to see a deer," said Chris Lund, of Miles City. "I've been close to forty years hunting in the country and it's changed a lot over that time. I can remember hunting with an old Model A. My dad had an old blacksmith cut out the rumbleseat and put in a pickup box. A rancher friend of ours had a place out in the Sonnett country. That old Model A went on a lot of hunting trips out there.

"The mule deer started coming back in '47, '48," he added. "I can remember in 1949, I shot one that was a monstrous thing. With skin, hide and head off, he weighed about 215 pounds."

The deer recovery at that time was dependent on the rough terrain and the timbered hills scattered throughout this part of Montana, which provided secure strongholds for the species. Those same core areas come into play today during periods of decline. When mule deer build back to sufficient numbers in the core areas, they spill out into the surrounding countryside.

"This part of Montana is a mixture of sagebrush prairie, grassland-agriculture type, ponderosa pine hills and ponderosa pine and juniper breaks," said Heidi Youmans, wildlife biologist for Fish, Wildlife and Parks at Forsyth. "But this part of the state is also a land of extremes. We have wide population fluctuations. You don't have the average, you have the booms and busts.

"When the populations are up, you have high populations everywhere. When we're short, we'll be short in those prairie habitats because they're not as secure. It's our pine habitats and the breaks that you might call our core areas. Even when the deer populations are down, you're going to have pretty good populations in those core areas," she said. "The deer are a lot more protected there. They have the topography and the food source and, in some areas, they have the agricultural areas as a buffer to carry them through even if you do have a devastating winter. The rougher topography offers the best habitat for mule deer."

Not surprisingly, the deep cuts of those rough breaks and the pine hills are also among the best places to look for big mule deer year-in and year-out. "Mule deer are notorious for using topography," Youmans said. "Some of the ugliest, most barren-looking, rugged places are where you'll find the big bucks."

One way to hunt is to take advantage of the deer moving between these rugged hiding places and nearby agricultural areas during the early morning and evening as they go out to feed. "They'll come out at night and feed on the fields," Lund said. "You try to pick feeding grounds in morning and evening but during the day I like to hunt that rough stuff, just walk the ridges and hunt the points out. They'll be bedded about two-thirds of the way up the hill in those cuts. It depends on what the weather is like as to where they'll be. If it's hot, they'll be in the shade. If it's cold, they'll be in the sun. And they don't like wind."

The really big bucks might present other problems, however. In a relatively wide-open environment compared to the timbered security of

Mule deer thrive in most years in the timbered areas of eastern Montana. Michael Sample photo.

the mountains, darkness becomes their biggest ally and the hunter who wants to take the big bucks has to be there at the first hint of light.

"It's getting out there early and taking binoculars and scoping the other side of the hill until you see something suspicious," said Dennis Loreth, of Forsyth, who heads for the hills for his mule deer, searching rough country on foot for big bucks. "Getting out early means going out about a month ahead of the season. The other part of that early would be getting up early in the morning so I'll be there in the dark.

"I like to get up to a point where I can observe the skyline and the tops of the ridges. Most of the big mule deer will be leaving the low meadows at daybreak. They're going to take their does with them and head back into the hills. If you get into that high country before they get there, that gives you an advantage. You've got to be up looking down at them. They key then is to move very little, scan a whole lot," he said. "I like to hunt from sunup to about 11:00, then knock off and start again at about 3:30. About the only thing you accomplish walking for them during the daytime is to wear yourself out. I might go after varmints. I might do some photography."

Camping in hunting country can help a hunter to be back in the hills early enough to intercept the deer. But even then, it's going to take some work if the hunter wants a big buck, one with an antler spread of twenty-eight to thirty-four inches.

"My biggest buck went thirty-two inches," Loreth said. "We were camped back up in the pines and it was the third day of our hunt. We knew there was a good mule deer buck in that area. We had just about walked the bottoms off a good pair of hunting boots and blinded one eye from looking through a spotting scope but hadn't found him yet.

"That morning, we drove about a half-mile toward where we were going to hunt when we spotted him. He was coming off the meadow and just starting to take his does and move them up. We caught him flat-footed. His mind was on the ladies."

Using that rutting time weakness is often essential to finding the biggest old bucks. "A lot of guys will go out in the beginning of the season and think they're going to get a good mule deer. But they're still pretty wily then," he said. "You'll be able to have greater success on getting a big mule deer if you wait until later in the season. They're so busy fighting off the smaller bucks and keeping the ladies in line, you can get up on them.

"You also have to be willing to get out and walk," Loreth said. "Your average hunter will only get his big bucks through luck. Very few hunters care to throw on their canteen, pack an apple and some Granola bars and work the backcountry."

While a hunter looking for good bucks should concentrate on the

Mule deer are notorious for using topography like deep weathered cuts. Mark Henckel photo.

wrinkles in the landscape and on the timbered hills rather than the open range, Cattle Country is still long-range country for the mule deer hunter. That means a person should be prepared with a good set of binoculars or a spotting scope to size up his deer and have a rifle ready to shoot at those distances.

"I try to sight in for about two hundred yards," Lund said. "And you may have to shoot further than that. You can't shoot offhand in those situations. You've got to drop to a knee or get something for a rest to be accurate."

"You've got to be able to determine how big that buck is and how wide his antlers are," added Loreth. "One way to tell is if the deer has his ears straight out like he's sensing something. Their ears from tip to tip, on an average, run twenty-five inches. If you use that as a gauge, you can tell when you're getting into a trophy-class deer. But you don't just go out and get a real big deer like that every year. I figure I manage to get one real nice mule deer buck every three to four years. In between that time, he's winning and I'm walking."

While mule deer numbers rise and fall in Cattle Country depending on natural cycles and the severity of the winters, one of the basic keys to success is finding a place to hunt in the first place.

"Southeastern Montana is seventy-five percent private land and it comes down to landowner tolerance," Youmans said. "As far as available deer to harvest in this country, that is in a direct balance between a tolerance of the landowner for deer numbers and hunter numbers. When deer numbers go down, lands will close again. When they're up, more land will be open."

Lund said finding a place to hunt has always been the single most important factor in going after mule deer in Cattle Country but many hunters aren't willing these days to prepare in the off-season for the days when they want to hunt their bucks.

"The most important thing is to get to know a farmer or rancher," Lund said. "It used to be that a guy would go out at other times and maybe give them a hand with the chores. A farmer or rancher appreciates that. Anybody that lives in these smaller towns, there's no reason if you want to go hunting, you can't get to know a farmer or rancher."

One last note about mule deer in Cattle Country is that because of the rise and fall in deer numbers and the variable of landowner tolerance, hunters would be well-advised to learn about their relative abundance in any given season before planning a hunt here.

In the years of few deer and tough access, finding a buck and a place to hunt for him can be extremely difficult, even in the best of habitat situations. On the other hand, when the deer population is booming, access can be a breeze and it's possible to get multiple tags where your freezer can be literally lined with doe steaks by the season's end.

That variable also means that in some years, like those in the late 1970s, it was primarily bucks-only seasons. On the other end of the spectrum in deer-rich 1984, a hunter could purchase up to five doe tags to go along with his general license and the harvest was estimated at over fifty thousand deer in Fish, Wildlife and Parks Region Seven alone.

It's unlikely, barring catastrophic weather conditions or wholesale changes in land use practices, that mule deer will ever again become so

In years of plenty, there are multiple tag opportunities for antlerless mule deer. Frank Martin photo.

rare in Cattle Country that it takes a boy twelve years of growing before he sees his first deer.

But the boom and bust existence of mule deer here and the tendency of big bucks to hide out in the roughest places is still very much the rule. It's the hunter who learns how to play the population game here, and to search out the places those big bucks hide, who can find both quantity and quality in the mule deer of Cattle Country.

White-tailed Deer

It seems to take a special breed of hunter to chase big whitetail bucks in Cattle Country. It takes someone who loves the hunt as well as the venison at the end of it. And it requires slow patience to beat big whitetails at their own game.

The prairie whitetails found here are not the creatures of the wide-open spaces like their mule deer cousins of the higher ground. And they're not the denizens of the foothill hardwoods or the low mountain conifers like others of their kind further west in Montana.

Instead, they have grown up rubbing shoulders with man in the river and creek bottoms, honing their natural skills to elude riflemen's bullets and bowhunters' arrows.

"You just have to go in there and live with them. You have to observe what they do and how they do it. You have to have an extreme amount of patience," said Neil Martin, regional wildlife manager for Fish, Wildlife and Parks in Miles City. "I like to hunt them on the river bottoms. There are a lot of whitetails and you can shoot some of the does or the small bucks almost anytime, but the larger bucks are something else. They know their home a lot better than you do. They have evolved with man. These

147

guys live right in your backyard and you don't even know they're there."

Martin's jaunts on the Yellowstone River bottoms aren't tied to secret places. In fact, he goes to places frequented by other hunters and public ground where everyone is welcome.

"We're shooting those big bucks right in the heaviest-hunted parts of this state. I generally go where anyone else can go," he said. "We just spend time at it and we go at the time of the year when things are most in our favor, when there is snow on the ground and as late as we can when they're rutty."

The key is how Martin hunts the river bottoms and the years of experience he has put in at the game. "My dad and son and I, three generations, will go in there and we do very well at it. We move about five steps and stop or maybe a step and stop. We go through it very slow, very, very quietly. We move into one of those thickets or a big river island and what we're trying to do is not run them out into somebody else but move them in between us. We just work in unison. That takes lots of time and concentration. One of us is always stopped when the other one is moving. If you've got the deer moving and you're standing still, you've got an advantage. If they make a mistake, you've got an opportunity," he said.

"It's tough hunting. They are extremely adept at giving you the slip. They've got almost everything on their side in the river bottoms. We just go in there and spend hours and hours. If you put in enough time and pay attention, you can learn a lot from them. Dad's got sixty years in. I've got at least forty years in. My son has at least fifteen years in. That's a hundred fifteen man years of hunting effort between the three of us. When you spend that much time at it, just killing something is not the goal. Hunting is hunting. It's the challenge."

Despite the amount of hunting that goes on in the Yellowstone River bottoms of Cattle Country, the big bucks rarely are affected. Their defenses are just so well-refined that it takes a chance meeting between hunter and hunted for the big bucks to fall.

"I have actually watched them," Martin said. "I've been within a matter of feet of them. I remember a buck when one of my partners was coming through and he was making a lot of noise. That deer wasn't over fifteen feet away. I was standing in some thick stuff and he couldn't see me. I watched him crawl under a big thicket of rosebushes and actually stretch out under there. I watched him let that hunter walk right by him and when the guy went on by, he got up and slipped out the other side. They're tough as an old rooster pheasant. They'll lay there and let you go by."

Martin's method is to move slowly enough and quietly enough to be able to pick up on those deer movements. "That's the key to the whole thing, moving as slowly as you can," he said. "Don't go to the Yellowstone bottom unless you've got a lot of time, lots of experience, and the right kind of equipment. You need some kind of boat to get on the islands. You have to be prepared for the worst if you get frozen in out there, a sleeping bag and some matches. And you need lots of wool clothing, quiet kind of clothing. Anything nylon makes too much noise. If you've got one of those orange plastic things, put a match to it. Plastic on those rosebushes are just like somebody running their fingernails up and down a chalkboard, you can hear it for a hundred miles. You have to wear wool clothing. Even when you're driving, you don't need to worry about letting them know where you are. They know where you are when you step out of the boat."

148

Whitetails are plentiful on the privately-owned river bottoms of Cattle Country. Mark Henckel photo.

While deer drives aren't generally successful on moving the bigger deer on the Yellowstone bottoms, they can be an effective tool in other parts of Cattle Country.

In the Long Pines area near Ekalaka, for example, they can be extremely effective when carried out properly. The Long Pines, made up of dense stands of ponderosa pine at its center interspersed with brushy hardwood draws, is one of the few upland areas where whitetails thrive in Cattle Country.

"Some of the most successful hunters are guys that come here from Minnesota," said Steve Knapp, wildlife biologist for Fish, Wildlife and Parks at Broadus. "They come in and push the deer like they do at home and do well on them. That's often the most effective way because of the deer's behavior. Those deer have areas they live in and they're going to circle around."

"You can make a pretty decent drive with a half-dozen guys," added John Ramsey, game warden for Fish, Wildlife and Parks at Baker. "They drive those draws and it seems to work well. The good whitetail bucks are nice big deer here. And there are mule deer in the area, too, especially around the fringes.

"Another good time to hunt them here is late in the season during the rut. It always seems to make me a lot smarter as a hunter when the deer are in the rut," Ramsey laughed.

In recent years when mild winter weather has smiled on the species, whitetails have expanded their range into other upland areas, but whether they'll stick there in the face of more severe weather conditions is open to conjecture.

Their most secure areas here remain the creek and river bottoms where their numbers can be counted on to be high season after season. And while it's possible to fill tags on smaller bucks and does there with relative ease, hunting big bucks in the bottoms is never going to be easy in Cattle Country.

"It's almost impossible to get the big bucks in those heavily-hunted areas," Martin said. "I know what they're going to do, they know about me, and you can chase them exactly where they want to go. It's tough hunting and that's what makes it fun."

Antelope

Finding antelope in Cattle Country is no problem, no problem at all. But hitting them can be. For some reason, pronghorns annually provide fits of shooting apoplexy that no other species can even come close to causing.

Just a few years ago, it was a hunting friend, John Kremer, who succumbed to what I like to call the "Cartridge Man of the Year" syndrome while hunting the country north of Ekalaka. Antelope were everywhere, and Kremer was everywhere spotting them, stalking them, and shooting at them. He missed high. He missed low. He missed close shots. He missed long shots. In all, he missed twenty-nine times before he called a halt to his folly and collapsed back in the four-wheel drive for the long ride home.

It was such a painful, humiliating, soul-searching experience that it took almost the entire rough and dusty length of the Mizpah Road before I saw fit to comment on the exhibition. "That was some shooting there. That was a lot of shooting there," I said. "I don't suppose it matters to you now, but I do believe I'm going to nominate you for an award for that performance. You're a cinch to win it—Federal Cartridge Man of the Year, the individual most responsible for keeping the company showing a profit this hunting season."

It was while relating this tale to others that I heard about a woman who fired nearly four boxes of ammunition one season at antelope and missed with every shot, then turned around the next year and fired just three rounds, taking a buck deer, buck antelope, and cow elk.

"That's one of the most enjoyable things about hunting antelope. You're hunting a visible animal. When you're hunting them, you're seeing a couple hundred or three hundred animals in a day. You can see a lot of them," said Jamie Byrne, an outfitter from Mill Iron who has taken both Boone and Crockett and Pope and Young pronghorns from Carter County.

"To me, they're one of the most enjoyable animals to hunt. And if a person takes his time and looks for them, his chances of getting a real respectable trophy are real good," he said.

The key is to look over as many animals as possible, and that requires some help from the terrain and good optics. "We travel around in a pickup on the back roads until we get up on some high point, then use binoculars," Byrne said. "We look the country over until we spot a band of antelope, then we use a spotting scope to see if there's anything worthwhile. That saves some time because you don't have to get as close.

"We limit our numbers of hunters quite a bit so that we can get the size animals we do every year. For a fifteen-inch antelope, you'd have to look over approximately a hundred to a hundred fifty antelope early in the

Antelope can disappear in an instant if they spot the hunter in mid-stalk. Michael Sample photo.

season. On the last day of the season, it would be four hundred to five hundred to six hundred head. You go until you find a respectable buck you're interested in. After we spot them, we get out and stalk," Byrne said.

Stalking in southeastern Montana depends quite a bit on the type of terrain: the rougher the area, the easier the stalking. "The country is a little rougher down here," he said. "If there's enough cover, you can crawl up a draw or get behind some available cover for a reasonable shot."

Even in more open country, a successful stalk can be made if a hunter is willing to move slowly and keep his head down. "My son and I have spent all morning crawling on our bellies to look at a buck that was out on a flat," said Neil Martin, regional wildlife manager for Fish, Wildlife and Parks in Miles City.

"For everyone from a novice to an old hunter, they're fun to stalk," he added. "In the beginning of the season when they're coming out of the rut and haven't been messed with much, they're not much of a challenge. But you wait until after they've been hunted, later in the season, then test your mettle. It's a lot of fun. If you're very confident and adept at that kind of maneuvering, you can hunt them in places where it doesn't seem like there's any cover at all."

As for finding antelope, that's not really much of a problem unless the population has bottomed out. It's not even too site specific as to where in Cattle Country the trophies can be found.

"In eastern Montana, no one county is better than another for trophy antelope," said Mitch Howe, a Forsyth taxidermist who outfits in the fall. "We've got Boone and Crockett heads coming locally, coming from down south and from up north. The hardest part is to judge the antelope in the field. A guy who is absolutely looking for a Boone and Crockett antelope has to know what he's looking at before he pulls the trigger.

"I use the length of the head to judge an antelope. The ears vary but the length of the head averages about fourteen to fourteen and a half inches. If you're looking at horns about as long as the head and if they've got a good long hook to them, you're looking at a sixteen-inch-plus antelope," Howe said. "About two percent of the population may be trophy class but as for fifteen-to-sixteen-inch antelope, there are quite a few of them."

Howe relies on a spotting scope in making his final analysis of a head in the field. "A spotting scope, that's the trick to the whole thing," he said. "The strongest you can use is the best but normally, because of the flat conditions and the heat waves coming off of it, twenty power is about the most you can use. I can't accurately judge a head until I'm within two hundred or three hundred yards. When you get up that close, that's about the only time I can guess within a quarter of an inch and with the minimum scores for Boone and Crockett, you've got to be right on the money."

While Cattle Country could be considered the heartland for antelope in Montana, that doesn't mean the herds are always plentiful. The ravages of a tough winter can cut deeply into their numbers. The strength of the species, however, is in its ability to bounce back from these catastrophes quickly.

"The capacity of these populations to expand is beyond our comprehension," said Martin. "In the winters of 1978 and 1979, we virtually lost ninety percent of the antelope in some of these areas. In two years time, some of those areas increased in numbers to what we had before those two winters. With the exception of one or two places, they all bounced back. The animals responded very quickly with multiple births, twins and triplets. Bingo, we were right back in business.

"There are two things that are responsible for their well-being," he said. "One is overprotection by too conservative seasons. The other is weather conditions. If you don't harvest enough, you get an overpopulation that's resulting from overproduction. You end up with very weak, poor animals in the population. Then you don't even have to have a bad winter. You just have a moderate winter and they're going to die.

"If you keep the herd in good shape, they can respond even when the winters are as tough as those in 1978 and 1979. The remainder of the herd was in good shape and the land was in good shape," Martin said. "They are products of the land. They are not products of protection."

It should also be pointed out that in years of plenty, antelope tags are relatively easy to come by. Though these, too, are awarded in the computer drawings each summer along with tags for bighorn sheep, mountain goat, and moose, there are often leftovers available in Cattle Country because these hunting districts are so far removed from the population centers of Montana.

With good antelope numbers there and tags relatively easy to come by, Cattle Country is possibly the best of choices for hunters interested in taking a pronghorn. The antelope certainly are here. Just as long as you pack enough cartridges to hit one.

Turkeys

Turkey hunters would gladly bargain away many things for fine weather in spring. Take away their white Christmas. Bring rain on the Fourth of July. Drop a blizzard on the St. Patrick's Day parade. Frost their tomatoes on Labor Day. But please, Lord, make it clear and calm and warm in those final days of April and the first days of May.

"This is one of the key factors in spring turkey hunting. If you have good weather, it's going to increase your odds," said Ken Walcheck, information officer for Fish, Wildlife and Parks in Miles City.

Walcheck certainly ranks among the more avid turkey hunters to stalk the pine-covered ridges of Cattle Country during the spring gobbler season and seek out the big birds in fall. As such, he is part of a growing legion who have discovered that wild turkeys in Montana can spruce up a Thanksgiving dinner table and provide a new field of operations just as a winter's worth of cabin fever is becoming unbearable. But having the weather cooperate is of paramount importance for the turkey hunter in spring.

"What you want is quiet days and fairly warm days," Walcheck said. "This really turns the turkeys on and they do their thing out there as far as their courtship rituals. If it's blustery out, cold and snowy, the internal machinery is not turned on and they don't cooperate."

It's in the pre-dawn darkness of those beautiful spring mornings that he likes to be up and about, listening for the toms to sound off from their roost trees.

"You get up real early in the morning, about 4:30, especially if you have a good full moon. What those gobblers will do is start gobbling when it's pitch dark. You can sit in one location and mark those gobblers as to where they're calling from. You may have four or five toms in different areas so pinpoint the closest one and work him first. A gobbler further out is more difficult to pinpoint," he said.

"What you want to do is not get too close, no closer than 150 yards. The natural tendency is to get a little closer but many hunters make a mistake

Gobblers strut their stuff for the hens when the weather cooperates.
Bob Krumm photo.

because they get too close and they get spotted. Turkeys have a tendency to come down to the caller rather than going uphill so be on the same ridge either downhill or parallel to him and sit with your back against a good tree," Walcheck continued.

"If you have the tom in the tree, you don't want to produce the love yelp on your call yet because it's a little too early and he's not interested in that yet. I usually give out a couple of sleepy hen clucks just to let him know the hen is on the ground, then you wait for him to come down. Sometimes you can hear him fly from the roost or, if he's on the ground, you can tell from the location of the call that he has moved. Then use the hen yelps. The key is to get the right rhythm, not so much the sound, but the rhythm. I like to give out a fairly fast and snappy yelp. Usually I run a series of three or four yelps. Then I'll stop and I'll do it again. Then I put the call down and I don't do anything. Then the whole show is in his corner as far as what he wants to do. If he has any hens around, chances are he'll gobble back but won't come to you. You want to hope that you have a jake there or an older tom that has not acquired any hens yet. That's where your best success lies. I usually don't yelp anymore. I cluck with the box call. Sometimes, you can whine with it, too, just a scrape across the lid. Usually the cluck is the most consistent type of call to use. I really only concentrate with the two calls, the yelp and the cluck. They're not that bad to learn. The main thing is to get the rhythm."

While the system sounds simple enough, turkeys annually provide some of the more bizarre experiences to be found in hunting. At times, it can be extremely tough to bring in a bird. At others, it seems too easy.

"Two years ago, a friend came and we went out hunting," said Bill Schwarzkoph, of Forsyth. "We got out of the camper and I heard one gobble so we walked out in front of the truck a ways and called to him. But it seemed like the bird was moving around pretty quick. Then I saw him out of range, but my friend wanted to I take him now. I told him to wait. I kept calling and the bird got a little closer. Then my friend said he was going to take him and shot. I wondered why, because that bird was just barely in range. It turned out there were two birds and his was awfully close. I was watching one bird, he was watching another. I guess we could have had two at one time if I had known what was going on."

Walcheck also found out that the action could be unpredictable. "If you're working on a jake, I've had them almost run over the top of me, just barrel in so fast, then put on the skids. When you're working with an older mature tom, he's going to be very, very wary," he said.

It's those wary toms that a hunter has to be prepared for, he added. "The first thing on a turkey you see is the head. It's rotating and turning. He's looking all over the place for the hen. Once you see your turkey, the real key is to not bat an eyelash, be perfectly motionless. When I'm not going to call anymore, I'll put my gun on my lap and have a finger in the trigger guard. When I'm ready to shoot, I want to do it real fast. If you lose a millisecond, you're out of luck. Once that turkey sees you, watch out. They'll put on a disappearing act like you wouldn't believe."

Both Walcheck and Schwarzkoph advise 12-gauge shotguns that can shoot three-inch magnum shells for the big birds. "They can be extremely tough to kill," Walcheck said. "I would compare them to a miniature tank running around, heavily armored with all those feathers. Line up on the

Hunters must be able to distinguish between gobblers like this one and the hens in spring. Michael Sample photo.

head and neck, that's the area to shoot for and use forty yards as your outside range. And don't get too excited and shoot too quick and miss the turkey. Everybody has done that, including me. That really hurts. You go through all this work and you blow your opportunity and you start all over again."

To increase a hunter's odds, he should plan on going after them for more than a day at a time, however. "It would be nice to have a good three-day weekend at least," Schwarzkoph said. "The more time you spend out there, the more apt you are to find some birds or hear some birds. I like to camp overnight and be there early in the morning to hunt. And the evening is a good time to scout around and find out what area they're roosting in so you can be there the next morning."

But hunters who measure their success just by the number of turkeys they have taken over the years are missing the point of the spring season.

"I think a spring gobbler season is a quality type hunt," Schwarzkoph said. "Bagging a turkey isn't the number one thing. Hearing a gobbler gobble and answer your call is the most exciting thing. Everytime he gobbles, he's getting closer and closer. When he gobbles to your call, it makes your heart jump up in your throat pretty quick. That's more exciting than the actual killing of the bird."

Hunters should remember that the spring season is for gobblers only and they should be able to distinguish between the toms and hens. Among the characteristics are the tom's beard; breast feathers that are an irridescent black on the tom compared to the white-tipped fringe of the hen's breast feathers; and the head of the tom that is covered with caruncles and wattles which are gorged with blood and range in color between red and blue.

In years past, the spring season was relatively restricted to several areas by the simple fact that turkey populations were far less widespread than they are today. The Long Pines, near Ekalaka, the pine hills around Ashland and the rough breaks of Garfield County are still good places to look for birds. But the turkey population has found other homes as well.

"There are mainly two habitats they fill today. One is the river bottom birds. The other place would be in the pine hills," said Steve Knapp, wildlife biologist for Fish, Wildlife and Parks at Broadus.

During the spring season, it's relatively easy to locate the birds through their gobbling but a hunter doesn't have that going for him during the fall. "In the fall, it's mostly the opportunity of hunters coming across the birds when they're deer hunting," Knapp said. "In the river bottoms, finding them isn't too difficult. In the pine hills, it's a little more difficult to find them. If there are agricultural areas in the pine forests, they prefer that. They also prefer some areas with brushy, deciduous cover in the coulees. You'll also find them in ponderosa pine that has an understory of fruit berries like Oregon grape, snowberry, and rose. In the fall and winter, they also love ponderosa pine seeds when they can find them."

But hunters shouldn't expect to find a great deal of competition with others seeking turkeys in Montana. "Compared to other states, they're not hunted hard," Knapp said. "But numbers of turkey hunters over the past five or six years have been increasing. There seems to be more interest in turkeys."

And spring hunting has been the most interesting of all in recent years, just as long as the hunter has the weather to perk up the turkeys. That spring weather is worth everything, even if it means hail has to hammer your mother-in-law's petunias, once a week, every week, all summer long.

Waterfowl

Canada geese are providing a relatively new target for shotgunners along the Yellowstone River of Cattle Country. There have always been some geese along the river, of course. But over the past decade, the gunning has been getting better and better.

Part of the reason for the new opportunity is changing land use patterns along the river. The rest can be attributed to a rising goose population which is moving through the area.

"I think the hunting has been better in recent years," said Dennis Hoovestal, a native of Sanders now living in Billings. "There are fewer and fewer sugar beets being raised in the valley and a lot more corn and grain.

"My folks have owned the general store and run the post office at Sanders since the 1930s," he said. "The first goose I got was when I was in the fifth or sixth grade. There were very few guys that hunted geese back then. Now, every year there are more and more of them."

Those goose hunters have found plenty of reasons to come back. Though the river itself has been closed to hunting from the mouth of the Bighorn River downstream to the Custer County-Rosebud County line, access in the surrounding fields hasn't been too difficult to obtain. And the numbers of geese in some years has been astounding.

"The hunting has been excellent," said Tom Hinz, Central Flyway waterfowl biologist for Fish, Wildlife and Parks in Miles City. "The goose population on the river is fairly stable but the population of geese that uses the area, primarily the Hi-line Canada goose population, has been increasing for twenty years. A lot of geese are being raised north of the Yellowstone in the Hi-line area and in the stock pond country. The fall flight of the Hi-line Canada geese is about a hundred fifty thousand. It's a big bunch of birds and they're augmented by the Shortgrass Prairie Canada goose population. They come down through the same area. Those are the smaller geese and the preseason population on them is over two hundred thousand."

Exactly how well hunters do on these migrating honkers depends on the weather. Given a long warm fall and an easy transition to winter, the chances of holding the birds here are excellent. When winter storms in quickly and the thermometer dips below zero and stays there, the opportunities are more limited.

"The main thing is the fall weather," Hinz said. "Last year was an excellent year. We had that zero weather before Halloween. A lot of the geese were pushed off their staging areas further north. They came on down here and our weather warmed up and a lot of the birds stayed. In terms of availability of geese for the hunter, the weather is a major factor."

Hunting is generally confined to the river valley during this part of the season, though the geese may venture further out on their morning and evening feeding flights.

"You just watch for two or three days and see what fields they are feeding in," Hoovestal said. "If they've been in there and haven't been bothered, we go out and set up there about daylight. We never dig any pits, just use tarps and a bale of straw or corn stalks. We use about twenty-four to thirty-six decoys. I have seen guys who put out a hundred or a hundred fifty, but if they've been coming in, I don't know if you'd need any decoys.

"At that time of year, sometimes you get flocks of five thousand geese in a field," Hoovestal added. "Later in the year, they tend to break down in smaller groups. One group will drop in, then another and another until you've got a field full of them. They're a smart bird and a tough bird to bring down. I have a 10 gauge double that takes 3 1/2-inch magnums that I use sometimes and it's kind of like a bomber taking flak into them and they keep on going. But if you get a good shot in the heart or head or break a wing, they'll come down."

If the weather cooperates, hunters may also get some shooting off stock ponds and reservoirs in the wheat country adjacent to the river. "I've seen them fly as far as eight or ten miles to feed and I've heard of them going further than that," Hinz said. "Winter wheat is being grown in little patches away from the river in a lot of the outlying areas. Frequently those are some of the best places to hunt. Once those geese travel out that far, they'll generally seek out a stock pond nearby to loaf on during the day. They'll try to avoid a routine of long flights back to the river."

The Yellowstone River has also traditionally been a good place to go for mallards, but declines in the continental population have cut into that in recent times and few hunters have ever tried field shooting for them.

"The duck hunting is more sporadic. The mallard population is declining. Compared to ten years ago, the mallard population is less than half of what it was," Hinz said. "Generally they jump them off the open drain ditches but you can field hunt for them along the river, too.

"The best thing to do is pick out an area where you know there are mallards around and find a nearby picked cornfield which is fairly good-sized. Go out in mid-afternoon and build yourself a pile of corn shucks to lay under and set some duck decoys between the rows," he said. "If it's really mild, a lot of times those birds don't come out to feed until after sundown. If you can wait until it gets colder, ten to twenty degrees above zero or colder, they'll come out during earlier parts of the day. They'll come out in flocks of a hundred to five hundred or more and they'll circle the field. Sometimes, I've had them walking around me in the blind.

"The key is to find a field the ducks are using. If you're going to a field you chose, you may not be able to draw them in with a hundred decoys. If you've seen them circling there at sundown, you can do it with two dozen decoys," Hinz said. "Try to bring the birds into a field they're not accustomed to using and there's a lot of lack of success in that kind of endeavor."

While access is still considered to be good along the Yellowstone River, the increasing pressure could change that as landowner tolerance begins to swing away from the hunter and in favor of the ducks and geese.

"In the thirteen years since I've lived here, there's a real noticeable increase in hunters and the vast majority of it is on the weekends," Hinz said. "It may require you to do some scouting around and you may have to ask some farmers before you find a place to hunt. If you get to know the farmer, he may save some hunting for you.

"But the most important thing is the weather. We've had two or three good years in a row because we've had some fairly mild weather. In a more normal year, we'd have them move in in early November and they'd be gone in a couple of weeks. You can have an excellent season here," Hinz concluded. "But you've got to have the weather on your side."

Upland Birds

They say big game offers the best opportunities for the serious hunter in Montana. Upland bird hunting is just for fun. If that's the case, there's a good time that's waiting to be enjoyed in Cattle Country.

"There are some bona fide bird hunters, but the percentage is drastically different than with bona fide big game hunters," said Neil Martin,

Pheasants tend to hold tighter in the snow and offer tracking possibilities for the hunter. Mark Henckel photo.

regional wildlife manager for Fish, Wildlife and Parks in Miles City. "People generally are not willing to put out the effort. You take things like sage grouse and sharptails and most people take them incidentally. A guy is out there hunting antelope and takes his shotgun along and if he sees sage grouse, he takes them."

There are a few serious bird hunters in Cattle Country, however, and their wingshooting trips can be excellent. Pheasants annually attract the most interest, finishing ahead of species like sharptails, sage grouse, and Hungarian partridge in the hunters' hearts.

"The pheasant hunting here is as good as it is anywhere in Montana," said Clif Youmans, of Forsyth. "It's not as good as when this area had more small farms and there were more dispersed cover types. But I have seen flocks of thirty and forty pheasants in this area."

Pheasant hunters should head to the agricultural areas and the brushy creek bottoms to find their birds in Cattle Country. "Look for the river bottoms, creek bottoms or the irrigated uplands where there are small grains planted," Youmans said. "The best places to look are on the agricultural fields where there are a lot of weeds. That's one place they like to be.

"If it's early in the season and the pheasants are not being taxed for food, they often head into the cornfields. The best way to hunt them is to have two or three people walk through the cornfield and have one or two people posted at the end. They'll almost always flush well out in front of you," he said. "My personal favorite hunting conditions are when there's a fresh snow on the ground. It holds the birds tighter and you can track them. The birds are also a lot more active because they have to be out looking for food."

That cold-weather hunting extends to the most bitter conditions that can be found in Cattle Country. "In really, really cold weather, when the temperature is in the low teens and zero area, the best areas are along the thick willows," he said. "They get in there and it's almost impenetrable for people to get in there. The best way to hunt those is to have people on either side and try to work a dog through the middle."

But a pheasant hunter has to be versatile when hunting the bottoms. He has to be able to read the signs and know what type of habitat the birds are likely to be hiding in.

"When I'm walking, I like to look for the little dust bowls they make. Pheasants like to take dust baths," Youmans said. "Pheasants actually have their own runways through the rosebushes and snowberry when they're really heavy. There are certain times of the day when the pheasants come to the roads looking for gravel. You're out in the brush beating around and they're out on the road. If you're having a slow day, it might behoove you to look for pheasant tracks in the road dust.

"Pheasants move around," he added. "They have a routine. They're in the cornfields at a certain time, they're going to be taking their gravel or they're going to be taking their dust baths at a certain time. You have to be able to read the signs and figure out when they're doing it. If they're not there now, they're going to be there. They might be coming back later."

With the number of pheasants that can be found in some drainages of Cattle Country, it's hard to believe that there were once more of them around. Yet Harold Miller, who has lived on the same farm near Sanders for the past seventy-four years, can attest to the fact that the hunting was better.

"The pheasant hunting is not as good as it used to be. There's not the birds we had twenty years ago," he said. "It's mostly the loss of habitat. We've lost twenty acres of good habitat through land leveling and getting rid of brush on our place. But we've still got quite a lot of habitat. Now everything is also fall-plowed. It didn't used to be. The farm practices have changed here in the Yellowstone bottom. Up on the creeks, it hasn't changed so much.

"We have also had a lot more hunting pressure. But most everybody gets a few birds," he said. "You get a lot of people hunting pheasants, but not very many hunting grouse."

One hunter who still hits the prairies for birds on a regular basis is Al Lee, who ranches north of Forsyth. Most often seen with a single-barrel muzzleloading shotgun, Lee said sage grouse, sharptails, and Hungarian partridge provide plenty of fun for the upland bird hunter.

"I like to get my deer hunting done early so I can go out and enjoy birds," he said. "I hunt almost entirely with black powder. You have to swing a little different because your shot is a little slower. You have to lead a little bit more. If I'm hunting in a party, I take a regular shotgun. But if I'm out for the fun of it, I go out with a muzzleloader."

Lee said he likes to hunt during the middle of the day for his sharptails and partridge. "I'm not much of an early morning bird hunter. I never try to go out and hunt them early in the morning. They're out feeding and they're very alert," he said. "I wait until the middle of the day when they're in their cover. I look for a brushy draw that's not too far from a grain field.

"An individual grouse isn't a smart bird," he added. "A covey is smart. If you find a whole covey out in the open, you're not going to get close to them as often. But if you can get a covey scattered down a brushy draw in the middle of the day, you can get a limit that way sometimes."

Sage grouse simply require the expenditure of some boot leather, walking the sagebrush until a bunch is located. "I walk sagebrush flats and try to find where their droppings are. I just hunt areas that show the sign of sage hens," he said. "When you jump them, you also watch where they go. But I've seen sage hens fly two miles. You think you know where they land but you go right to where you figure they should be and can't find them. The earth seems to swallow them up sometimes."

Lee said a dog is a big help in hunting both prairie grouse, Huns, and pheasants in Cattle Country. "You don't always find all those birds you knock down without a dog," he said. "A dog always helps."

He added that a bird hunter should always be prepared. "The cardinal rule for hunting these birds is always be ready to shoot. More birds are missed by hunters who are not mentally ready to shoot than by any other reason. This shows up in sloppy gun carrying, improper foot placement and being totally surprised when a bird takes off. That gives the bird quite an advantage, doesn't it?" Lee said.

But just like with every other huntable species in Cattle Country, bird numbers can vary from year to year. In the years of good hatches, the shotgun hunter may fill his limit every time he heads into the field. In the years of few birds, it may take many miles of walking to put feathers in your game pouch.

"At times, it's really good. It runs in cycles," Lee said. "But whether there are a lot of birds or not so many, it's always fun to hunt them here."

Peak and Prairie Country

Hunting season is a visitor with many faces when it pays its respects to Peak and Prairie Country each fall. It can arrive as friendly as a warm September breeze drifting over the sagebrush or as hostile as an equinox storm raging through the high country. It's big flocks of stiff-winged Canada geese setting into the October grain stubble and mule deer bucks driven down from high places by the urges of the November rut. And it's mallards clinging to the open rivers in the face of zero cold and chukar partridge huddling in the snow.

But hunting opportunities certainly don't end there. This is the land of the long season in Montana, less affected by the ravages of winter than many other parts of the Treasure State and better blessed with diversity for the hunter willing to alter his tactics and change his prey.

It doesn't hold the big elk herds that other parts of Montana can boast of, but there are some bulls here. It isn't the heartland of the moose and mountain lion, but there are representatives of these species, along with black bear, mountain goat, bighorn sheep, turkeys, waterfowl, and every huntable upland bird species except spruce grouse.

Peak and Prairie Country is just that, a mixture of high country and low where mule deer, whitetails, and antelope are the undeniable stars of the big game scene and shotgun hunters can see action on everything from sage grouse and sharptails in September to chukars, Huns, honkers, and mallards by the time the New Year arrives.

In its varied parts, it offers the highest peaks in Montana in the Beartooth Mountains and such island ranges as the Snowies, Bulls, and Pryors. There are the sagebrush flats and rolling grasslands where antelope, sage grouse and sharptails can be sought under a broad blue sky. And whitetail hunters can find trophy-class bucks in river courses like the Yellowstone, Musselshell, Clark's Fork, and Bighorn.

Public land is scarcer here than in parts of Montana further to the west, but there are some Forest Service and BLM tracts to be found by the person who can read a map and know exactly where he's standing. The bulk of Peaks and Prairie Country, however, and much of the richness of its hunting opportunities, rest with the private landowner. Asking permission is the undeniable rule here and with Billings, the largest city in Montana, at its heart, gaining access can be a problem because of sheer hunter numbers.

But that doesn't take away from the rich wildlife and multiple opportunities that Peak and Prairie Country has to offer. It's rich enough, in fact, that though a hunter may experience his season in many ways here from September through December, he can rarely do it all. But that doesn't keep him from trying, and hunting, and trying some more when next season rolls around.

Mule Deer

There's a certain ridge far back in the mountains that Rob Seelye likes to visit when the archery season beckons in September. It's a place where few other hunters tread but where big mule deer bucks have been spotted season after season by the Laurel bowhunter.

"You find big mule deer in the same places every year," Seelye said. "You look for an area that's rough enough to provide secure bedding areas. They're the hard-to-get-to places that take time to walk in to. It's high open ridges, headwalls of creeks. The big bucks have got to have good feed and they like to bed where they can see and watch the valley below."

When a hunter locates such an area, it can be an annual source of big antlers and, at times, too easy a hunt for those who value the experience as much as the mule deer buck in hand. "After we located it, we hunted that spot the first morning of the rifle season and got three big bucks in an hour, all of them four-points, and the biggest one had an inside spread of twenty-eight inches," Seelye said. "We had them figured out and it was a piece of cake. They use the same escape routes every year. But it's a small area and if you hunt it right, you could take them all. That was in 1979 and we've been hunting it ever since with bows. We hunt it only one or two days a year and take our chances."

Despite stacking the odds in the deer's favor, Seelye knows that trophy-class mule deer are the most difficult target an archer can face in Montana. "It's tough to get a big muley with a rifle or bow. With a rifle, it's a lot easier but it's still inaccessible country where they live. And most people with a bow aren't accurate enough out past forty yards. There are not very many guys successful at doing it consistently with a bow."

His contention that a person has to locate big buck areas and learn them well stands up, however, no matter where a hunter heads in Peak and Prairie Country. And the popular notion that mule deer bucks are easy to come by isn't necessarily so.

"Muleys are different than whitetails. A muley will often bound off a certain distance and stop and look at you, but there are some pretty clever mule deer. The older they get, the smarter they get," said Jay Archer, of Billings. "Those old muleys are crafty. They are smart. I've pushed some of those big deer for hours and just gotten glimpses of them. I've tracked them half a day and never got a chance at a shot. Once you start pursuing them on their own ground, on their own terms, they can be darn elusive."

The answer is to get to know an area well and observe the habits of the deer that live there. Season after season, mule deer will do the same things, hide in the same places, and feel hunter pressure in the same ways.

"I used to hunt 15 miles east of Billings," Archer said. "You can't do it anymore because of population. But back then, I could tell you what the deer were going to do. I could tell you exactly where they were going. When a person is out hunting and they spook deer, the hunter's attention is soon somewhere else because they feel those deer are long gone. But if you learn the country, the terrain, you can learn those deer's habits pretty easy."

Figuring out the haunts and habits of deer is a necessity for big buck hunters no matter what part of Peak and Prairie Country a person chooses to hunt. In the mountains, Seelye learned his high ridge and the paths of the bucks that lived there. Rich Stevenson, of Livingston, did the same thing in the years he was growing up in Billings and hunting the broad prairie country toward the Snowy Mountains.

The prairie affords a different look for the mule deer hunter, however, in that there's more of a mixture of habitats to be unraveled. "There's prairie grassland, sagebrush, sandstone and pine ridges, and dry creek beds running down the valleys," Stevenson said. "In the old days, you used to just drive the trails anywhere and it was pretty easy. That was the most popular way of hunting deer in the 1950s and '60s. At that time, if you saw a rancher, he was happy to see you. You were someone to talk to. There's more still hunting in a smaller area now, watching the deer crossing the ridges or getting them going to feed and water.

"You walk for them, quietly, just like you'd hunt pheasants. You can walk for them by yourself or, with partners, you can put one guy on the bottom of a dry wash coulee and a guy up on each side," Stevenson said. "A lot of times when you're still hunting, when a mule deer buck sees you, he's surprised and he'll just lie there and look at you. You can shoot it in its bed. Or, he'll stand up and you can get a shot. But a smart old buck that's been nicked a few times, when he sees you, he's just up and gone. You might have a snap shot and you might not."

Much of the hunting centers on land features that can offer a buck some cover in the midst of his wide-open surroundings. "They'll use these dry washes for routes of travel so they can't be seen. They'll bed on the ridgetops where they have a good look at the land around them and where they have a good escape route so that if trouble comes, they can get out of there," he said. "The big bucks will bed where they're less likely to be disturbed."

But hunters should also be aware that prairie and mountain mule deer were not created equally. Depending on the year, people should be prepared to change their hunting destinations to match the current population picture for the species.

"The prairies are far more productive in terms of turning out deer, but they're also more vulnerable," said Charlie Eustace, regional wildlife

Some areas hold big mule deer bucks which use the same escape routes year after year. Michael Sample photo.

manager with Fish, Wildlife and Parks in Billings. "Because of the easier terrain and the relative lack of cover, mule deer there are fairly easy to get to. They're easy to see. But their life expectancy is not nearly as long from hunting pressure and natural causes."

In years of plenty, mule deer numbers on the prairie can be truly unbelievable. But when the population is on a downhill slide, their scarcity can be equally surprising. The mountains of Peak and Prairie Country provide more stable environments for mule deer and seem to weather the boom and bust cycle with less variation in numbers.

In a species which takes a number of years to produce a good set of antlers, that may mean the mountains would be a more logical choice for the hunter heading after big bucks. "The longevity of deer on the prairie just doesn't match up to the mountains," Eustace said. "In the mountains, there seems to be areas that characteristically carry big bucks. Cover does help them get that way. Even in the prairie areas, we have older age-class bucks where you get into more rugged topography and better cover for them. The other areas where I have always observed big bucks are in areas where access is either limited through the landowner or the terrain."

The boom and bust cycle of mule deer can also be extreme. And in the worst of times, a hunter may have to really work at it to get his deer.

Glenn Saunders, of Columbus, can remember the leanest of hunting situations back in the 1930s. "When I was a kid, you hunted and hunted hard and you didn't pass up a legal buck," he said. "The only place you had deer was way back in the high country, back on the Forest Service land in the Beartooths. We went back there on horses and set up a camp to hunt. We'd take the track of an animal and stay with him all day, because that might be the only animal you'd see all day. We became adept at going after them and walking them up in their bedding grounds."

While that has certainly changed and mule deer have come back in a big way to repopulate the lowlands, it still gives a peek at the secure habitats where mule deer will thrive when the going gets tough elsewhere. It's also a sure bet that those areas will hold big deer today.

"If you want to go back into the high country, way back on the ridges, you'll find big bucks," Saunders said. "There are a lot of them in that country but they're real cagey. We've taken some two hundred thirty and two hundred forty-pounders. That's rough-dressed, weighed weight. We used to weigh deer a lot. We also prided ourselves in our ability to judge their weight within five pounds. Their bodies are just tremendous and they're in great shape in the fall. I've taken several deer that were really tough to get on and after we got them, they were just as tough to get out of the country."

That difficulty is one of the reasons why mountain mule deer bucks tend to grow older and bigger than their counterparts on the prairie. But that difficulty is also the basis for many hunters forsaking the public ground of the high country for the private lands down low where the deer, though generally smaller, are easier to find, easier to hunt and easier to get back home once they're taken.

That necessitates getting permission of the landowner, of course, which isn't always easy to come by. It takes an effort on the part of the hunter both in and out of season. And the hunter who does the best landowner-sportsman relations work is the one most likely to get the big buck.

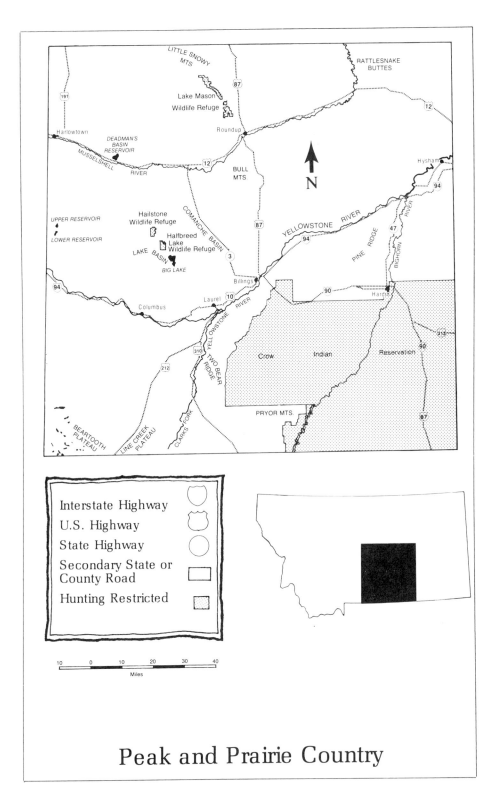

10   0   10   20   30   40
Miles

Peak and Prairie Country

"It's best to get permission in late summer or early fall, not on the opening day of the hunting season," Archer said. "You stop at a few places, introduce yourself, get permission long in advance. Then all it often takes in the hunting season is a note on the door to let them know you're there.

"I don't think there's anything more frustrating to these farmers and ranchers than to have sixty or eighty people coming to their door on the opening day of the hunting season. You drive them crazy. Contact these people ahead of time, get to known them and they'll welcome you a lot more than being the twenty-seventh guy on opening morning to knock on their door."

White-tailed Deer

In many ways, big whitetail bucks are the last hunting frontier in Peak and Prairie Country. That's something that can't be said for the species elsewhere in Montana.

In the Northeast, whitetails are the most common target of deer hunters. In the Northwest, they're the deer of choice. And even in central Montana, availability makes them a popular prey.

But in Peak and Prairie Country, they've become almost a sideshow to the mule deer hunting that surrounds them. Tougher to get in the crosshairs, more difficult to locate, and generally found only in areas of private land where access takes a little more effort, whitetails definitely don't attract the hunting pressure that their big-eared cousins do.

Perhaps that's the reason that in recent years, hunters searching for big bucks are increasingly looking to whitetails. In areas like the Yellowstone, Bighorn, and Musselshell river bottoms and their tributaries, a new field of operations has been opened simply because trophy-class whitetails have been found there.

"There are lots of big bucks, lots of cover and quite a bit of pressure around towns," said Bill Butler, of Billings. "But most of the big bucks still die of old age. A lot of game species are not very wary, it's just getting to where they're at, but a big whitetail can live right there under your nose year-round and you can't get him. If you don't believe it, just go down to the river bottoms in spring and you'll find big antlers. They kill some big ones, but a lot of them just die of old age.

"Once a whitetail gets into his fifth season, you kill him when you make a mistake," Butler added. "He's got you programmed and when you do something else, he runs into you."

Whitetails do take more specialized techniques than mule deer, where all a hunter often has to do is walk through suitable cover, spot his buck, and shoot him. Whitetail hunting just isn't that way. "If you just get out and walk through, you're not going to see much of whitetails except for the flash of a tail," said Tom Butts, wildlife biologist for Fish, Wildlife and Parks in Roundup. "The average Montanan just doesn't have the knowledge of tactics to hunt them in thick brushy situations. Little drives or stand hunting seems to work the best. I've killed two whitetail bucks in the last three years and I've gotten both of them essentially stand hunting. I'd pick a spot near a saddle early in the morning or late in the evening and just wait and they'd come by."

Merl Schruder, of Laurel, is another stand hunter who goes after big bucks in the Yellowstone River bottomlands in both the archery and gun seasons. "I like to hunt islands but with those whitetails, usually when you see them is usually when they're gone," he said. "That's why they call them the white-tailed ghosts."

To get the big bucks, Schruder feels scouting is essential and the more time and effort a person puts into his deer hunting, the better his chances at downing a trophy-class deer. "About two weeks before the bow season, I scope out and binocular it all, then I sit down and mark it on a map basically where I saw the majority of the bucks that were four-points or better. I have a whole map of the Yellowstone and I mark and number the buck on how big he is and where I've seen him and every time I've seen him," he said. "I also do my PR work at that time and get permission to get a tree stand in or get in stacked hay. You can sit back in the stacked hay and observe as much as you can from a tree stand."

As a two-season hunter, the knowledge gained on the archery outings often can be put to use when rifle time rolls around. But even without the rifle season, the bow season can bring some thrills.

"I remember one time when I was hunting this big whitetail," Schruder said. "About ten minutes before dusk, I was sitting there in a haystack and there were a couple of spikes and some does out in front of me and they started snorting. I heard deer behind me doing the same thing so I turned around real cautious and here's that big buck just five yards behind me.

When pressured in the bottoms, whitetails often move away from the river onto higher ground. Mark Henckel photo.

They're so sharp, you never even hear them coming. But he heard something and jumped out to thirty yards. I nocked an arrow and let it fly and it went over him. On the second arrow, I cut hair underneath him. He jumped up on that one, but just came back and sniffed the arrow. I just quit. I couldn't believe it."

Hunting techniques on whitetails often depend on how many hunters are in the group. For the lone hunter, stands are generally considered to work the best. If there are three people hunting together, drives can be effective.

"I prefer to hunt by myself," Butler said. "I build myself a tree stand and I go across to islands either afoot or in a canoe. I've come back in the pitch dark in a canoe but I always have a life jacket on—I don't fool around.

"If you've got three guys, you can move everything on a medium-sized island," he added. "You go to the downwind end of the island and have one guy go up the center a little ways and get into a good tree where he can see well. The other two go around the outside of the island to the other end. When they do that, they push everything to the center. Then they come back down the island right through the middle. The whitetails are not going to go where you've already been. The only way they've got to go is back and you'll push everything right back down the island under that tree."

Bigger islands take a little different technique which gathers its strength from the fact that whitetails would rather sneak around a hunter than move out in front of him. "On a big island, you can get one guy out in front with the other two about a hundred yards back. The bucks will get up and be coming around the first guy and the guys on his flanks will kill the deer," Butler said. "Another way on a big island where you're not going to move them off of it, is to put two guys on stands on each end of the island and the rest of the guys just get in there and mill them around. The big bucks will just sneak and sneak and sneak around the guys on the island until one of the guys on stand spots them."

While the bottomlands are undeniably the secure home ranges of whitetails and they can sneak past a lot of hunters there, hunting season can change deer distribution. Deer, especially the big bucks, will move out if pressure gets too great and pull into the coulees and tributary creeks that feed into the bottoms.

"Once the bird season starts, the best bucks go up in the breaks," Butler said. "I've seen them ten miles from the river. I've killed them up with the mule deer does."

Butts said the whitetails in his country also move up into the hills. "They are moving into the Bull Mountains," he said. "Most of them are within four miles of the Musselshell but they use that ponderosa pine woodland extensively in the hunting season. Even without the hunting pressure, I find that during the late summer and early fall, they move out into the hills more on their own."

No matter which drainage a hunter chooses, there are excellent opportunities to take a big whitetail buck. "There are some humongous non-typical whitetails," Schruder said. "There are many nice four-points with eighteen and twenty-inch inside spreads and some that are bigger than that. I've got four that are twenty inches or bigger and I've got one on the wall that is twenty-four inches. The big problem is access. You have to get permission from the rancher and farmer, that's the big thing.

"The big bucks are there," he added. "But you're not going to just walk out and shoot them. You've got to do your homework first and then know how to get them."

Antelope

There's a hurry-up rush associated with the opening day of the general antelope season that remains something of a mystery to veteran prong-horn hunters. Maybe it's the fact that the October opening is the first chance for the majority of the rifle hunters to break out their .270s and .30-06s. Perhaps it's the notion that if a hunter doesn't get that buck right away, someone else will take it away from him. Whatever the reason, that opener can be guaranteed to put long strings of headlights on the highways in the predawn hours and have antelope herds running wild by mid-morning.

Part of the credit for this phenomenon has to go to Peak and Prairie Country itself and its rich antelope population which generates plenty of tags for the hunters. The rest of it may just be opening-day enthusiasm. But in either event, it's not necessarily the best way to get a good antelope buck or to foster better landowner-sportsman relations.

"I always hunt antelope in mid-season," confided Tom Butts, wildlife biologist for Fish, Wildlife and Parks in Roundup. "There's less hunters and easier access. If a rancher wants hunters in the first place, on the opening two weekends they take as many as they can cram onto a place. Each rancher has his own tolerance, whether it's five hunters or fifty. But at mid-week or in mid-season, there's almost no antelope hunters out."

The notion that antelope will be too spooky if a hunter doesn't get out there on opening day is debatable. "Their flightiness varies almost from day to day," Butts said. "A lot of it has to do with wind and weather. At times, I have seen big bucks just after the season that are relatively easy to stalk. Other times, on opening day you can't get within two miles of them."

The big advantage of going out at mid-season is that in avoiding the other hunters, you also dispose of the possibility of other hunters ruining a well-designed stalk by opening long-range fire from somewhere in the next county or driving their pickup over a ridge and spooking the buck toward parts unknown.

It's often in pulling off a difficult stalk that antelope hunters obtain the most satisfaction. Being creatures of the wide-open prairie and with visual capabilities far exceeding that of man, getting within range can be a challenge.

"The system I have always used is to drive and glass and once I have spotted the antelope, I get out and start the stalk," said Charlie Eustace, regional wildlife manager for Fish, Wildlife and Parks in Billings. "If a person will take the time to stalk them and use a few rudimentary prin-ciples, they can get up within good range of a good buck. If at all possible, keep the sun to your back and have it in the antelope's eyes, the wind in your face and if you can get those two together, great. Take a little bit of time to analyze the terrain and how you're going to get to the antelope. Even in the flattest country, there is usually some relief you can use to your advantage.

During mid-season, there are fewer hunters out to spoil a stalk on a nice antelope buck. Michael Sample photo.

"I do a great deal of crawling on my belly, particularly the last couple hundred yards. It's essential that you crawl," he added. "Anytime you have made a successful stalk, the rest of the antelope will have no idea you're there. They'll mill around the dead antelope. One time, I almost got run over when they finally ran out of there. They passed within a couple of yards. If the stalk is a good one, they have no idea what you are or where you are."

Not that all that crawling across the prairie doesn't have its hazards. "There was one time when the first thing I did was sit down to shoot and I sat on a cactus. Then I jumped up and knelt on a cactus. Then I just let the antelope go," Eustace said.

While the middle of the season will provide a hunter with more access and less competition, it should be pointed out that waiting too long can also present problems for a hunter looking for a big buck. Antelope have black shiny horns composed of cornified hair which are shed every year just about the time the pronghorn season winds down, leaving a bony core on which next year's horns will grow.

"By late season, they're losing their horns," Butts said. "I can remember going out once with a day or two left before the season ended. I had a friend with me and we found this herd with two respectable bucks in it. They ran off and made a big U and when they came back, she shot one of the bucks, but between the time she shot him and he hit the ground he lost his horns. And we couldn't find them."

Another way to beat the crowds is to hunt the archery season which opens in early September and coincides with the breeding time for the species. Rodger Warwick, of Billings, has chased antelope in the archery season for years and considers the rut a mixed blessing.

172

"The rut's a bonus because the bucks are out and active chasing the does," Warwick said. "But it's a minus because they're usually in bigger bunches and you've got all those eyes watching you. The bucks may be preoccupied, but the does aren't."

Warwick stalks antelope with a bow, but said that method is extremely difficult because the hunter must get so close to the animal. "It's easier if you can let them come to you," he said. Warwick has taken antelope on a creek where they crossed between feeding and bedding grounds; in brush near a watering hole; and even along fenceline crossings, using tumbleweeds wedged against the fence as cover. He has a Pope and Young buck to prove such strategies work.

For the serious antelope hunter who wants to shoot a truly good buck, the season should start early with trips into the field to locate trophy-class animals. "I do most of my scouting in the summer," Warwick said. "By the time the season comes, I've got my antelope located. I think you waste a lot of hunting time if you don't do your scouting before the season."

And hunters who want a trophy buck in Peak and Prairie Country should realize that it's not necessarily the numbers of animals which determine size—the age of individuals is more important.

"Some of the larger antelope we have here are in areas where we do not put out a great number of permits," Eustace said. "A greater proportion of the males will live longer because we harvest them at a lower rate."

It takes a certain number of years before a buck gets big. "A yearling is going to have horns about seven inches," Eustace said. "On a two-year-old, you're going to be running ten to twelve inches. It's a minimum of three years before you get up to that fourteen-inch class and four years before you get over that. You always hear about sixteen-, seventeen-, eighteen-inchers that hunters see, but there aren't very many of them."

While those giants may be rare, there are certainly respectable bucks to be found throughout the season in Peak and Prairie Country. The most important ingredient for a successful hunt is not to fret about whether the big ones will all be gone by the time you get there. Instead, a hunter should plan his outing to avoid the pressure of other hunters and rely on his stalking and standing skills to get the job done. To that end, a mid-season or archery trip just might be the perfect answer.

As Butts put it, "You don't need to worry, the big bucks don't all get killed on opening day."

Bighorn Sheep and Mountain Goats

Winter arrives early in the high country of the Beartooths, the tallest mountain range in Montana with peaks that kiss the clouds at more than twelve thousand feet in elevation. Equinox storms of September and October blow in with a fury, dumping snow by the foot on the high plateaus and ragged ridges while the valleys below may still be basking in the glow of autumn. It's a rough time in a rough country, but it's also the best of places to be a bighorn sheep or mountain goat hunter, glassing the alpine basins and scanning the rock faces in search of these creatures of the high and wild.

Peak and Prairie Country offers some of the few hunting districts anywhere in the country where a person can obtain a sheep permit simply by applying for one. Further to the west in Headwaters Country, there are Districts 300, 301, 302, and 303, while Peak and Prairie Country counters with 500, 501, and 502 in the Beartooths. In these unlimited areas, a tag is issued to anyone who asks for it and the season ends when a quota of legal rams is reached for each hunting district.

"Montana is the only place in the U.S. that offers this opportunity," said Shawn Stewart, wildlife biologist with Fish, Wildlife and Parks in Red Lodge. "Everyplace else, sheep hunting is on a limited-draw basis. The odds of drawing those permits is horrid. The state averages about one-in-fifty odds. In some areas, it's more like one-in-two hundred. We do provide an opportunity for a guy to get out and hunt sheep. It's been my experience that anybody who wants it bad enough and is willing to put the time into it will eventually kill a sheep. It's just a matter of sticking to it.

"The most successful hunters spend a lot of time out there in the summertime," he added. "In 500 and 501, the guys that get out there in July and August have a fair chance of taking them very early in the season. If they don't do that, the middle part of the season generally isn't very good. The rams, after a while, get into the most terrible country that they can, stuff that's very tough to hunt in, very rugged rock walls, steep, cliffy areas that are three thousand feet tall. Even if you do find one, how are you going to get to them? In 502, the sheep have to migrate back into Montana from Wyoming before we can shoot them."

None of the districts should be considered as easy for the sheep hunter. "That's why it's an unlimited area," Stewart said. "There is a lot of country out there and most of it is pretty rugged. There are not a lot of sheep and they can be scattered in two or three little bunches in five hundred square miles."

With that kind of area to cover, it takes a long time before a hunter can say he honestly has figured out the habits of the sheep that live there. Bruce Saunders, of Columbus, for example, has put in as many as forty days in a season since he began hunting the high country for sheep in 1970. "Don't expect to get one quick," he said. "It took me seven years to get to know what the sheep were doing. And even if you're really good at what you're doing, you still won't always get into them."

Saunders added that sheep hunters looking for rams with forty-inch curls would be better off to wait until the draw smiles on them with a tag for the Rock Creek herd in western Montana, Thompson Falls, Sun River or other limited districts. "We're not hunting major rams. We're not hunting record book rams in the Beartooths. We're hunting smaller rams," he said. "There are not many big rams in these units. There are only a couple in each herd that are worth their salt. A thirty-three-inch ram is a good one here. If you get into one that's thirty-five or thirty-six inches, that's a real trophy ram. At thirty-six, they're full curl. Our hunting for record rams isn't great. But it's a place for a man who hasn't drawn a tag anywhere else to be able to go after them."

All but a few hunters will leave the Beartooths with just that to show for their efforts. But there are some natural tendencies among the sheep, and types of country where they're more likely to be found. "In September, they'll be running tree lines and below tree line," Saunders said. "The later you get, the better your chance of getting into the higher areas. The

Until the equinox storms, bighorn sheep stay in the timber in the unlimited hunting districts. Michael Sample photo.

equinox storms, the big storms, is the time to hunt the big rams. They come out of the timber and go to the high plateaus where you can see them. When they get into the timber, you can't find them. When they're on top of the mountain, they're easier to hunt but the sheep are pretty smart, they won't come out unless a storm hits."

Hunting the stormy season can be demanding on a hunter, however, and necessitates good equipment to be able to weather the cold and snow. "It's a tough man's area to hunt," Saunders said. "You had better be ready to take everything the Beartooths is ready to throw at you. You can pay your dues real quickly in this country. But I love to hunt them in November. That's the time when they're making a graphic change of area. You can see them coming back to the tops of the ridges. In November, you've got them in migration. If you're a good enough hunter and strong enough, you can get into the bigger rams. What you're looking for is the rams coming home. That may be the big ram you're looking for."

Hunters should remember that the good rams are relatively scarce, however, and even under the best of conditions, they can be tough to find. "In a good year, you can see five, maybe six legal rams. That's a lucky, lucky year when you've had at least twenty days of hunting," he said. "If you're not an excellent spotter, an excellent walker and have a real good definition of how to track an animal, how to follow him, you're not going to do well here."

Tracking bighorns is one technique that hunters in the Beartooths should concentrate on, he added. "Ray Hertzler, of Absarokee, he trails

Mountain goat country is easy to reach in September, but can be deadly in November. Michael Sample photo.

rams," Saunders said. "He likes it when the snow is on the ground. He'll trail them and trail them and trail them three and four days. Learn to hunt with the tracks. Know if it's a bigger ram or a smaller ram. Use that ram track and track him."

And finally, hunters accustomed to waiting for the sheep to reach the winter range in order to find them more easily should be aware that Saunders doesn't feel the truly big rams go there. "The bigger rams are smarter," he said. "They get themselves in harder country. They stay on areas that aren't fit for a man to work with. Then, when they do move, they get into another area that may be almost as tough to reach. Some of the older, bigger rams don't come to the winter range. They stay away from the winter range. They'll get on the wind-blows and spend the winter up high on the ridges and plateaus."

Mountain goats in the Beartooths are generally easier to locate but hunters should be prepared to weather the same type of physical conditions. "They're a lot easier to hunt than sheep are. They tend to be visible from a lot further away," said Stewart. "We have a fair number of goats in the Beartooths. The last couple of years, I've been able to count in excess of three hundred goats in a single census flight. If I flew it very intensively, I don't know how many goats I'd find."

The goat hunting opportunities in the Beartooths are available in four hunting districts with a limited number of permits available in each. "We don't put near as much pressure on the goats. Hunter pressure does not affect distribution of goats like it does sheep," Stewart said. "If you're hunting early in the season, it generally takes quite a bit of walking to get back where the goats are. As the season progresses and winter progresses, a lot of the winter ranges are in more accessible areas. But there's a lot more snow on those rock walls if you wait until later and getting around on them isn't as easy.

"Goats use the steep rock walls and alpine areas. They don't seem to utilize timber as much in the Beartooths as they do in other areas of Montana. Typically, when a guy is hunting them, they're in the alpine areas," he said. "Most of the time, you're going to catch them on steep rock walls. A goat is a tough critter to kill and they tend to get into bad situations. You have to pick one that is not going to roll ten thousand feet after you shoot him. A friend of mine shot one two or three times with a .270 out on a plateau and it kept walking and walking right over the edge. He picked it up sixteen hundred feet later. The fall didn't break either horn, but it didn't have any hair on it either. You get a lot of goat hunters bringing in hornless goats."

The trade-off for most goat hunters, then, seems to be the relative ease of going after them in September or the alternative of rough weather in November. "The earlier you kill one, the shorter the fur is. The later you wait, the more chance you have to be up to your butt in snow far back in the mountains," said Randy Smith, game warden for Fish, Wildlife and Parks in Columbus. "The hunting gets tougher the later you wait, but the prize gets better."

Each hunter will respond to that trade-off in his own way, but Smith warned that hunters heading into the high country shouldn't underestimate the forces of nature that can be unleashed in the Beartooths. "People live in the low country where it's fifty-five and sixty degrees at that time of year," he said. "They go wandering up in the mountains and it's a different world up there. They don't realize that several times around September 15th, we've had four or five or six feet of snow up there. It's instantaneous winter. You're up there in your blue jeans and a couple of shirts and light coat and you're in a world of hurt. People should bear in mind that they're going into something that's the dead of winter.

"We had one of those September storms one year and a guide had a sheep hunter up there on the Fishtail Plateau when they got four-and-a-half feet of snow. He was eight miles back in and it took him four days to get out. That's about two miles per day," he said. "The best thing to do if you're going in is to tell somebody where you're going to be and how long you expect to be there. Take the right kind of equipment so you can weather the storms, more food than you think you're going to need, more and better quality sleeping equipment, and more clothing.

"It's a whole lot better to have more than you need in there than not enough," Smith said. "If something does happen, a hunter can hold out. In flat country, a guy can take off and panic. Up there in the Beartooths, there aren't too many places you can run."

Waterfowl

It's really anyone's guess how often Roger Fliger can be found waterfowl hunting in fall. Just pick a number and the guess still might be low. It isn't that Fliger, regional supervisor for Fish, Wildlife and Parks in Billings, doesn't go after deer, elk, antelope, upland birds and even squeeze in a fall fishing trip, but waterfowl occupy a special place in his heart.

"I start out hunting the small shallow-water ponds and lakes during the wet years. On the bigger ones, I use a small boat," he began. "I field hunt along the Yellowstone for geese and field shoot around those lakes in the wheat stubble. After those areas freeze up about mid-November, I hunt just a little on the Yellowstone for a day or two and I hunt on the Bighorn. That can be field shooting for honkers, or quite often it's pass shooting for ducks and geese. When I'm out antelope hunting, I might jump-shoot ponds and reservoirs. I've walked rivers like the Musselshell jump-shooting. I've hunted as much as I could, as often as I could all my life and tried to maintain a reasonable kind of life."

In Peak and Prairie Country, Fliger has found a field of operations that's been vastly underrated as a waterfowl hunting area over the years. There are big alkali waters like Lake Mason and Big Lake, major rivers like the Yellowstone and Bighorn, and countless smaller ponds, reservoirs, streams, and creeks. It's also an area that's been improving for waterfowl over the years, especially for geese.

"In the fourteen years I've been here, the goose hunting has been getting better and better all the time," Fliger said. "Back then, Buck Compton and I figured the goose population on the Yellowstone between Billings and the mouth of the Bighorn at one nesting pair of honkers per mile and we were elated. Years ago, there were very few. Now, I'm sure there are probably five to seven nesting pairs per mile in this stretch and they're nesting up the Clark's Fork, Boulder, Stillwater, and Musselshell. You've got a tremendous population of nesting geese building here."

Not all of them can be counted on to remain here during the hunting season, however. "The goose populations are mobile," he said. "Just as soon as the geese on the river get airborne, they'll move out onto large reservoirs and alkali lakes. Some geese that have been banded by our personnel as young of the year have even been taken in southern Saskatchewan."

It's on the reservoirs and alkali lakes closer to home that Fliger takes advantage of the growing goose flock. "I find out where the geese are staging and where they're feeding and I try to get myself in between if I want to pass shoot," he said. "If I can, I also try to get into an area where they're feeding in the fields and set up my decoys."

His field shooting strategies are much the same as those in use elsewhere in Montana, with a few new wrinkles. He watches the flocks as they leave their watery resting places and follows them to the stubble fields where they feed, pinpointing the location down to the exact wheat strip. Then he returns in the predawn hours to set up five dozen or more goose shells and wait for the birds to come in to feed.

"For years, the only way you did it was with pits. You didn't go out and hunt geese unless you dug a real healthy pit. It was like a big glorified foxhole," he said. "I haven't found it necessary to do that in recent years. For one thing, it takes a lot of time and effort and a lot of farmers and ranchers don't want you digging holes in their land. There are usually irrigation ditches along alfalfa fields or corn fields. They stack their straw in piles. Or you can use an area where the wheat stubble is a foot deep. The most we do for digging now would be lowering about a six-inch pit. I use marsh mat a lot, laying that over us. Put a piece of plastic underneath us and that's about it."

Fliger also likes to hunt geese over water on the bigger reservoirs. "I enjoy hunting them over water. There's always so much more action," he said. "I've used as many as three dozen floaters and if I'm in shallow water, I'll set out some shells with the floaters, too. When I hunt the water, I wait until they go out and I don't shoot at any ducks until the geese are gone. Usually, the geese will go out a little after daylight and come back about 10 a.m. In between, I may get some duck shooting. When the geese are coming back in, I try to call them. Most of the good goose hunting over the water is between 10 a.m. and 2 p.m. but when it's blustery, they may come and go at any time of day."

While geese are undeniably a favorite, ducks also get their fair share of attention early in the season on the big alkali lakes. Among the items in his waterfowl hunting equipment is a low-riding layout boat. It's one of the few boats of its kind to be found in Montana where a man can lie back and have the entire profile of the boat be only about a foot above water level.

"I dearly love to hunt mallards, but I like to hunt a variety of things," Fliger said. "Early in the season, I like to hunt blue-winged teal. In wet years, we produce a lot of bluebills and there are good concentrations of bluebills and quite a few redheads. When you're shooting for bluebills, you get into goldeneyes. I like to shoot diving ducks. It's really exciting. They fly fast and they come in in flocks."

His tactics for divers often include the layout boat and spreads of 75 to 125 bluebill decoys far out in the open water. "I'm in the boat upwind of the decoys and the scaup usually come in over the decoys and set up upwind of them," he said. "The other way is to find an island or a long point that goes out into the lake, put your decoys out and get whatever cover you can find."

It's finding that cover which can be the biggest problem and remains the big eliminator for waterfowl hunters on most of Montana's big alkali lakes. "These shallow water lakes are tough to hunt because there's hardly any cover at all," Fliger said. "Most guys will just walk up and down the

Late in the season, ducks gather in bigger flocks and can be extremely wary. Mark Henckel photo.

shoreline a while and give up. You have to find something to break up your outline, an island, a reef, seaweed, Russian thistle, greasewood. You've really got to have some kind of cover."

But even with the waterfowl hunters who have figured out the early season methods to put ducks and geese in the bag, hunting pressure still couldn't be termed excessive. "You'll have some guys who will hunt pretty hard the first weekend or two. But then the big game seasons start opening and you've got such a wide variety of things to hunt that most of them go elsewhere," Fliger said. "Waterfowl hunting never will be the popular thing here it is in the Midwest."

While interest in waterfowl wanes during the middle of the season when deer, elk, antelope and pheasants take hunters to other places, ducks and geese come into focus again in Peak and Prairie Country in late November and December. After freeze-up, the mallards and geese will pull into open-water areas on all the creeks and rivers but no place will bring in as many of them as the Bighorn River downstream from Fort Smith to its confluence with the Yellowstone.

Rusty Rokita, of Hardin, hunts the Bighorn throughout the season for ducks and geese and said it's a fair river for ducks anytime in the season.

"It can be good for teal early in the season, then at the mid-part of the season, the ducks really start coming back to the river and then later in the year they get tougher to hunt and are in bigger groups," he said. "We've had days, though, when we've had five-hundred to a thousand ducks come in."

The goose hunting also tends to go in stages on the Bighorn, he said. "There are three kinds of goose hunting. Early on in the season, it takes about two or three days before they learn and you get shooting on the locals. Then the next flight of goose hunting is mid-November. We'll hear the geese honking at night as they come in from Canada. They're in smaller bunches at that point and are easy to decoy. Then, when you break into that last phase, geese get into flocks of two hundred or three hundred and the rule of thumb is that they avoid decoys. They're tough to bring in."

On the river, it's the mallard hunting late in the season which attracts the most attention. "We hunt the islands and set up for ducks. Because the river never freezes, it's excellent for mallards," Rokita said. "Twenty to thirty magnum duck decoys is about what you need. There just isn't enough room on most parts of the river to set up any more than that and twenty to thirty magnums work as well as spreading out fifty or sixty regular decoys. We've put out five and six dozen and it really works but we've also used as few as a dozen. It's only later in the year that those big sets have a lot to do with your success.

"One thing about the Bighorn is that because of the lack of islands, a dog is almost a necessity. The water is deeper than it used to be, the channels are swifter. Dogs have always been a help, but they're even more valuable today than they were before," he said. "It's a good place for Chesapeakes and Labs. Smaller dogs have a tougher time in the current."

But though the hunting has held up in recent years despite the growing popularity of the Bighorn, there is trouble brewing on the river and the waterfowl picture is changing. "It used to be that goose hunting on the river was the place to go, it isn't that way anymore," he said. "More people are putting in with jet boats and float boats. The jet boats especially have made people a lot more mobile and guys will run the river to stir up ducks and geese. Now, a lot of times, the geese are off the water just at daylight and they don't come back until dark."

While the traffic on the river may move some ducks, the mallard population that winters there soon gets wise to the tactics as well and holes up in backwaters where the hunters can't reach them or moves off into the fields out of range of hunters' guns.

"The best hunting we've had is when it's pretty cold and there isn't so much activity on the river," Rokita said. "If it's warm, they're not up moving around. When it gets cold, they're flying the river more and getting up more to feed. You also pick up a lot of movement after storms."

With the changing picture of waterfowl hunting on the Bighorn and elsewhere in Peak and Prairie Country, it's a sure bet that the hunters willing to study waterfowl and learn their habits will be the ones most successful on them in the future. Just as individual flocks alter their habits as the season progresses, the hunters must be versatile as well.

"Just change your tactics as the time goes on," Rokita said. "The hunting can be excellent, if you just change your tactics."

Upland Birds

Peak and Prairie Country is a bird hunter's paradise. Not that there are more blue grouse, sage grouse, sharp-tailed grouse, ruffed grouse, pheasants, or Hungarian partridge than in other parts of Montana, but you can find good numbers of all of them here along with the only abundant population of chukar partridge in Montana.

It's also the area of the long bird season in Montana where shotgun hunters could uncase their 12-gauge in early September and keep it in action until the New Year arrives if they keep changing species.

While it's possible to do it all here, the best strategy could be to plan your seasons by the calendar, taking each species in its own time, varying the prey only enough to add a little spice along the way. For the calendar-wise bird hunter, that would necessitate heading to the mountains early in the season to take advantage of the mountain grouse hunting there before the onset of winter.

Rich Johnson, of Lewistown, has hunted the high country of the Peak and Prairie Country for blue grouse since his days stationed with the U.S. Fish and Wildlife Service in Billings. "I like to hunt high and I like to hunt the open ridges," he said. "If you have a little juniper, they like that and they eat grasshoppers and berries."

Johnson believes in using a pointing dog on blues and feels that a shotgun hunter without a dog is probably walking past most of the birds. "He points them and I walk in and they flush. A lot of people say blues will just sit there but I find that's true only twenty to twenty-five percent of the time. The rest of the time, they'll flush and they'll fly down off the ridge and you get one quick shot," he said. "My own personal opinion is that they're the most sporty upland bird in the state. The only one I'd say is close to it is the chukar. But you really should have a dog. With the birds' coloration, without a dog, you'll walk past seventy-five percent of the blue grouse out there. Their natural thing is to sit there, but with a dog, he'll point them and they'll flush."

While blue grouse abound in the mountains in the years of good hatches, they're still ignored for the most part by hunters. "Very few people know how to hunt blues," Johnson said. "They just drive the roads and jump out and shoot them. Probably eighty percent of their habitat isn't hunted at all."

Ruffed grouse are also ignored, even by most hunters who may have grown up hunting them in other parts of the country before moving to Montana. "The ruffed grouse here are a lot less sporty than in the Great Lakes states," he said. "That's probably because they're not hunted as much and aren't as smart as the ones back there. But there are some ruffed grouse around. If you've got a clump of aspen with a spring in it and some berries around, I'll bet you there are going to be ruffed grouse."

The season on mountain grouse generally runs through the end of the big game season, but the wise hunter would be one who moved on to prairie grouse when the calendar read October. With that kind of shift, a hunter could still get in on the action before the birds gathered into their big winter flocks and get in a little gunning before big game season stole his attention. While both are birds of the wide-open prairie, their habitat preferences vary a bit.

"The sharptail is a native of the shrub grassland," said Charlie Eustace, regional wildlife manager for Fish, Wildlife and Parks in Billings. "They like a mixture of grassland and shrubby draws, preferably with something like buffaloberry, chokecherry or some other berry-bearing bush. Any of this in association with grain crops would be a bonus.

"Sage grouse and sagebrush, say one and you've said them both," he added. "This is the only game species we have that is tied so close to a single plant species. There is no time of the year the birds don't use sagebrush. It is most important in fall and winter when it makes up almost one hundred percent of the birds' diet. In the summer, they will go to insects and forbs a lot more, like dandelion and wild lettuce."

While all sharptails are considered to be good table fare, it would be wise for a sage grouse hunter to be a little particular. The rule of thumb when a flock goes up is to aim for the little ones. "On the rise, it takes a

Big male sage grouse can be tough to eat without a good seal on the pressure cooker. Michael Sample photo.

sharp eye to pick out the little ones but if a person can tell them apart, particularly on the ground before they flush, they will be by far the best eating," Eustace said. "In the hunting season, the hens and juveniles will usually be by themselves and the males are generally segregated into what they call a cock flock."

Just so there's no mistaking the difference, understand that a big male can weigh up to 8 1/2 pounds, mature hens will run 3-4 pounds, and yearling males can even average 5 1/2 pounds.

"If you've got a good seal on your pressure cooker, those old males are satisfactory," he said. "The young ones you can fry and they're good, but the old ones you don't fry. They look like small turkeys. You've got to watch out for those big bull grouse in the alfalfa."

One final piece of advice on sage grouse, and sharptails to a lesser degree, is that the gunning isn't necessarily over when the flock goes up. "There are always the late-time Charlies," Eustace said. "After the flock gets up, there is often one or more stragglers. If you've emptied your gun, it's best to reload again before taking a single step."

By late October, the pheasant season has opened in Peak and Prairie Country and the colorful cocks of this species are by far the most sought-after bird in Montana, though hunting for them has changed over the years.

"I think their habits have changed," said Jay Archer, of Billings. "It used to be that we knew the stubble areas, the alfalfa fields, the less-dense ditches you could walk and flush birds. Now they have moved into much heavier cover and if you want to get them, you had better have a good dog and a couple of guys and be willing to hit the brush."

Some of this can be traced to changing agricultural practices in valleys like the Yellowstone. "I don't know if they're leaving as much cover for the birds as they used to," Archer said. "I think they're plowing up more of the ground. A lot of these guys are burning the weeds or spraying them. What they used to call natural cover is being depleted."

There are some things that haven't changed, of course, and one of these is the pheasants' tendency to run rather than flush. Give them half a chance to run away from danger and these birds will kick it into high gear and go. "Their instinct is to run," he said. "When four of us used to hunt a stretch of cover, we'd break it down into two hundred or three hundred-yard segments. We'd drop two guys off at the beginning and those guys would talk and throw rocks and the other two guys would push the birds toward them. When we'd get within a certain distance of one another, that's when the birds would flush. That was the only way you could get the birds up.

"It worked great but you couldn't always find three other guys to go hunting with you. That's when I came up with the transistor radio idea. That would make a lot of noise, too, so I'd put the radio in the ditch, circle back a distance and then walk the cover toward the radio. That worked great, too," Archer said.

Often, the later in the season a hunter goes after them, the tighter the birds will hold. "They'll run if they can, but the further into the season you get, the tighter they're going to hold," he said. "They know what's going to happen if they fly."

For the strong of leg who still have some bird hunting left in them as the calendar year winds down, there has been a late chukar and Hungarian partridge season open in the southern reaches of Peak and Prairie Country. While Huns can be found over a wide range in Montana, those chukars are something special because this is the only part of the Treasure State where the birds are really thriving.

"Once you've learned their system and you want to work for them, there are a lot more chukars here than most people realize," said Tom Ringo, of Belfry. Ringo hunts chukars in the Belfry country throughout the season among his other outings for big game and birds and said that the chukars' habits change as the environment around them changes.

"Early in the year when it's dry, they'll roost on the ridgetops and between 9:00 and 10:30, they'll come down to water. After they water in the morning, they tend to scatter and feed," he said. "But if you find water in a likely-looking area, you can walk the edge and look for chukar tracks. They'll come down in the same areas and a lot of times, they'll come down the same ridge. If you find tracks at the bottom of the ridge, you'll find birds up above there sooner or later.

"The best place to find chukars is on the open hillsides in real steep country. Look for a lot of cheatgrass and some available water within a ridge of where they're hanging out."

Chukars are definitely birds of the ridges and a hunter who goes after them should be prepared to do some climbing of the steep arid hills which make this country unique. "If you run into them on the lower part of the hill and they fly up onto the hillside, you might as well not figure on catching up to them until they hit the top of the ridge," Ringo said. "The only time you'll catch them before the top is if there's a layer of small cliffs. Generally, after you shoot, you go to the top. Most of the time, they'll hold for you there, but sometimes they might just go over the top on the other side of the ridge a little ways, usually no more than twenty-five yards."

In the late season, hunting for the birds usually improves, Ringo said. "When the snow flies, the hunting gets a lot better. For one thing, you can track them. For another thing, they bunch up a lot more. It's not unusual to see fifty to sixty or maybe as many as a hundred in a bunch. I've found them to be more down toward the bottoms of the hills then, the bottom quarter of the ridges."

A dog is a definite advantage in chukar hunting. "A dog helps a lot, especially for retrieving. You also want a close-working dog," he said. "Your chukars do hold a lot better than Huns or pheasants. Once you get to where they're going to stop, they hold."

Ringo added that hunters would do well to stop and listen on the quiet mornings to help them in their searches for birds. "Once you split the coveys up, if you're quiet for a while, they might start talking to regroup," he said. "Also, you can hear them in the morning but their sound is real deceptive. Binoculars can sometimes help you, too. Look at all the ridgetops, everything on the skyline and they'll stand out on those rocks and watch you. Look a little closer and you'll see the others meandering down the hillside."

By the time the last of your chukar hunts in late December or early January is completed, the bird hunter who believes in careful calendar planning should be able to survey his freezer and find packages wearing the labels of two mountain grouse, two prairie grouse and two partridge species tucked amid all the pheasants.

That may not seem like much of a precious cargo for big game hunters, but for the hard-core shotgunner, that's Peak and Prairie paradise.

Odds and Ends

Mountain Lions

There is a dedicated group of dog men who anxiously wait for the snows of winter to come to the mountains. In the tracking snows of mid-winter, they run hounds in search of mountain lions and participate in one of the more grueling seasons that Montana has to offer.

In recent years, it's become an increasingly bloodless sport, however, with the thrill of the chase most often the hunter's only reward.

"Every morning, I drive up a canyon and check for tracks," said Mick Iten, of Hamilton. "Then, on a weekend, you take a truck with your hounds or a snowmobile and dog trailer and travel, looking in the snow for tracks. Male mountain lions can go thirty miles in a day or two so they can cover a lot of country. They're somewhat like fish in that they'll encompass their area. You can go hours and days without seeing a track. When you cut one, you go up to the next drainage and try to cut it again."

If the track is fresh and the general location pinpointed, it's time for the chase to begin. "When you turn the dogs loose, it's no return," Iten said. "You've got to catch them. Very rarely will the chase ever be less than a mile. The average is about five miles. We've treed them within a quarter-mile or as far as thirteen miles. That's about as far as you can go in a day."

The lion hunter follows his dogs by ear, listening to the barks and howls of the hounds and slogging through the mountain snows of winter.

"When they tree it, there's a whole different sound from those dogs. You can hear that from about a mile away," he said. "After a day of chasing them, there it is. There's something of a thrill in looking up at the animal. He can leave anytime but he's scared of that bark. You gasp, chain up the

Mountain lions can offer the thrill of the chase during the winter months. Jon Cates photo.

dogs to a tree and take a picture. You talk a little bit and go back home."

Iten has killed mountain lions after the chase, but very few of them. "Two out of ten would be a keeper, something you could kill, but mostly I just like to chase them," he said. "We like to tree ten in a season. Last year, we got six or something like that. Mostly, we just like to tree them and take pictures."

It's a sport for the fit who are able to cover a lot of ground in the winter mountains and a game that has a price to pay for those who are serious about it. "You put up with barking dogs all year long and you have to feed them," Iten said. "They're void of all charisma and class. They're meant to bark. Your neighbors and you put up with them for the rest of the year just for the thrill of the chases in winter."

Grizzly Bears

Montana boasts of some of the last strongholds of the grizzly bear in the lower forty-eight states. It can also claim the final hunting seasons on the great bears in the lower forty-eight. But it's a tenuous and limited hunting opportunity at best, which realistically could end anytime.

Grizzlies inhabit the backcountry of northwestern Montana stretching southward from Glacier National Park to the rugged mountains which surround Yellowstone National Park. The Yellowstone ecosystem has been closed to grizzly hunting for some time, but hunting seasons for the threatened species have been held in northwestern Montana where a quota of twenty-five man-caused grizzly mortalities by any means has been in effect. That would include grizzlies hit by cars or trains, killed in damage situations, or taken by hunters.

The season has drawn mixed reviews both in and out of the hunting community.

Some hunters are happy for the opportunity to still take a bear and claim that having an open season on grizzlies is valid because the populations can stand it. Even non-hunters agree that hunting keeps them in the public eye and continues to pump sportsmen's dollars into the cause to save grizzlies from extinction in the state. Still others claim that having a hunting season on grizzlies keeps them wary, makes the bears fearful of man and prevents man-bear confrontations which the bears invariably lose because they face the threat of getting a problem bear label and being eliminated.

On the other side of the issue, people argue that the species has taken all the pressure from man that it can stand and adding hunting mortalities into its fight for survival is more than the grizzlies can stand. With increasing numbers of hikers and backpackers heading into the remaining shreds of wilderness which the bears need to survive, man-bear confrontations are inevitable. And with all the other hunting opportunities available in Montana, why is grizzly bear hunting necessary in the first place?

It's an emotional issue being battled in the courts, in the world of

Montana's grizzly season has drawn mixed reviews both inside and outside of the hunting community. Michael Sample photo.

wildlife research, and on the street corners of grizzly bear country. If there's a final answer available in all the verbiage, it has yet to be agreed on by all parties in the dispute.

The only common ground that all share on the issue is that grizzly bears need wilderness, either designated or non-designated, to survive and that kind of country is a rare commodity, even in Montana. They also know the great bears never again will roam the open prairie like they did in the last century or become residents of mountain country far beyond where they're found today.

But even hunters who have no desire to kill one must be aware of the bears' presence when they head into grizzly country. Care must be taken with food around camp, and supplies and big game animals kept there should be suspended from a tall meatpole. Big game carcasses left for a time in the mountains should be approached with care so that a grizzly or black bear which may happen onto the kill isn't surprised into defending his newly-discovered meal. And hunters should realize that in all but a miniscule percentage of cases—these usually involving cubs, food caches, or den sites which are being protected—grizzlies will try to avoid man at all costs. They should also know that even in country which is loaded with grizzlies, very few are ever seen.

As far as opportunities to hunt them are concerned, however, suffice it to say that as of this writing, there's still a grizzly bear season for those who are willing to seek them out in the backcountry of northwestern Montana. But that hunt could be restricted, expanded, or even become extinct, at any time.

Mourning Doves

At least Montana has progressed past the rubber chicken stage when it comes to mourning doves. For years, the rubber chickens would be hauled out at the State Capitol and the legislature would treat it as a joke when a bill was introduced to put doves on the game bird list.

Such uproarious humor was finally overcome, they made the game bird list, and Montana offered a dove hunt in 1983 for the first time in recent history. But the birds really haven't attracted too much attention from hunters who already have three species of mountain grouse, two species of prairie grouse and partridge and pheasants to hunt. Compounding the problem is the fact that while Montana raises an incredible number of doves, they head south with the first frosts of fall and even an early September season doesn't give too much time for hunters to get after them.

"I saw a few doves in Montana really late last year but it seems like they're on the move as soon as it starts getting cold at night," said Dave Books, of Helena, editor of *Montana Outdoors*. "The southeastern corner of the state has the best shot at them and the longest shot at them here."

Books has taken advantage of the season here and hunted them in other states as well and feels that many Montana hunters haven't given them a chance to show why they're among the more popular targets of shotgun hunters across the country.

"They can probably be the toughest game bird of all under certain conditions. When they want to, they can really do some fancy flying and maneuvering," he said. "If they're coming into water, it seems like they're not as hard. But if you're on a pass and the wind is blowing, it can be tough."

Mourning doves nest in Montana, but head south with the first frosts of fall. Frank Martin photo.

Dove hunters generally can take three approaches depending on the birds' movement patterns and the time of day. "If there are a lot of birds, they'll find either a field where there are some birds coming in on a regular basis to feed or a water hole where they're coming in at morning or evening to get water," Books said. "If you watch the flight patterns, you can see what the birds are doing and then just pick a good spot where the birds are passing over. Or, you can walk them up. Generally, they'll feed in the morning and evening and after they're done feeding, you can just walk a shelter belt or a field that has some birds in it."

Because of their small size, he recommended using size 7 1/2 or 8 shot. Choke bore on the shotgun is a bit more difficult to choose. "They're a small bird, so it's kind of a trade-off. If you have too open a choke, it's possible for them to sneak through the pattern. If it's too tight, they're going to be tougher to hit," he said. "You wouldn't want any tighter than a modified choke for most hunting. If you're getting pretty close to them, an improved cylinder would be better."

While Montana hunters probably never will get a chance at the big flocks that shotgunners in states further south enjoy, the doves do open up new possibilities.

"We're never going to have much of an opportunity here. The majority of them are on the move as soon as it gets cold and the birds here are spread out for breeding. We don't get the big flocks here," Books said. "But they're kind of fun. Sometimes, they can be easy targets. Other times, they're incredibly tough."

Rabbits

All it takes to get a game species ignored is to offer a wide-open season on them. If you don't belive it, take the case of rabbits in Montana.

In most states, there is a season on cottontail rabbits, snowshoe hares, and jackrabbits, but Montana offers a year-round season and no bag limit on them. As a result, there is no impetus to get after them and rabbit hunting here is viewed more as a lark than a serious venture.

Cottontails can be found throughout eastern Montana in areas where thick stands of sagebrush and rock outcrops provide cover for them. Unlike rabbits in other parts of the country, most cottontails here are not found in the brushy bottoms or in hardwood tree areas.

Jackrabbits will often be found in the same type of habitat, but are more prevalent in the open grasslands. Pressed flat to the ground, they often surprise a hunter because they wait until the final moment to take off in bounding flight and the startled gunner can't believe that he didn't see it lying there before it took off.

Snowshoe hares are creatures of the mountains, where they inhabit the areas of heavy timber and play hide-and-seek amid the deadfall with big game hunters in search of deer and elk.

Populations of all three species vary widely depending on whether it's boom or bust time in the cycles. During the peak times, they seem to be everywhere. During the low population periods, hunters can walk all day and rarely see one.

Because of the wide-open nature of the season, the only time hunters ever get after them to any degree is during mid-winter when warm afternoons stir an interest in getting outdoors for something, anything, to cure cabin fever. They'll hunt them with shotguns, small caliber rifles, pistols, or bows and arrows and put as much of a premium on getting shots as putting rabbits in the bag.

There's no great interest among most hunters here for putting many away in the freezer. After all, in Montana where there are so many other big game and upland bird species to hunt, they're only rabbits.

Outfitters

If your pocketbook can stand it and your dreams for a trophy animal are strong enough, an outfitter just might be for you.

Nonresidents coming to Montana, or even residents who may not know the country they're planning to head into, would be wise to consider a guided hunt.

"It's a quality experience. You see good scenery, have good equipment, good food and a good camp," said Bill Maloit, supervisor of outfitting for Fish, Wildlife and Parks in Helena. "If you get an elk or a sheep, that's a bonus. If a hunter is looking for an exceptional trophy, the average nonresident would have better success going on a guided hunt."

There are some species where an outfitter is more advantageous, of course. Hunting mule deer, whitetails, antelope, waterfowl or upland birds can be accomplished just as easily without a guide, unless a hunter is looking for a trophy-class animal. For elk, bighorn sheep, mountain goat or moose, on the other hand, a guide can provide a hunter with the benefit of years of experience and a knowledge of the country which can boost his success.

"Hunter success on elk averages fourteen percent for all hunters, eighteen percent for nonresidents, and twenty-five percent for guided hunters. About a third of the nonresidents use outfitters," Maloit said. "The majority of them provide a good service."

That doesn't mean a hunter shouldn't shop for his outfitter carefully. "They should be especially aware of anybody who advertises a high hunter success. You should see what they have to offer, the price, the length of the hunt, whether ten hunter days includes the day going in and going out, and whether there are any extra charges for picking the hunter up at the airport or other transportation? Are there extra charges for taking care of trophies? Are scabbards and saddlebags furnished or do you have to buy them? How many guides do they have per hunter? For the best success on bugling elk, a one-on-one guide-to-hunter ratio is best. It's usually more expensive, but there's better success. Later in the season, you could go two-on-one, but no more than that."

Hunters can obtain a list of Montana outfitters through Fish, Wildlife and Parks headquarters in Helena, and written or telephone communications with those on the list can answer some of those questions. But Maloit advised checking on references as well. "They want to make sure they're getting a cross-section of references," he said. "They should get a credit reference from the outfitters' bank. If they're respectable businessmen, that shouldn't be a problem. They should also ask for previous client references from the immediate past year."

Hunters should understand, as well, that only licensed outfitters may charge a fee for a guided hunt in Montana. And to get that status, they have to earn it.

"Outfitters have to file an application, they have to pass a comprehensive written examination, carry liability insurance, have the necessary equipment to provide the service, and those operating on federal lands have to have a special use permit," Maloit said.

"If they're preparing for a hunt in Montana, they should start a year in advance. A lot of your better outfitters are booked a year in advance," he added. "You should also have a written contract or agreement as to what the outfitter is going to provide and what services he is expected to perform. There is usually a deposit fee, between a third and fifty percent is what most outfitters want. And the contract should state what happens if there is an illness or death in the family. If there is something of that nature, an outfitter may carry you over to the next year. But he may keep part of the deposit. If the licenses are filled for that year, there is no opportunity for them to fill that vacancy."

An outfitted hunt isn't cheap, of course, but the hunter has to remember that the season isn't very long and the outfitters' overhead can be high.

"For elk hunting, I would recommend not less than a ten-day hunt," Maloit said. "That should run about $2,000 and that doesn't include the license. If they want a quality hunting experience, they're going to have to pay for it. If a fellow buys a cheap hunt, that's what he's going to get. It won't be of the quality that a hunter travels to Montana to find."

Fair Fees

It's a widely-known fact which defies the laws of nature that a big game animal on the ground expands in size and weight in direct proportion to how far it must be packed out of the mountains. The farther you have to pack it, the bigger and heavier it becomes until shrinking again when it's safely tucked away in the freezer.

Take an elk, for example. Days, weeks, and sometimes years of hunting have gone into shooting a nice bull and there's an immediate feeling of exhilaration when a hunter shoots one. But then the hunter looks around, realizes he has downed it in horrible deadfall, understands there is a five-hundred to eight-hundred-pound load to be moved a mile or miles back to his vehicle, and the onset of depression begins.

The first answer that pops into his mind is "Horse!" Yet relatively few hunters have them at their disposal and the decision is made to try their friendly, neighborhood rancher. Then, they are immediately shocked by what they feel is an excessive fee for getting that beast out of the back-country.

"If I had the time, I would pack an elk out for $100," said Larry Clark, a rancher on Rock Creek in western Montana who also guides during elk season. "That may sound like a lot of money, but it's not."

He told a tale of two hunters who heard his fee and thought it was excessive. "They decided it was too much. So they both laid off a day of work and made two round trips, four miles one way, to get the elk out packing a quarter each on each trip. They were beat at the end of the day and I'm sure they lost more money than the $100 by laying off. Add it all up and the $100 is a bargain," Clark said.

"When you figure it out, you're looking at at least three horses, one for me to ride and two more to pack the elk. It would be four horses if the guy would want to come along. Then there's a chainsaw to get to the elk and my time. There might be some elk you'd bring out where $100 would be high, but there would be a lot more where it really wouldn't be enough."

Packing Them Out

Every elk hunter should have a Glenn and a Bruce. If you don't believe it, just ask Ralph.

Ralph Saunders, of Billings, hunts elk in southwestern Montana every season and honestly feels he has the problem of elk hunting all figured out. "My father, Glenn, is an elk magnet and my younger brother, Bruce, is a pack animal. How can you lose?" Saunders laughed. "I've got the best of both worlds. We've brought out twenty animals this way."

While few hunters would dispute the need for Glenn on these outings, it's Bruce who is a rare and wonderful commodity when it comes to packing out a downed animal. "A person can pack a lot of weight, but from my own experience, I feel when you get over fifty percent of your body weight on your back, you're talking about a heavy load. Except for Bruce."

Bruce, a former jockey, weighs just 105 pounds, but can make that slender body do amazing things with a pack frame. "He's not the only one in our party ready to tie into a downed animal, but he'll pack his weight," Saunders said. "He eats a heck of a lot less than a horse and he's a lot easier to keep, but he can carry quite a load."

In many hunting instances in Montana, packing an animal out on your back isn't necessary. Often it's possible to drive your car to the kill site while at other times, it's close enough to a road that a short drag will get the animal there. But there are some places where long-distance travel is necessary and for that kind of move, there's no substitute for a pack frame.

While strength is an undeniable factor in moving heavy loads on your

It takes some experience and a system to pack an animal like an elk back to your vehicle without difficulty. Bill McRae photo.

back, part of the reason for the Saunders family's success in moving those animals is the fact that they have figured out an effective system to transport an elk from the kill site to their vehicle. And that knowledge has even helped them when it comes to getting the elk in the first place.

"I'm firmly convinced that a lot of people don't get into the backcountry to hunt elk because they're worried about how they're going to get the animal out. And they're right to worry," Saunders said. "A lot of it is learning a little bit about the tools they need to get an animal out of there.

You can pack an animal many, many miles on your back but it's so time-consuming and energy-consuming. Unless a person is in real excellent condition, a person shouldn't pack an animal more than a couple of miles."

The tools needed include a sharp knife for field dressing, a good saw for cutting the animal into pieces, a strong pack frame, fifty feet of cotton rope, half a bed sheet, and an extra hunter orange vest.

"One of the major tools is a good saw," Saunders said. "The one we use is the Knapp saw. When you get an elk down, you don't usually have the convenience of being able to hang him up in the air. And with that saw, you can cut through the meat and the hide with the elk lying down. The sharp edge on the end of the blade is what makes the difference.

"If we have cool weather, we keep the hide on. The hide keeps the meat clean and it insulates it from warm weather if it gets warmer later. It also keeps the meat fresh and keeps the animal from drying out," he said. "You've also got to have the pieces there to prove sex. The head is the best method of proving identification of the animal so we take out one of the front quarters of the animal with the top portion of the skull attached."

Splitting the animal isn't easy even with the best of saws. "We start at the neck and take him right down the middle of the spine. Right between the front legs is the toughest part, it's the deepest part of the animal. Once you get past that, it goes pretty fast and you take it right down the tailbone," Saunders said. "When you've got him in two halves, you have to decide the weight of the quarters you want to pack. If you want the front quarters and the hind quarters to weigh the same, about seventy pounds on a yearling bull, you've got to cut them on about the third rib. We like to make the front quarters heavier and the hind quarters lighter by cutting them right at the base of the ribs. That will make the front quarters about ten pounds heavier. That's so I can give Bruce the front quarter and I can take the hind quarter.

"The front quarters are harder to pack. They're bulkier. They're a little broader and they don't fit on the pack as well as the hind quarter. A hind quarter is more compact," he said.

Saunders' hunting party uses old Army pack boards, which are heavier than some of the modern alloy frames, but won't bend under the stresses of a heavy load. This is also when the bed sheets, rope and hunter orange material come into play.

"The sheet goes around the meat to keep it clean. I'll wrap most of it around the lower end of the quarter. It soaks up the blood," said Saunders. "We also put the hide side of the quarter against our backs and that helps keep the blood away from us. Then I'll take a garbage sack and put that on the side against me and will curl the garbage sack up around the bottom to pool the blood. There's nothing worse than having that blood soak down your back and your wool pants."

The quarter is lashed leg up to the pack with cotton, not stretchable nylon, clothesline-type rope, leaving a tail of about ten feet of rope at the end. "After that is strapped on good and tight, you take your spare, netting-type, hunter orange vest and it goes up over the leg and is spread out over the quarter and you use that ten feet of rope to tie it down," he said. "I've never been shot at by anybody, but that's something you want to insure against."

This method keeps the meat, bones, and hide intact, as opposed to boning the meat out, which may be practical if a hunter has a long distance to travel. "We have boned them out before in the field. I feel that is an alternative if you're a long, long way in. Hauling out bones is heavy," he said. "But you've got to have a good knife to bone them out. It also takes a long time. The animal is also warm and the meat is not that easy to cut. And if you're going to carry them out that way with the meat in a regular pack bag, the meat has got to be thoroughly cool."

Another secret to moving the animals easily is having a good pair of hiking boots. "You want a real stiff-walled, stiff-soled boot," he said. "When you put an additional seventy-five pounds on your back and start going downhill, it's hard on the feet and ankles. A real soft shoe will twist underneath you. It can almost be dangerous going down a real steep hill. Often I'll take more than one pair of boots along, keep a heavy pair in the outfit and when Bruce takes that first load out, I'll have him bring them back with him."

While it may sound like Bruce is used and abused on those trips, rest assured that the work isn't quite as one-sided as Saunders portrays it. But it does point to the final fact about packing game out on your backs, and that fact is that Bruce is really the best able to handle it.

"Above all is being in shape and Bruce is in shape," Saunders said. "If a guy isn't prepared for something like that, he shouldn't be doing it."

Field to Table

Too many big game animals go from good meat in the field to bad meat on the table. Though there certainly may be some tough old bucks out there, and beasts that are a bit gamey, the way the meat is handled is most often the cause of poor table fare.

"There's only about one in two hundred that comes in dressed exactly right. That means I get two a year that are really done right," admitted Leo Stepper, who owns the Park City Locker and has processed every species of big game animal found in Montana.

The principles of good field care are relatively simple, however, and well worth remembering.

"The first thing, if at all possible, is to get a good bleed on them," he said. "Then the warmer the weather, the sooner the hide should come off. If you're interested in good meat, you should also keep them clean. And, if it's warm, you have to keep the flies away from it."

While that sounds simple enough, it's surprising how individual habits vary among hunters and how much meat is tainted because they aren't careful with it.

"After you dress it out, you should skin them right away if you're interested in good meat and can keep them clean. If you skin them real fresh, it will pull right off," he said. "The sooner your meat cools out, the better the meat can be. About eighty percent of the hunters don't cool out the meat quick enough. About fifty percent of the elk have some spoilage on them. Especially if the weather is warm, I get a lot of them that are bone sour. They'll get that way from the time it's killed to four hours later if you don't get them cooled down."

The next most common abuse comes when the animal is transported. "They throw a deer in the back of the pickup and prop it open and you've got the dust and whatever else is back there that can affect the meat," Stepper said. "You can take a tarp and cover it up after it's cool and that will keep it clean. Game bags (made of cheesecloth) are also a good investment. Those keep flies away from it as well as foreign particles and the heat can still pass through them."

Once the animals are home, many hunters believe that aging will help make their wild game tender. While that may be true, care should be taken here as well.

"You have to have it cool, but it can't be too dry. The average animal that's skinned and hung, you're going to start losing meat in about three days because of the air drying it out," he said. "If it's under forty degrees, you can put a plastic bag over it to keep the moisture in. But it's got to be that cold because they'll get moldy in two days if it gets above forty degrees."

While the majority of Montana hunters cut up their own animals, locker plants and butcher shops are available in most cities and towns in the state and they can help you in several ways. If it's warm outside and they have space available, they can hang your deer, antelope or elk quarters in a cooler. If you want them to do the meat-cutting, they can also provide that service. And it's even possible for them to ship meat across the country for hunters far from home.

"I have air freighted a lot of it," Stepper said. "It will get there in one or two days and costs about $23 per hundred pounds. An average deer costs about $15 to anywhere in the U.S. A sixty-pound box is the heaviest they'll allow you to ship. I use a heavy insulated box, then line it with either newspaper or brown paper, and stack the frozen meat in as tight as I can. If it's going to take two days or more, I put a five-pound block of dry ice on it. Dry ice will last about two days so you've got three days to get it there.

"There are some hunting parties that buy a trailer and an old chest freezer," he added. "When they stay overnight someplace, they plug it in and that keeps it frozen for the next day until they plug it in again. That's about the sharpest way to do it. This way you never have to go back and pick up your meat someplace. You've got it with you."

The cost of having animals cut, wrapped, and frozen varies in different parts of Montana, but Stepper said that the average cost on an elk would be $60 to $75 for about two hundred pounds of finished meat. The cost of flying it out air freight would be another $35 to $40. For deer, the cost of cutting, freezing and wrapping would be about $20 to $30 for about fifty to fifty-five pounds of meat while an antelope would run $15 to $25 for about thirty pounds of finished meat.

"People should allow about a week's time for processing depending on how rushed the season is and if they know when they're leaving the area, they should let them know that, too," he said.

But even though a professional butcher can make all the right cuts that the home grown variety may not, the fate of that meat may have been decided long before it ever gets to the chopping block. Taken care of properly from the start, wild game can be excellent table fare. Taken care of poorly, it can be a nightmare. And it's up to the hunter to decide the way he wants it.

Giardia

Water in the high mountain lakes and streams of Montana may look like a safe bet to drink, but looks can be deceiving. A miniscule protozoan parasite, called Giardia Lamblia, is found throughout the waters of Montana and may turn that drink into weeks of illness.

Giardia, or "Backpacker's Disease," is caused by someone drinking the dormant cyst of Giardia Lamblia. Though it's possible for a person to drink water in the mountains for a long time and never contract the disease, all it takes is one drink from the wrong place and Giardia will develop. The cyst then attaches itself to the small intestine, becomes active and reproduces. Symptoms may appear from a few days to a few weeks after ingestion and include severe diarrhea, weight loss, "rotten egg" belches, fatigue and cramps.

Some people will be affected more severely than others, but it takes a doctor's treatment to cure anyone of the disease. And once it is in the environment, it's difficult to get out. The parasite is spread by the excrement of dogs, cats, horses, cattle, beavers, rabbits, marmots, ground squirrels, elk, and people.

Hunters and hikers in the mountains can help slow the spread of Giardia by making sure they dispose of feces by digging a hole at least two hundred feet from any water course and covering the waste with six inches of soil.

The surest way to protect yourself from contracting Giardia is to boil your drinking water at least a minute, or longer if above 6,000 feet in elevation because water boils at a lower temperature there. If that is impractical, get your water from springs which are less likely to be contaminated. Or, you may purchase a water purifying kit which relies on a filtration device that will trap the cysts and take them out of the water.

While all of these methods are relatively time-consuming for a hunter who would rather grab a quick drink and head on down the trail, they may prevent a case of Giardia which could put a premature end to a wonderful hunt.

Fishing

The hunter who forgets to pack a fishing rod along during hunting season is missing a good bet and denying himself an excellent excuse for physical recovery.

Montana's general fishing season runs through November, yet there are hundreds of miles of empty trout streams and countless lightly-used reservoirs at this time of year. It seems that from the time the first gunshot is fired, sportsmen tend to put their rods and reels away in a closet.

Despite the lack of interest, fall fishing can be outstanding. During the first weeks of autumn, before the big frosts hit, grasshoppers abound in the river valleys and fly fishermen floating big patterns can catch a creelful. There are also some afternoon hatches on the streams during this season of crisp mornings and warm afternoons.

Later in the fall, the brook trout are wearing their bright spawning colors and browns have begun to make the move that will carry them to riffles further upstream. Flashy lures and big streamers pulled past these lovesick trout can bring vicious strikes and wrist-wearying fights on fish that have grown fat in a summer of good feeding.

While the stream fishing of western Montana is well known, the reservoir fishing in the eastern part of the state can also be good. In these rich waters, stocked rainbows grow quickly and trout planted in May at three or four inches long may be pushing a pound and a half in the best reservoirs by fall.

These fall fish can provide some variety in the menu of a hunting camp

Trout can add variety to your menu and provide a well-deserved rest after days of hard hunting. Mark Henckel photo.

and some spice to an outing. But even more important than that, they can provide a respectable remedy to too many days spent hiking in the mountains. When your leg muscles are too sore to climb another slope and your back is too tight to face another forced march in the predawn darkness, it's perfectly acceptable for the hunter to explain that he'd really like to be hitting that high country again tomorrow, but someone has to catch the fish for dinner and he's not only the best hunter in the bunch, but the best fisherman as well.

198

Sources

Montana has been blessed with bountiful big game, waterfowl and upland bird populations and a wealth of public and private lands to hunt them on. But putting those two factors together and making it a successful hunt isn't always so easy to accomplish.

This book has been understandably vague in terms of telling a hunter exactly which drainage, mountain range, or patch of prairie to hunt. For one thing, directing all hunters to one particular location would quickly spoil it for everyone. For another, game habits change and an area that was dynamite last year may just be a firecracker or a fizzle by the coming fall. And finally, the hunters who shared their knowledge of tactics and insights in this book deserve a bit of protection. They've already given the reader the benefit of their experience. They shouldn't have to provide their hunting spots, too.

But there are ways to get a lead on good hunting, whether you are a lifelong resident of Montana looking for a new area or someone who has never set foot in the Treasure State before. One way is to study game distribution maps, public land maps, and topographic maps. Most maps these days are not free and it may take a letter or call to determine the amount of money to include. But then, hunters can follow up their map studies with telephone calls or written inquiries to public agencies or area chambers of commerce which could direct their efforts and give them some guidance.

Here are some sources that might come in handy for maps and information on hunting in Montana. All phone numbers are area code 406.

**Montana Department of Fish,
  Wildlife and Parks**

Headquarters and supervisor of
  outfitting:
Department of Fish, Willdlife and Parks
1420 E. Sixth Ave.
Helena, Mont. 59620
444-2535

Regional Offices:
Department of Fish, Wildlife and Parks
Region One
490 North Meridian Road
Kalispell, Mont. 59901
725-5501

Department of Fish, Wildlife and Parks
Region Two
3201 Spurgin Road
Missoula, Mont. 59801
542-5500

Department of Fish, Wildlife and Parks
Region Three
1400 South 19th
Bozeman, Mont. 59715
994-4042/4043

Department of Fish, Wildlife and Parks
Region Four
4600 Giant Springs Road
P.O. Box 6609
Great Falls, Mont. 59406
454-3441/3442

Department of Fish, Wildlife and Parks
Region Five
2300 Lake Elmo Drive
Billings, Mont. 59105
252-4654/4655

Department of Fish, Wildlife and Parks
Region Six
Rural Route 1 - 4210
Glasgow, Mont. 59230
228-9347/9348

Department of Fish, Wildlife and Parks
Region Seven
Rural Route 1, Box 2004
Miles City, Mont. 59301
232-4365/4366

Department of Fish, Wildlife and Parks
Region Eight
1404 8th Ave.
Helena, Mont. 59620
444-4720

U.S. Forest Service:

Information Office
Northern Region
Federal Building
200 East Broadway Street
P.O. Box 7669
Missoula, Mont. 59807
329-3511

Beaverhead National Forest
610 North Montana Street
Dillon, Mont. 59725
683-3900

Bitterroot National Forest
316 North 3rd Street
Hamilton, Mont. 59804
363-3131

Custer National Forest
2602 1st Ave. North
Billings, Mont. 59103
657-6361

Deerlodge National Forest
Federal Building
P.O. Box 400
Butte, Mont. 59703
496-3400

Flathead National Forest
1935 3rd Ave. East
Kalispell, Mont. 59901
755-5401

Gallatin National Forest
Federal Building
10 East Babcock Street
P.O. Box 130
Bozeman, Mont. 59771
587-6701

Helena National Forest
Federal Building
301 South Park, Room 334
Drawer 10014
Helena, Mont. 59626
449-5201

Knotenai National Forest
506 U.S. Highway 2 West
Libby, Mont. 59923
293-6211

Lewis and Clark National Forest
1104 15th Street North
P.O. Box 871
Great Falls, Mont. 59403
791-7700

Lolo National Forest
Building 24
Fort Missoula
Missoula, Mont. 59801
329-3750

U.S. Bureau of Land Management:

Montana State Office
222 North 32nd Street
P.O. Box 36800
Billings, Mont. 59701-6800
255-2913

Miles City District Office
Garryowen Road
P.O. Box 940
Miles City, Mont. 59301-0940
232-4331

Powder River Resource Area
Miles City Plaza
Miles City, Mont. 59301-2844
232-7000

Big Dry Resource Area
Miles City Plaza
Miles City, Mont. 59301-2844
232-7000

Billings Resource Area
810 East Main Street
Billings, Mont. 59105-3395
657-6262

Lewistown District Office
Airport Road
P.O. Box 1160
Lewistown, Mont. 59457-1160
538-7461

Valley Resource Area
Route 1 - 4775
Glasgow, Mont. 59230-9796
228-4316

Havre Resource Area
West 2nd Street
Drawer 911
Havre, Mont. 59501-0911
265-5891

Phillips Rersource Area
501 South 2nd Street, East
P.O. Box B
Malta, Mont. 59538-0047
654-1240

Judith Resource Area
Airport Road
Lewistown, Mont. 59457-1300
538-7461

Great Falls Resource Area
812 14th Street North
Great Falls, Mont. 59401
727-0503

Butte District Office
106 North Parkmont
P.O. Box 3388
Butte, Mont. 59702-3388
494-5059

Dillon Resource Area
1005 Selway Drive
Dillon, Mont. 59725
683-2337

Garnet Resource Area
3255 Fort Missoula Road
Missoula, Mont. 59801-7293
329-3914
Headwaters Resource Area
106 North Parkmont
P.O. Box 3388
Butte, Mont. 59702-3388
494-5059

National Wildlife Refuges:

Benton Lake National Wildlife Refuge
Box 450
Black Eagle, Mont. 59414
727-7400

Bowdin National Wildlife Refuge
Box J
Malta, Mont. 59538
654-2836

Charles M. Russel National Wildlife
  Refuge
Box 110
Lewistown, Mont. 59457
586-8706

Lee Metcalf National Wildlife Refuge
Box 257
Stevensville, Mont. 59870
777-5552

Medicine Lake National Wildlife Refuge
HC 51, Box 2
Medicine Lake, Mont. 59247
789-2305

National Bison Range
Moiese, Mont. 59824
644-2211

Red Rock Lakes National Wildlife Refuge
Monida Star Route, Box 15
Lima, Mont. 59739
276-3347

U.S. Geological Survey topographic maps:

Branch of Distribution
U.S. Geological Survey
1200 South Eads Street
Arlington, Va. 22202

Chamber of Commerce and travel information:

Montana Chamber of Commerce
2030 11th Avenue
Helena, Mont. 59601
442-2405

Travel Promotion Bureau
Department of Commerce
1424 9th Avenue
Helena, Mont. 59620
444-2654

Game Distribution Maps

The following eighteen maps showing general distribution of Montana's big game mammals and upland game birds are reprinted by permission of *Montana Outdoors* magazine and are based on those from "Game Management in Montana" (Montana Fish and Game Department; Helena, Mont., 1971), updated by Dr. P.D. Skaar of Montana State University, Bozeman. These maps are only approximations, because animals may travel extensively, especially in response to droughts or severe winters, and ranges are constantly increasing or decreasing. Individual animals may also be found occasionally far outside the normal range of a species.

Mule Deer
(Odocoileus hemionus)

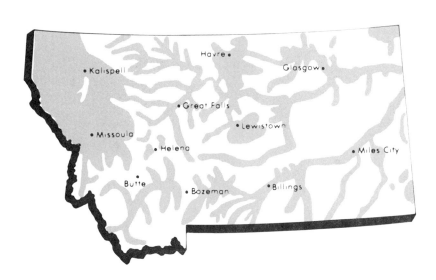

White-tailed Deer
(Odocoileus virginianus)

Elk
(Cervus elaphus)

Pronghorn
(Antilocapra americana)

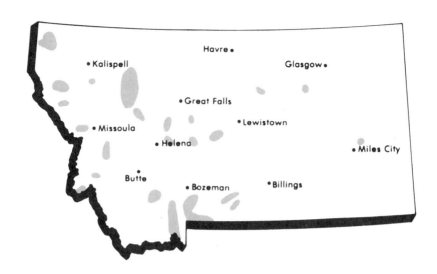

Bighorn Sheep
(Ovis canadensis)

Mountain Goat
(Oreamnos americanus)

Grizzly Bear
(Ursus arctos)

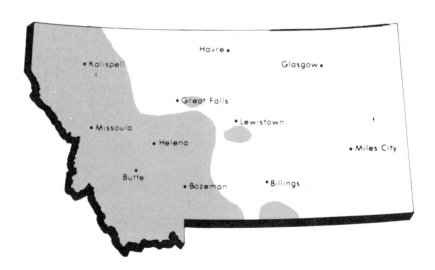

Black Bear
(Ursus americanus)

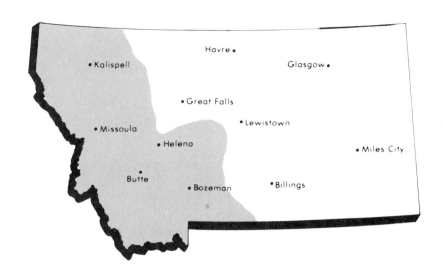

Moose
(Alces alces)

Mountain Lion
(Felis concolor)

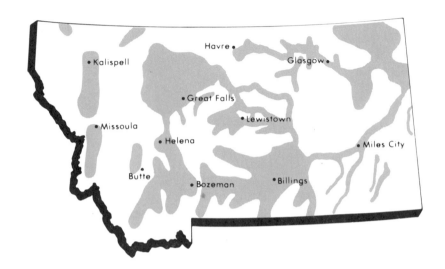

Ring-necked Pheasant
(Phasianus colchicus)

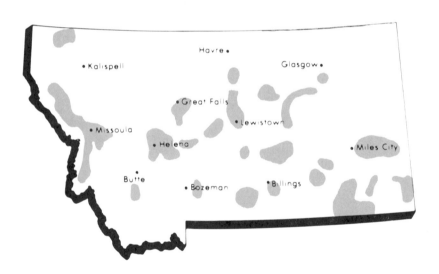

Merriam's Turkey
(Meleagris gallopavo merriami)

Sage Grouse
(Centrocercus urophasianus)

Blue Grouse
(Dendragapus obscurus)

Spruce (Franklin) Grouse
(Canachites canadensis franklinii)

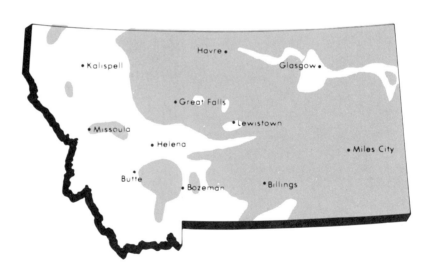

Sharp-tailed Grouse
(Pedioecetes phasianellus)

Ruffed Grouse
(Bonasa umbellus)

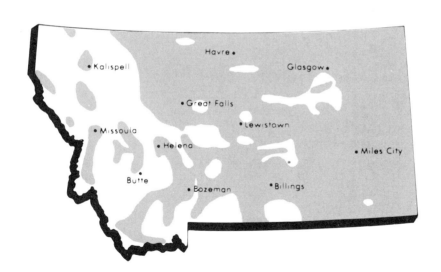

Hungarian (Gray) Partridge
(Perdix perdix)

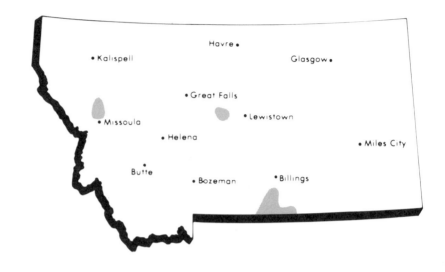

Chukar Partridge
(Alectoris chukar)

More Recreation Guides from Falcon Press

The Angler's Guide to Montana
The Traveler's Guide to Montana
The Floater's Guide to Montana
The Floater's Guide to Colorado
The Hiker's Guide to Montana—Revised
The Hiker's Guide to Utah
The Hiker's Guide to Idaho
The Hiker's Guide to Colorado
The Nordic Skier's Guide to Montana
The Bicyclist's Guide to Yellowstone National Park
The Rockhound's Guide to Montana
The Beartooth Fishing Guide

Falcon Press is steadily expanding its list of recreational guidebooks using the
same general format as this book. You can order extra copies of this book
and get information and prices for the books listed above by writing Falcon
Press, P.O. Box 279-A, Billings, MT 59103. Also, please ask for a free copy
of our current catalog.